Kiran Babcock

The WHISPER

of God

Awaken Your Heart to God's Presence

D1608058

Dr. T. S. Wise

Author of *Leaving Religion Finding God*
and *Every Scar a Treasure*

The Whisper of God: Awaken Your Heart to God's Presence

Scripture quotations are taken from the New Revised Standard Version Updated Edition. Copyright © 2021 National Council of Churches of Christ in the United States of America. Used by permission. All rights reserved worldwide.

ISBN: 978-0-9860613-6-3

Published by
Dr. Terry S. Wise
With kind assistance from Servant Communications, Inc.
Jefferson City, Missouri 65101

Cover picture background photo: File ID 43113837 | © Sikth | Dreamstime.com
Used with permission.

Cover graphic: Designed by macrovector / Freepik.
Used with permission.

Cover and Interior Design: Terry S. Wise and Lissa Auciello-Brogan
Cover and Interior Setup: Lissa Auciello-Brogan

Printed in the United States of America.

14 13 12 11 10 / 10 9 8 7 6 5 4 3 2 1

DEDICATION

THIS BOOK IS DEDICATED TO ALL WHO LONG FOR more than what organized religion has to offer. It is dedicated to those who are willing to swim in deeper waters, where whispers abound and the heart is stirred.

This book is also dedicated to four wonderful friends, who happen to be dogs. They serve as the sacred presence of God in my life.

To Coaster, my illustrious, purebred golden retriever, who taught me a great deal about the unfathomable love of God. Coaster's devotion blessed me for ten glorious years before he passed. To this day, his love and loyalty thrill my heart.

To Lottie, my charming, amber-eyed, rescued chocolate Labrador mix, who taught me a great deal about patience, trust, and investing in myself and others. She was my kind and constant sidekick for fourteen years before succumbing to cancer. To this day, her calm demeanor reminds me to relax, for only one thing is really necessary.

To my whippet puppies, Finnian and ilo, who impart new life to my weary soul. Though my patience is tested with their boundless energy, they are teaching my heart to smile with renewed joy and peace. Grow, young Finnian and ilo, and teach me all you can about the divine. Your student is ready to learn.

TABLE OF CONTENTS

The Perspective

1. The Yearning Within   3

2. Invitation to Intimacy   11

3. Walking into Mystery   25

4. Living in God   37

5. Welcoming Resistance   47

6. Means & Ends   59

7. A Way of Life   63

The Pathway

8. Solitude & Silence   75

9. Simplicity & Surrender   95

10. Prayer & Scripture   121

11. Pain & Pleasure   141

12. Margin & Challenge   171

13. Odds & Ends   195

14. The Primacy of Love   225

PREFACE

DOES YOUR HEART LONG FOR GOD? ARE YOU WORN out and disillu-sioned by the church? Have you ever said to yourself, "There has to be more to the Christian faith than what I am currently experiencing"? If so, this book may help renew your connection to the peace, power, and presence of God!

This is a book about intimacy—divine intimacy. It was written to help us practice the presence of God in our lives. I love that term—*practice the presence of God*—for isn't that what our hearts long for: to know God personally and intimately in a way that draws us toward deeper faith? How do we practice God's presence? Is it even possible? Maybe this hope of ours is just another empty cloud flirting with our heart, promis-ing rain and quickly disappearing. But drawing closer to God is possible. We *can* experience God, sense divine whispers, and walk in step with the Spirit. We *can* practice the presence of God each moment of the day.

This belief that God exists and can be known in the real world of daily living is what I am most interested in—experiencing God—not explain-ing God, debating God, pleading with God to advance my cause, or arguing about God like children fighting over who has the best toy in the sandbox. That's the lot of organized religion and human ego, not the sort of thing I ache for. My heart seeks to touch the One who beckons from within, and that beckoning moves me to write this book. Is the Spirit whispering to you? Do you yearn to know the living God in real, authentic, tangible ways? If so, then join me on this journey into the mystery of God.

God has been a strong presence in my life ever since my introduction to spiritual realities back in sixth grade. For more than fifty years, this sacred presence has whispered for me to come closer, enter deeper waters, travel unknown roads, and see with my heart instead of my eyes. It has been a thrilling journey over all sorts of terrain, and if my experience tells me anything, it is that God is real, powerful, and discoverable in this journey called life. Take heart—the moisture-filled clouds are about to rain upon you, for the Spirit is whispering to your spirit.

Elevating the experience of divine intimacy over proper statements of belief is frightening to those who champion legalistic adherence to correct doctrinal statements, right religious rituals, and the holy rule book as the way to know God. Let me save you some painful road miles: Those who diminish divine intimacy hang out on a dead-end street where disillusionment, shriveled souls, and dust-drinkers congregate. Devoid of hope, it is the place where death looms. Life, on the other hand, is associated with awareness and sensitivity to the Spirit's moving. For far too long, we have confused the whispers of a still-speaking God with religion, ritual, and right belief, and doing so has sucked the life right out of us. These days, are you drinking dust or living water from the well of God?

This book will increase your awareness of and sensitivity to the sacred presence that is within you, beside you, under you, over you, and beyond you. As the created image of God, you already possess the life and Spirit of God. There is no need to get more of God, learn some new creedal formula, attend more church meetings, or earn divine brownie points. The issue is one of awareness and sensitivity to what is already yours. I want nothing more than for you to genuinely experience the presence of God in your life.

This book is organized into two main sections: perspectives and pathways. The first section (perspectives) sets the foundation for divine experiences. Without a proper foundational perspective, we will be hard-pressed to experience divine intimacy—yes, it is that important.

Often, we enter our search for divine intimacy with preconceived ideas about how everything should unfold. When our experiences don't go as planned, we jettison the quest and return to drinking dust, much like the desert Hebrews who longed for a return to Egyptian bondage. In essence, when the movement of God is restrained to the limits of our preconceived ideas and unrealistic expectations, we refuse to walk into a mystery that we cannot control. It is a recipe for failure because our perspective is way off base.

This perspective section places the train on the right track so we have a better chance of arriving at our intended destination—intimacy with God. It shores up our mind and heart for divine encounters so the winds of God can blow freely and fully.

The second section (pathways) presents various practical avenues that move us toward greater awareness of spiritual realities. They are conduits through which divine intimacy flows, but as helpful as they are, they are merely a means to divine intimacy, not the intimacy itself. The two must never be confused. Many true and tried roads can enhance our whisper-hearing abilities, and many of them are addressed in this book. In our quest for divine intimacy, perspectives and pathways are intricately linked.

I wrote this book for myself and you, with the high hope that it would become a catalyst for the whisper of God to our souls. The Spirit is constantly calling us to go deeper, love more expansively, enlarge our vision, and live in union with the divine. As we travel this journey together into the mystery of God, we can drink all the living water we need. Let's set aside our preconceived notions and let the winds of God blow freely in our lives. Let's take the time to set a proper foundational perspective upon which to build our God experiences. Are you with me? The yearning within you is real. It is from God. Let's see where it takes us.

TSW

Ft. Myers, Florida 2024

The Perspective

1. The Yearning Within   3

2. Invitation to Intimacy   11

3. Walking into Mystery   25

4. Living in God   37

5. Welcoming Resistance   47

6. Means & Ends   59

7. A Way of Life   63

1

THE YEARNING WITHIN

WITHIN THE DEEPEST CHAMBERS OF MY BEING, there is a yearning to know my creator. I can't explain it; it's just there—silent and loud, profound and simple, mysterious and recognizable at the same time. I wonder whether you sense it, too, a desire to connect with something beyond the physical world that surrounds us.

The concept of God entered my life when I was a tender adolescent and my family began attending church. Prior to that, I was simply unaware, lost in my own little world with absolutely no awareness of God. The church, however, opened my eyes to a reality beyond the one I was currently experiencing—a spiritual dimension to life that I had never before considered. With my eyes opened, my ears bent forward, and my heart quickened, I set my sails toward experiencing this new reality. The yearning that arose in my adolescent years has never gone away. I doubt it ever will. Although it is constantly present, my awareness of it ebbs and flows to differing degrees, depending on the shifting winds blowing across the landscape of my life.

I am now at a point in my life when there is more past behind me than there is future in front of me. My journey has generated its fair share of scars from the numerous and diverse battles that have befallen me, but I consider them trophies of God's grace—gentle reminders that I am not alone. My voyage through life has changed me. I am profoundly different than when I began: softer in some ways and harder in other ways. Accumulating so many road miles has helped me narrow down what is worth dying for and what isn't. I have benefitted from greater maturity, balance, and introspection, and I am no longer prone to quick judgments. The wear and tear of life has bestowed upon me rich perspectives that I would otherwise never have contemplated. Yet the more seeking I do, the less certainty I obtain, and I am okay with that. I have come to accept life's many ambiguities. These days, solid conclusions are not easy to come by.

Adjusting the Price Tags

Much of life is what you make of it, and I don't make a great deal of materialism, wealth, status, and all the things that seem to matter to people these days. For instance, I have purchased some high-quality pieces of wood furniture over the years—not heirlooms or valuable antiques, but certainly not the cheap hand-me-down furnishings of my early adult years. I own a massive armoire that I call it "The Beast." Moving it so many times has wreaked havoc on my back, and I have the MRI to prove it! I believed in buying once and buying well. I really like these well-built pieces, but in all honesty, they don't hold the value for me that they once did.

From my current vantage point, an end table is an end table is an end table, simply meant to hold such things as a lamp, a beverage, or all the knickknack clutter with which people adorn their homes. Quite frankly, whether end tables are made of wood, plastic, or cardboard seems trivial and inconsequential to me. I am not against having nice things—not at all. I own some lovely possessions for which I am grateful, but the difference now is that my heart no longer pursues them as though they could somehow assuage my deepest yearning for the divine.

Chasing after that which cannot satisfy my ultimate longing is a colossal waste of time and energy. *Things* are merely items made by human hands, not the "something more" I value and pursue. It is as though my value system has been turned inside out and upside down. Instead of loving things, I esteem people. Instead of seeking status, I treasure service. Instead of pursuing wealth, I cherish generosity. That which the world finds worthless, I highly esteem. I am beginning to value that which is truly priceless, and find myself adjusting the price tags in my life.

I long for that which touches my soul and has the sustaining power to transform me from the inside out. Instead of owning more things, I want to be more than I currently am. As a living, breathing human being crafted in the image of God, I seek to touch the divine and see with my soul instead of my eyes. I am not a mistake or an accident but a real person living a real life in a real world, trying to touch the *ultimate reality* from which everything exists. I ache to experience the source of life within me.

Some boldly declare that no deity exists, while others promote such a warped view of God as to be repulsive to the modern mind. As for me, I ask, "Why is there something rather than nothing?" The answer to that question leads me to something beyond myself—to God, a power and presence unlike all else. I yearn to experience this sacred presence even though I cannot fully articulate what "something beyond myself" is. And yet I know it to be real in my own life.

I have been a Christian for nearly fifty years, and you would think that I would have everything down pat by now. That's certainly plenty of time to learn religious doctrine, how the church functions, and all the pious jargon that makes us feel spiritually superior to others. Oh, I have *those things* down pat, but they are ancillary items that often detract from the desires of my heart. No, I am referring to something much different than all the religious entanglements we associate with God—those annoying barnacles that produce excess weight and drag by attaching themselves to the hull of our ship.

What I *don't* have down pat is my understanding and experience of God. Quite simply, I don't understand God. I can't describe or explain God to my own satisfaction, and I realize that I never will. The dilemma is one in which the very thing I am unable to grasp is the very thing my soul longs to experience.

I suspect that you may be in the same boat, for we never arrive in this voyage of ours. As we journey into the great cloud of mystery, we are in constant motion, always moving forward to new vistas and more enlightened views of our self, our world, and God. We spend the first half of our lives building, acquiring, and producing without the wisdom of time and experience. In one sense, it is nothing more than barnacle building. It is often in the second half of life that these barnacles are scraped away and we begin to feel comfortable in our own skin, to discover our place in life, to function with less arrogance, and to learn what matters and what doesn't. God becomes more precious than we ever imagined.

We are like leather that has finally been broken in and is now soft and pliable. In the first half of my life, I did a lot of talking. Now, I do a lot of listening. In the first half of my life, I engaged in a great deal of barnacle building, and now, after scraping them away, I realize that there is something far more valuable than the crustaceans that once fascinated me—a ship that is actually worth sailing. Today, I am a better version of myself, with ears to hear and a heart primed for dancing with the divine.

I have had my fill of religious jargon, religious games, religious lists of do's and don'ts, and the smug, judgmental attitudes associated with those who believe that their halos are larger than everyone else's. In many ways, I have become numb to the constant sting of disappointment offered up by the church—a place that can make you feel as though you never measure up, you never do enough for God, and you never meet the expectations of all those "holier than thou" religious folks. "Enough!" my heart cries out. "Where is the abundant life Jesus spoke about?"

It finally dawned on me that my internal exhaustion and spiritual let-downs stemmed from the fact that religion and God are not the same thing. The barnacles clinging to my ship arose from a religious system crafted of human hands, where we *do things for God* instead of *living in God*. This human-made religious scaffolding clouded my vision and experience of the divine. In many ways, my quest for God was nothing more than learning how to function and survive within a religious system. I became adept at articulating God within the confines of my denominational upbringing, trying to live up to its religious ideals, and promoting the system to others. In essence, I was a pretty good soldier and had advanced through the ranks to a leadership role. In reality, I was nothing more than a skilled religious system builder who was not well versed in actually experiencing God.

After a while, you begin to wonder whether this is all there is to spirituality and the pursuit of God. Is following God about learning how to function within a religious system plush with its doctrines, practices, and lingo? What happens when you learn a system, master a body of knowledge, and become adept at leading others into and through the system, but are spiritually exhausted all the time? Is that of God? Should we strive harder? Surely, the fault lay at our own feet! That's what the system wants you to think, for the system never blames itself. At all costs, its goal is to protect and perpetuate its own existence. Self-preservation becomes the overarching goal.

Despite all of my hard work within my preferred religious environment, the yearning within me was still smoldering. It could not be extinguished, for it was built deep within—an essential part of my very existence as a human. The religious system didn't quench my thirst for God; instead, it tried to replace it and trick me into thinking that it *was* God. As each year passed, my devotion waned to the point of irrelevance. Although I still loved God and would forever remain a follower, the human-made religious system was choking the very life out of me. Would another system work better, another religion, another denomination? Absolutely not, for no religious system can produce the abundant life my heart desired, for God is beyond all religions, denominations, and churches. This is the God I long to know.

Is There Something More?

"This can't be right," I finally gathered the courage to say out loud. "Following God should be easy, not hard." Jesus said, "Come to me, all you that are weary and are carrying heavy burdens, and I will give you rest. Take my yoke upon you, and learn from me, for I am gentle and humble in heart, and you will find rest for your souls. For my yoke is easy, and my burden is light" (Matt. 11:28–30, NRSVue). The way of Jesus stood in stark contrast with the religious elite of his day, who made following God a difficult burden. Speaking of the Pharisees, Jesus said, "Do not do as they do, for they do not practice what they teach. They tie up heavy burdens, hard to bear, and lay them on the shoulders of others, but they themselves are unwilling to lift a finger to move them" (Matt. 23:3b–4, NRSVue).

The contrast between Jesus and religion is glaring. They couldn't be more different. It is not that churches and denominations are inherently evil, for they can bring a great amount of good into this world. The problem is that they are merely tools that should *lead us* to God, not become obstacles that *prevent us* from experiencing God. They can never impart life to us; they can only point us toward life—and they don't even do that very well. Unfortunately, Christianity is experienced as a *burden to bear* rather than the *abundant life of God* coursing through our veins. When we substitute religions, churches, denominations, doctrines, or religious practices for God, we are burdened, mistaken, and sorely disillusioned. We are, in essence, *practicing idolatry*. Oh, we would never call it "idolatry," but in the real world of everyday living, that is exactly what it is. By mistaking the tools for the reality itself and elevating the symbols of our faith over the substance of our faith, we usurp God's primacy in our life. Religious systems have a tendency to become corrupt, oppressive, and disillusioning—an unfortunate self-serving end unto themselves.

I was good at system life, but I was poor at experiencing God. Do you relate to that statement? The church does little to distinguish between the two. It is the difference between butter and margarine. One is the real deal, while the other is a cheap, unhealthy, human-made imitation. I yearn for real butter, not religious margarine. I long for the reality of God, not a system that corrupts, distorts, and diminishes that reality.

Do you sense a beckoning from within to experience God personally, wholly, and consistently? Are you stuck in a religious system where exhaustion and disillusionment prevail? Ever feel like throwing it all out the window? If so, I shout, "Hallelujah!" My friend, you are on the brink of discovering a new way of connecting with God. You are approaching a state of readiness, hope, and expectation for something more. You are primed to receive the planting of new seed in the fertile soil of your softened heart.

In many ways, the church has created what I refer to as "hollow Christians"—those who outwardly play the part but are inwardly empty and lifeless. Where do you turn when this happens to you? Have you experienced this very phenomenon? Your heart is sincere and your desire is real, but you just keep going through the motions, hoping for a different outcome. Do you aspire to drink deeply and often from the refreshing waters of life so you will never thirst again—as Jesus promised his living water could do for the Samaritan women in John 4? If so, I hear the cry of your heart, for I have been there and done that. I am with you.

When our gaze moves beyond a religious system to the sacred presence that transcends all systems, we are well on our way to recognizing that God is in us, over us, beside us, under us, through us, and beyond us. It is time to scrape away those stubborn barnacles that prevent us from experiencing the great mystery of God—a mystery that offers peace, power, perspective, and presence. It is time for God to become a precious reality that we treasure rather than a barnacle-entangled deity. I desire nothing more than to experience the sacred presence of God in my life. I want to go where the yearning within takes me, for there I will find the abundant life of which Jesus spoke. Are you with me?

In this book, I hope to close the gap between our yearning for God and our actual experience of God. It can't be that difficult, can it? Surely, we don't have to learn a new system to experience God. If we did, we would merely be exchanging one system for another, and another system is the last thing we need. I am experiencing the sacred presence of God to greater depths in my own life, and although I don't have all the answers, I invite you to explore this topic with me. Let's journey together for a season. Let's be real about where we are spiritually and where we want to go. Let's awaken our hearts and discover what it means to hear the whisper of God.

2

INVITATION TO INTIMACY

GIVEN THE PRECARIOUS NATURE OF RELIGION IN the postmodern age, we are surprised to learn that a divine invitation has been graciously extended to us and to all people everywhere—an offer of intimacy, relationship, communication, and communion with the divine. Much to our chagrin, we don't hear much about *that kind* of God—a God of gracious invitation. Instead, we are more likely to hear about a vengeful God who punishes temporal sins with eternal damnation and delights in our failure to measure up to the divine rules—rules that the church itself can't seem to agree on! That's not a God of intimacy but a celestial warrior of retribution—a rules and regulations kind of God—ever ready to hurl deadly lightning bolts our way. Who wants to cozy up to a God like that? No one, and yet that's the kind of God often portrayed by the church.

Let's be honest—that kind of God isn't calling us to intimacy but relishing the day we fail, for then that God can show us who is boss. Like so many who have turned their backs on institutionalized religion, I don't want anything to do with that kind of God. Who in their right mind would? Yet that is often the God Christians chase, only to fail over and over again in their pursuit of intimacy. After a while, the cause isn't worth the effort. More is said about the God who invites us in the coming chapter, but for now, let's marvel at this gracious invitation extended our way.

An Invitation to Dance

Are you surprised that a divine creator invites us to draw near? Each night, as the massive universe stares us down, we become keenly aware of our diminutive stature in the grand scheme of things—one person out of billions of people living on one single planet out of seven hundred quintillion planets. Yet a divine invitation goes forth to you, me, and all people to experience the sacred presence permeating life. To our delight and dismay, it appears that we aren't so insignificant after all, for we have been invited to the grand ballroom to dance with the divine. Absolutely amazing! The yearning deep within us is quickened at such an invitation.

It is nice to receive an invitation, but what exactly is the substance of the invitation? We know that we are headed to a ballroom, but to what kind of experience? What should we expect? What is this invitation to intimacy?

The invitation has gone forth throughout history, and many before us have experienced this divine dance. Although each moves a little differently to the rhythm of God's Spirit, each experiences the same divine presence. Think of dancing in the modern world. Some disco, some salsa, some tango, some fox-trot, some waltz, some ballet, and some have no clue what they are doing. They simply frolic about however the music inspires them. With misguided intentions, the focus of the institutionalized church has been upon getting everyone to dance the same dance and to do it just right. God's focus, however, is to get everyone to experience the thrill of dancing, whatever their dance moves may be. The two perspectives are totally different.

This gracious invitation is to simply dance with the divine, not to dance a specific dance in a specific way. God isn't a talent show celebrity judge critiquing the technicality of our dance moves. God is on the floor dancing with us! Some never experience the joy of dancing because they are too busy working out their choreography. For them, dancing with the divine is about doing it just right, learning all the technical steps, and critiquing themselves in the mirror. Unfortunately, they never make it to the grand ballroom and experience the thrill of God, for they are too busy pursuing the illusion of perfection. How can God be pleased with them when they just can't get the salsa down? They fail to realize that dancing with the divine is not about performing correct dance maneuvers but simply moving to the beat of the Spirit.

Others, however, have learned that intimacy isn't about the dance itself but about dancing. They have a smile on their face, joy in their heart, and a peace that passes all understanding as they move to the rhythm of God. It doesn't occur to them to dance just right, to get all the steps down, or to worry that God is somehow displeased at their dance floor gyrations. They simply move at the impulse of God, every day, all the time. For them, it is how life is lived, and it is how life *should* be lived—*with* the joy of God and *in* the joy of God.

Many Christians are deceived in thinking that life on this planet is to be spurned and endured until they are settled in heaven, where they can finally relax and enjoy streets of gold, pearly gates, and angelic choirs. If they can just make it through this life by the skin of their teeth, they plan to dance in the afterlife. What a dreadful outlook! They reject the invitation to intimacy in this life while clutching a ballroom ticket they hope to use someday in the future. But the music is playing now, and the dance has already begun, for the sacred music has been playing since eternity. God is actively present in this life, right here, today, on this Earth. To wait is to miss the joy and pleasure of God in this life. There is no reason to delay, for the invitation is in the present moment. Even Jesus lived each day in communion with the power and presence of God. He danced without delay in the here and now.

The dance has begun and is ongoing. It is never too late to begin moving to the rhythm of God. Now is the time to join in. Quit wasting precious time worrying about whether your dance moves are technically correct—just dance! Let go and let it rip. Get off of your spiritual laurels and have fun. Move that body and soul of yours and experience God's pleasure in you. God isn't a future blessing but a present reality to be experienced, and that is what the invitation is all about—experiencing the reality of God now, in this life.

A Loving Parent-God Invitation

A prevalent image of God found in Scripture is that of a parent. Some mistakenly interpret these images literally and miss the point entirely. God transcends gender definitions, for God is not a literal male father but a spiritual, figurative parental figure. It is merely a familiar human image that helps finite beings like us relate to the divine.

As the father of two grown children, I can say without hesitation that raising them was the delight of my heart and a privilege I will cherish forever. Although my father role has changed over the years, I am still in relationship with my children. Sure, there were times when I got caught up in *how* they were dancing, but there were plenty of other times when I was overcome with deep emotion and contagious joy simply from dancing with them in this life. To be in their presence, to have them in my life, to watch them grow and mature, to see them smile, laugh, and enjoy life is priceless. Dancing with my children brings joy to my heart. It doesn't matter what the moves are—we are dancing together and that is all that matters. The memories of years past and my time with them in the present bring joy to my heart and tears to my eyes. Even as I age and move at a slower pace, I am still kicking up my heels as the dance continues.

Can you imagine a loving parent-God whose pure joy is to delight in your very presence? Can you imagine a parent-God who relishes dancing with you? You are a precious child in the household of faith, and God delights in drawing you near. Have you ever danced with God in this way, or are you still looking in the mirror and checking out your dance moves?

Sadly, the prevailing caricature of God seems to be that of an angry deity who is never pleased with us and whose patience runs thin while trying to teach us thick-headed humans all the correct dance moves. Do yourself a huge favor and throw that perspective in the trash bin. Would your experience of God be different if you knew deep within your soul just how much God loves you, is proud of you, delights in your presence, and desires that you dance your heart out in the grand ballroom of life? What if God's invitation to intimacy is all about you experiencing joy, contentment, peace, and love in this life, not in the afterlife? Isn't it time to stop focusing on the dance moves themselves and simply start dancing under the watchful and caring eyes of a loving parent-God?

The music of God is playing for you. Do you hear it? Are you moving to its rhythm? Do you realize that life is meant for dancing, not standing with your back against the wall? For goodness' sake, life is far too short for you to be a mere spectator. Get up and dance! Enjoy God just as God enjoys you. This gracious invitation is about intimacy, love, trust, joy, peace, presence, relationship, and communion with the divine. To that end, let's examine some wonderful images in Scripture that shore up this divine invitation.

An Invitation to Sabbath Rest

From the very beginning of creation, God has offered us rest. Rest sure sounds appealing to those who are soul-weary and internally exhausted. We discover this invitation in the book of Genesis, when God rested after creating all that is. This isn't to be taken literally, as though the creative effort wore God out so badly that a day of lying in bed, eating junk food, and watching cartoons was in order. No, resting on the Sabbath conveyed something much deeper than a cartoon-laden Saturday. The Sabbath would become a key identifier of Jewish life, as seen in the fourth commandment of the Old Testament: "Remember the Sabbath day and keep it holy" (Exod. 20:8, NRSVue).

In the Hebrew language of the Old Testament, *Sabbath* referred to a cessation, a stoppage, a refreshing, or a complete rest. As a reminder of the rest found in Yahweh, the Jews set aside a day dedicated to the refreshment of their souls. In predictable fashion, however, the reminder itself replaced the intended refreshment it was to bring. Keeping the Sabbath became another item on the religious to-do list, while the religious elite argued over the definition of work. By the time of Jesus, extensive rules were in place, and ceasing physical labor had become the focus when a deeper, spiritual rest was envisioned.

The Sabbath is a tangible reminder to stop the cycle of frenzied hamster-wheel living. We focus on the trivial, we worry, and we strive to impress God. We feverishly work to be good enough to earn God's favor. Life becomes one great big task to check off our "pleasing-God" list. We focus on getting our dance moves down just right, when God invites us to cease from that kind of behavior, to stop striving and to discover what it feels like to dance in sacred rhythm with the divine. Although physical rest is important, it is the resting of the soul that calms our inner selves and helps us dance with joyful delight.

According to the book of Hebrews, this internal, spiritual rest is found in the Christ: "For we who have believed are entering that rest" (Heb. 4:3, NRSVue). The good news is that "a Sabbath rest still remains for the people of God" (Heb. 4:9, NRSVue), so "let us therefore make every effort to enter that rest" (Heb. 4:11, NRSVue).

Jesus is a prime example of someone who entered the Sabbath rest of God. In fact, we are told that "the Son of Man is lord of the Sabbath" (Matt. 12:8, NRSVue). The religious leaders of Jesus's day were upset with him, for he taught on the Sabbath, healed on the Sabbath, plucked grain on the Sabbath, traveled on the Sabbath, and actually did things that brought refreshment to himself and others on the Sabbath. From their perspective, he should have been in bed, watching reruns. The Pharisees were fastidiously concerned with correct dance moves, whereas Jesus simply danced to the beat of the Spirit.

It was Jesus's connection with the divine that was so attractive to others, for he simply danced with single-minded devotion. The invitation of God is to cease from the internal turmoil that overwhelms us and enjoy God's refreshing presence. Spiritual rest comes from dancing with the divine. That is what Sabbath rest is all about.

An Invitation to Shalom

Not only are we invited to spiritual rest; we are also invited to *shalom*, the Hebrew word for "peace." This overture is yet another invitation found in Scripture. Its basic meaning is "completion" or "wholeness." It means something more than the absence of war or violence; it implies a lack of fragmentation and a sense of spiritual completeness.

Jews often speak of Sabbath peace (*Shabbat shalom*) and greet one another in this manner on their holy day. Rest and peace go together. As we dance with God, we cease striving to earn divine favor, cease trying to perfect our dance moves, and cease doing things *for* God. Instead, we sense wholeness and the defragmentation of our internal hard drive. The book of Philippians reminds us of this very truth: "Do not be anxious about anything, but in everything by prayer and supplication with thanksgiving let your requests be made known to God. And the peace of God, which surpasses all understanding, will guard your hearts and your minds in Christ Jesus" (Phil. 4:6–7, NRSVue). We are invited to experience shalom.

An Invitation of Christ

The life and words of Jesus as portrayed in the Gospels are nothing more than one giant invitation to intimacy. As the central figure of Christianity, his life and teaching have become the prime example for us to follow. He was the Christ, a title that means "anointed." In other words, Jesus was someone who lived in the anointing of the Spirit. He didn't just talk about communion with God; he actually lived it, experienced it, and demonstrated it for us, and that's what made him so winsome. He was plugged into the divine in such a way that his life became a living example of what dancing is all about. Let's examine a few ways the gracious invitation of God is seen through the words and life of Jesus.

An Invitation to Abide

God's invitation to intimacy can be seen in the concept of abiding (John 15:4–5, 9–11, NRSVue):

> Abide in me as I abide in you. Just as the branch cannot bear fruit by itself unless it abides in the vine, neither can you unless you abide in me. I am the vine; you are the branches. Those who abide in me and I in them bear much fruit, because apart from me you can do nothing. As the Father has loved me, so I have loved you; abide in my love. If you keep my commandments, you will abide in my love, just as I have kept my Father's commandments and abide in his love. I have said these things to you so that my joy may be in you and that your joy may be complete.

The word *abide* resonates with me, for it relays the concept of permanency, connection, and life. Abiding, Jesus noted, is similar to a vine and its branches, which are connected to one another in a living and dynamic way. This vine-branch metaphor speaks of our symbiotic, life-giving relationship with the divine. In this life-giving relationship, we are in God, and God is in us, producing a dynamic connection that is quite different than the exhaustion and stagnation so many religious people seem to experience. Abiding is associated with growth, production, life, and connectivity. To know the power of Christ—the same anointing Jesus experienced—is to encounter intimacy with God. We are invited to experience this life-giving vine-branch connection.

An Invitation to Abundant Life

The Gospel of John placed these beautiful words upon the lips of Jesus: "The thief comes only to steal and kill and destroy. I came that they may have life and have it abundantly" (John 10:10, NRSVue). These words sum up what life is like when lived in communion with God. They are what the life and message of Jesus were all about, and they stand in stark contrast with the typical experience of institutionalized religion.

Rather than promoting organized religion, Jesus delighted in the sacred presence of God. He desired that his followers experience a similar life of abundance. Proponents of the infamous health-and-wealth gospel interpret this passage in terms of prosperity theology where fancy cars, fancy houses, fancy clothes, and fancy food are the expected norm for faithful followers. Fancy things are tangible proof of abundance. Fancy that!

This view defies all logic, however, for Jesus was all about serving and loving, not gathering and hoarding ostentatious possessions in a flashy, "look what God did for me" mentality. In reality, Jesus owned nothing but the clothes on his back. He didn't have a fancy bank account, a fancy 401(k) retirement plan, a fancy health insurance plan, a fancy Mercedes, or a fancy second home in Malibu. He had no place to call his own, for "foxes have holes, and birds of the air have nests, but the Son of Man has nowhere to lay his head" (Matt. 8:20, NRSVue).

The selfish elevation of himself and the hoarding of possessions weren't part of his theological framework. And yet, this simple man with nothing to call his own lived a life of abundance and helped others discover God's abundant life for themselves. What a contrast! Abundant life is found not in possessing things but in communing (abiding) with the Spirit of God. Over and over again, we have seen prosperous people with the means to go anywhere, do anything, and possess whatever they desire, wallowing in despair because their soul is dry as kindling wood, despite being surrounded by the bounty of "things."

God's gracious invitation to abundant living isn't about things but about personally experiencing the divine presence. The intimacy offered to us is life-giving, life-sustaining, and internal; it is about living with an abundance from within that always brings life, no matter the circumstances.

An Invitation to Living Water

On his way to Galilee from Judea, Jesus intentionally passed through Samaria, where he met a woman drawing water from Jacob's well. This story is interesting because of where Jesus was and to whom he was speaking. Comprised of Jews who married outside the faith, Samaria was a despised region of Palestine. In the eyes of "pure" Jews, Samaritans were half-breeds who diluted the true faith of Israel. Not only was Jesus in despised enemy territory; he also spoke publicly with a lowly female, for women held little standing in those days. Jewish males were cautious in their public dealings with females, and the fact that Jesus was fraternizing with a Samaritan of the opposite gender astounded even his disciples. Upon their return from the city, "they were astonished that he was speaking with a woman" (John 4:27, NRSVue). Jesus defied these cultural boundaries so that we might see the compassionate, welcoming heart of God.

Even the lowly Samaritan woman wondered why Jesus was speaking to her. His reply came in John 4:10 (NRSVue): "If you knew the gift of God and who it is that is saying to you, 'Give me a drink,' you would have asked him, and he would have given you living water." She couldn't figure out how Jesus would provide living water when he didn't even have a bucket with which to draw water. After all, *he* was the one who had asked *her* for a drink. Jesus, however, was speaking not literally but figuratively, for he was communicating something much deeper and far more satisfying than a temporal drink from Jacob's well.

Jesus expanded upon his remarks in John 4:13–14 (NRSVue): "Everyone who drinks of this water will be thirsty again, but those who drink of the water that I will give them will never be thirsty. The water that I will give will become in them a spring of water gushing up to eternal life." What an invitation—never thirsting again because of living water gushing up from within!

The issue is not of literal H_2O but of experiencing the divine in such a way that our soul is ever satisfied. Has that been your experience of God—full satisfaction? Christians long for this, but too few experience living water bubbling up from within. Most believers I know are tired of working on their dance moves and never getting to the dance itself. Internal soul satisfaction comes from drinking deeply from the living waters of God. What a beautiful image—never again to endure a parched soul as deep springs of faith rise from within.

An Invitation to Come

Additional words of invitation arose from Jesus in Matthew 11:28–30 (NRSVue): "Come to me, all you who are weary and are carrying heavy burdens, and I will give you rest. Take my yoke upon you, and learn from me, for I am gentle and humble in heart, and you will find rest for your souls. For my yoke is easy, and my burden is light." The offer is simply to come and experience rest for your soul. There are no preconditions, no status requirements, no creedal affirmations, and no political litmus tests—just come, and come just as you are. All are invited to the soul-satisfying rest of God.

Sooner or later, every religion seems to lose its way and get off track from its core teaching. Over time, religion has become a god unto itself, erecting barriers, creating rules and regulations, and establishing self-serving power structures. As a result, religion distances itself from the real reason for its existence. It happened in Jesus's day, and it happens in our day as well. Religious leaders of the early first century had commandeered Judaism into a hard task master. They turned a religion whose greatest commandment was to love God with all one's heart, soul, and might (Deut. 6:4–9), into their own chastisement. Jesus said of the Pharisees: "They tie up heavy burdens, hard to bear, and lay them on the shoulders of others, but they themselves are unwilling to lift a finger to move them" (Matt. 23:4, NRSVue).

Religion should *lead us to* God rather than *create barriers* to experiencing God. Jesus reminded his followers that God was gentle and humble in heart rather than harsh and overbearing. God has no desire to crush our spirit with heavy burdens. No, the invitation is simply to come just as you are, whoever you are and wherever you are on your faith journey. Just come and experience abundant life, joy, peace, and intimacy with the divine. Our souls yearn for this. It is the cry of our heart. What an invitation!

The Example of Jesus

The Gospels portray Jesus as someone intimately connected to the world of Spirit. He peered beyond the curtain of this world into the unseen dimension of life. He lived in constant awareness of the divine and demonstrated that communion with God is possible if we are willing to attend the ballroom dance. All that Jesus was, did, and said originated from his deep sensitivity to the Spirit. This is what attracted others to him. How do you think he knew where to go, what to say, and to whom to say it? He had no messiah manual to follow. Instead, Jesus simply danced to the rhythm of the Spirit in the grand ballroom of life. He prioritized time alone with God to ensure that this awareness and sensitivity remained on high alert. He became the human example of God's gracious invitation to participate in the divine dance.

Divine Breath

The first book of the Old Testament informs us that God breathed life into humankind: "the LORD God formed man from the dust of the ground and breathed into his nostrils the breath of life, and the man became a living being" (Gen. 2:7, NRSVue).

God breathed *nephesh* into human creation. This Hebrew word refers to "life." Adam became a living, breathing human being because the *nephesh* of God animated his body. The implication is that the very life of God is within you, and that life makes you a living, human being. You don't have to search for God, for the life of God is already within you. This living breath is what makes you human and spiritual at the same time. The issue is one not of obtaining or possessing God but of becoming aware of the divine presence that is built right within! The deep yearning we sense is the very life of God calling to us.

Be Still

A familiar verse is Psalm 46:10a (NRSVue): "Be still, and know that I am God!" One way we commune with God is through being still. This is quite a challenge in light of our frenzied lifestyle. It is hard to listen when so many distractions compete for our attention. Internal stillness provides the space we need to clear away the clutter and actually focus on the breath of God within us. It is one way the Spirit can freely move in our life.

Stillness as a way of communing with God is seen throughout the Bible. Old Testament prophets, for instance, often found their way to quiet places in the wilderness to hone their listening abilities. Jesus himself was led by the Spirit into the wilderness of listening and learning. Throughout his busy ministry, he stole away as a means of maintaining his intimate relationship with the divine. Paul did the same thing after his Damascus Road encounter with the Christ, and in solitude, he was taught by the Spirit.

The point isn't that we must literally go into a desert; instead, an invitation goes forth to know and experience God in powerful ways, if we will internally still ourselves long enough to hear the whispers of God. It is an issue of awareness that arises from quieting the inner self. God invites us to become aware of the divine presence within us!

Awaiting Your Response

Throughout Scripture, we discover God's gracious invitation to inti-macy, relationship, communication, and communion. What will you do with such an offer? Will you enter the grand ballroom and experience the thrill of dancing with the Holy One, or will you continue perfecting your dance-floor moves? One offers the thrill of the divine, while the other misses out on the sacred adventure.

There is a yearning deep within to know God—to go beyond the superficial and experience God's sacred presence fully and authenti-cally. That yearning is hardwired into us, for our soul is seeking to connect with its creator. There has to be more to Christianity than a hand-me-down religion that meets for one hour on a Sunday morning. God's gracious invitation to intimacy assures us that our yearning is real. If we would but dance our hearts out instead of perfecting our dance moves, we would experience the joy and satisfaction of divine commu-nion every moment of life. You have a yearning to *know God* and a divine invitation *from God* to pursue the intimacy you long for. What more could you ask for? The deep communion you seek is possible. It is my hope that this book will nudge you in that direction.

3

WALKING INTO MYSTERY

THIS DEEP DESIRE TO KNOW THE HOLY ONE IS hardwired in us by a God who also invites us to experience divine intimacy. The yearning within and the grand invitation encourage us to pursue this internal calling, but what exactly are we pursuing? Part of this question is answered in the previous chapter, as intimacy with God is about peace, rest, relationship, communication, and communion with the divine. But what is this divine presence?

For centuries, folks from all walks of life have wrestled with the question of what God is. Although I would love to provide a once-and-for-all definitive answer for you, I can't. No one can. If I could get my arms around God and understand all that God is, well—I would be greater than God. We are simply unable to fully explain, understand, or articulate the mystery of God.

You may not have expected or appreciated an answer like that, for finite humans prefer certainty over mystery, and where certainty is absent, we make up our own declarations of truth. It is easier to declare "Thus saith the Lord," than it is to walk into the unknown. If we are to experience intimacy with God, however, we will be walking into a cloud of mystery that is beyond our ability to decipher. God is not a mathematical equation to solve, a science project under the microscope, or a "thing" to dissect. God is what theologians call "transcendent"—far beyond our ability to comprehend.

Intimacy with the divine is a journey into mystery. That may be one reason why so many fail to experience God. They seek something to dissect, to solve, and to place under a microscope to evaluate and control. Good luck with that! Experiencing the divine isn't mapped out like a GPS route on our smartphones, and it isn't something we analyze and evaluate to determine its worth. God is something we experience, but nothing we direct or control. We don't put in a code and out pops our preferred spiritual journey. God really is a mystery beyond our comprehension. When we place parameters upon the God experiences we will accept, our expectations are dashed, and we question God's presence in our life.

The divine invitation is about experiencing peace, joy, intimacy, communication, and communion with the sacred presence of God. Although I may be able to provide helpful signposts along the way, I will never be able to explain the mystery to you or map out every twist and turn for your preapproval. That isn't within my power, and it certainly isn't within yours. In fact, the goal of this chapter is to move us from what we think the journey *should be* to what the journey *actually is*. In other words, I seek to move us from the certainty of our own prescribed expectations, which are always limiting and almost always wrong, to a journey filled with mysterious twists and turns—a journey that leads us toward dancing with the divine, no matter what lies ahead. In essence, we yearn to experience the presence of God, and Scripture invites us to walk into this great cloud of mystery. So, I will, and I do, walk by faith into the mystery of God, and it is my hope that you will also.

Seeking Certainty

Why do we seek certainty, anyway? Why is it that we always want some three-step formula that guarantees our preferred outcome? Our penchant for absolute certainty stems from our insecurity, our need for authority, and our desire for orthodoxy. Walking into mystery, on the other hand, is about faith and courage, for we journey among the many ambiguities of life. That is faith!

As far as I can tell, we are the only self-conscious beings on this planet, living in the shadow of a vast universe we don't understand or comprehend. This breeds fear and insecurity. In other words, we are aware of our own awareness, and that is frightening. Why are we here? Is there a God? How should we live? We ask all kinds of questions that other species don't, for they do not possess the self-consciousness of humans.

To assuage this lack of security, we seek some sort of authority that tells us what to do, how to do it, and why we should do it. When insecure people secure a source of authority, they can boldly claim that they are orthodox when others aren't. They follow the right path when others don't. They believe the right doctrines and do the right things when others falter. They alone are right when all others are wrong, for they have the absolute source of authority to prove it.

This is what Christianity has done with Scripture. To address our need for security, authority, and orthodoxy, the church has declared Scripture to be the inspired, inerrant, and authoritative words of God to humankind. There you have it. We sought security, declared Scripture to be directly from God, and, poof, just like that, we had our source of authority. Never mind that virtually all religions claim the same for their own holy writings. We can now align our life to God's will, claim to possess absolute truth, and judge all others according to our declared source of authority. We now become orthodox—that is, believing, doing, and following the "right way"—while all others are wrong. This attitude calms the fear generated by self-consciousness and provides the security we seek. Even if it is a false sense of security, it sure makes us feel better.

It seems to me that life is anything but certain. We have questions galore, and the increase of knowledge only generates more questions.

We will never reach a point in this life where all of our questions are answered. Even the concept of God is about as clear as muddy water. What do we mean by the term *God*? That depends upon where we live in the world, which religious system we find most attractive, and which historical period we live in. You and I aren't the only ones who sense this yearning deep within. The various religious systems are nothing more than human attempts to articulate a yearning for God.

It doesn't seem fair, does it, for me to point out the yearning within, describe the divine invitation, inform you that it's all one great big mystery, and then wave goodbye as I send you out into the fog to find your own way home. Is this some kind of a sick joke?

It is no joke, and I am not sending you into the fog without guidance. That's what this book is all about—helping you increase your spiritual sensitivity. But here is the thing that trips us up: We have a tendency to tell God what to do, how to do it, and when we want it done. In our mind, a spiritual journey should be just as we think it should be. In essence, we seek to control, restrain, direct, and manipulate the journey to our preferred pathway and outcome. You would think that God is somehow under our command and obligated to us. In the mind of some, God is nothing more than a celestial vending machine dispensing goodies when we put in enough spiritual quarters.

I happened to be in a used bookstore and ran across a published title that caught my attention. This author was writing about how to experience God, and the way to do it, according to this book, is through obedience. You obey, you get to experience God. Failure to obey means that you are out of luck. It is that simple. This is vending-machine theology, a quid pro quo approach to God's presence. If you put in the proper coins—in this case, obedience—the vending-machine God will supply you with blessing. If you don't, well, you are just plain out of luck.

By golly, you'd better obey every single one of the rules in Scripture, or you will miss out! With more than thirty thousand denominations throughout the world, we are in quite a quandary as to which doctrines are correct and which rules to obey. Too bad, so sad. I guess you will just have to live without the blessing and presence of God in your life. As you can tell, I am not a vending-machine-theology kind of guy. I don't see how anyone could be.

My point is that we earnestly desire to experience God, but we want to do so on our terms. That isn't how it works. We want to outline every step and every circumstance along the way so we can determine whether to begin the journey. Little faith is involved in that approach. My father was a loving and kind individual who was also risk-averse. He possessed great business ideas but lacked the courage to pull them off. He wanted to preapprove the journey and secure the outcome before assuming the risk. Wouldn't it be nice if we knew exactly how the stock market was going to perform before we invested our hard-earned money? It doesn't work that way in real life, and it doesn't work that way with God. We walk not into certainty but into mystery. We don't preapprove the journey but walk by faith into the great cloud of mystery.

Abraham was called to a pilgrimage of faith—to a land that God would only show him once he was on his way. The Hebrews sought freedom from slavery, but when their journey took them through a desert, they pleaded for a return to their former way of life. The disciples loved the notoriety of traveling with the popular Jesus, but when he was arrested, their dedication melted away in fear. Righteous Job was simply trying to live a life of faith and found himself tested with severe loss. One day, Isaiah was on a spiritual high after defeating the prophets of Baal, and the next day, wicked Queen Jezebel was hunting him down like a criminal on *America's Most Wanted*.

We want the outcome without the risk of the journey, but the journey transforms us, and the risk emboldens our faith. Abraham became the father of a great nation all because he walked into mystery. The Hebrew journey into the desert wasn't so much about getting out of Egypt as it was about getting Egypt out of the Hebrews. It was only after the death of Jesus that the disciples mustered up the courage to proclaim the message of Christ. Even after personal tragedy, Job's hope in God remained firm. After Isaiah's personal pity party, he encountered God on Mt. Horeb in a powerful way. There is no outcome of intimacy without a journey, and there is no gain without risk. There is no certainty, only mystery that offers us transformation.

Let's Be Crystal Clear

1. *God is no vending machine to be manipulated and controlled.*

   By necessity, dancing with the divine involves relinquishing our inclination for control. The Spirit moves as the Spirit wills, for mystery and certainty don't play well together. We do not manipulate the outcome or determine the path we travel. When we place "if, but, when" conditions upon the experiences we will accept, we are attempting to control God. Rather than dance with the divine, we bark out our demands and expect that God will dance to our rhythm, not the other way around. In essence, God is free to move in our life as long as God receives our permission and preapproval. This approach gets us nowhere and leads to exhaustion and disillusionment. In the end, God is no celestial vending machine, and our control tactics simply don't work.

2. *There is no worthwhile outcome without risk.*

   Yes, God is a mystery that cannot be controlled or adequately explained, yet our internal yearning, combined with the divine invitation to intimacy, nudges us to take risks and move forward in faith. Hearing the whisper of God requires that we risk a journey into mystery. As unnerving as it may seem, let go and allow the presence of God to envelope you like a cloud. It is the only way. Take a risk. Trust. Walk in faith, for the thrill of the journey will surprise and transform you.

3. *There is no quid pro quo relationship with God.*

God's presence is near us, within us, outside us, over us, beside us, under us, and beyond us. Because God is in us and we are in God, we live in the very presence of God. The issue isn't getting God, obtaining a blessing, or making God like us. We already have God and God already has us, for the very life of God resides within us. Stop trying to earn your way into the sacred presence. If you think that you must be more obedient, do more spiritual things, or believe right doctrine to experience God's presence, you are gravely mistaken. The invitation to journey with the divine is about becoming aware of this sacred presence that is already ours. The invitation is about opening our blind eyes, seeing with new vision, and living in the peace, power, and presence of God.

A Sacred Presence

Part of the problem is that our perspective is off kilter, and this influences our expectation of what the journey should be. Throughout this book, I refer to God as "divine," "the Spirit," or "a sacred presence." This choice, of course, is irritating to those who demand that I refer to God "properly" as a male father.

Scripture, however, uses all kinds of images for God. God is likened to a rock, a strong mighty tower, a shepherd, a mother, and a woman in labor. God even possesses a righteous right arm and other body parts while sitting on a throne in heaven. These depictions are not to be taken literally, for God is not in labor, isn't a literal rock, has no literal body parts, and isn't actually sitting on a literal throne. Think about it for a moment—the writers of Scripture experienced God's presence and tried to articulate that experience in the only terms they knew at the time. In a male-dominated world, the strong, in-charge, protective person was a male father, so God was described like that. The nurturing qualities they experienced can be seen in images of God as a mother or a shepherd.

Attributing humanlike qualities to God was the only way they knew how to share their God experiences in personal ways. It is the language of devotion and intimacy—human metaphors that help articulate sacred experiences that make sense to us. For instance, if someone says that God is watching over them or that they sense a warmth about them, it doesn't mean that God literally has a set of eyeballs or that God's temperature is warm as opposed to hot or cold. These are not literal descriptions of God, but metaphors and images that help us speak of the divine. God is mystery, and yet we have to speak of God somehow, so we use human images and human language to explain our experiences as best we can. We can only say that God is *like* this or that (simile), or use metaphors in our descriptions and explanations of God, but we can never say that God *is* this or that (certitude).

Focus on Experience

To me, it matters very little whether you refer to God as a shepherd, a father, a mother, a Spirit, or a sacred presence, for they are nothing more than metaphors of human language. Our culture may *prefer* certain images over others, but they are all merely *placeholders* for the concept of God, not the *essence* of Ultimate Reality. Christians spend enormous amounts of energy arguing and debating these things as if they have the corner on truth. Don't be fooled—God is a mystery and simply cannot be contained within the limits of human words.

About all that we can do is focus on our God experiences. Christianity isn't about believing correct doctrine but about experiencing the sacred presence of God. If the *nephesh* (life) of God is breathed into each of us, then all of us can experience this living presence within us. The issue is one of awareness of what is already ours.

Unfortunately, many Christians are caught up in the belief trap. They whip out a preferred interpretation of their authority source (Scripture) and work hard at believing the right things (getting their dance moves down) instead of experiencing God (dancing with the divine). If God is indescribable, unexplainable, and transcendent, then no articulation of God is wholly on target. Our focus, then, should be on experiencing the divine mystery, not on wasting precious time trying to figure out what can never be ascertained. God is beyond us and close to us at the same time, and although we are unable to explain the transcendent (beyondness) element, we can certainly experience the imminent (closeness) part.

Jesus was plugged into divine power, and although he expressed his experience in the cultural thought of his day, it was the anointing—his experience of the sacred presence of God—that he was attempting to convey. Although God is uncontrollable and indescribable, God is personally experienced, and that elicits the language of devotion and intimacy we find in Scripture. It prompts us to focus on *experiencing* the sacred presence of God, not on *explaining* that experience.

I AM

Assigned to be God's representative to the Egyptians, Moses asked God, "If I come to the Israelites and say to them, 'The God of your ancestors has sent me to you,' and they ask me, 'What is his name?' what shall I say to them?" God answered, "I AM WHO I AM" and further declared, "Thus you shall say to the Israelites, 'I AM has sent me to you'" (Exod. 3:13–14, NRSVue).

Is "I AM" the proper name of God, kind of like Bill, Jasmine, or Jayden? Does God even have a proper name, or is "I AM" trying to convey something deeper? Obviously, it is the latter. The phrase "I AM WHO I AM" refers to the fact that God is a ubiquitous sacred presence. Whatever term we use to name God (Lord, Adonai, Eternal One, and so forth) is merely a placeholder we have attached to the concept of God, not the proper name of a deity. God doesn't have a proper name because God isn't a "thing" wholly separate from the reality of our world. Rather, God is a sacred presence that permeates everything that is. How is that for a mystery too big for us to grasp? We want certainty, so we give God a name, but God isn't an entity like we are. God is more like a mysterious all-encompassing sacred presence that we walk into.

Spirit & Wind

Two images of God that I gravitate toward in Scripture are wind and spirit. In John 4:24 (NRSVue), Jesus informed the woman at the well that "God is spirit, and those who worship him must worship in spirit and truth." A spirit, by its very nature, is without physical body parts. God is nonphysical—a Spirit that moves and flows in our lives. The Old Testament likens God to wind (*ruach*) that is unseen and unconstrained, for it has no boundaries and moves however and wherever it pleases, and yet the *ruach* of God is profoundly experienced in our lives. This divine Spirit-wind hovered over creation in the book of Genesis. The point is that, like wind and Spirit that are unseen and unconstrained, God moves as God sees fit, and we personally experience this movement in our lives. Intimacy with God is about awareness, sensitivity, and connection to this blowing wind and moving spirit.

Love is another metaphor that we associate with God, as seen in 1 John 4:8 (NRSVue): "God is love." We say that God is love because we experience God in this way. We are, in effect, merely putting into human words and images an articulation of how we experience God. When we speak of God as Spirit or wind, we are using metaphors to say that we experience a mystery that is uncontrolled and unconstrained. The experience may be genuine, but the explanation is just that—a human attempt at describing a God experience.

Mystery

As Job endured tremendous suffering, his friend Zophar asked, "Can you find out the deep things of God? Can you find out the limit of the Almighty?" (Job 11:7, NRSVue). Paul recognized the mystery of God in

Romans 11:33–36 (NRSVue): "O the depth of the riches and wisdom and knowledge of God! How unsearchable are his judgments and how inscrutable his ways! 'For who has known the mind of the Lord? Or who has been his counselor? Or who has given a gift to him, to receive a gift in return?' For from him and through him and to him are all things. To him be the glory forever. Amen." Even the psalmist asked, "Who is like the LORD our God, who is seated on high?" (Ps. 113:5, NRSVue). The obvious answer is no one, no thing, nothing, nada. God is beyond us—a mystery. End of story. Period.

If God is a mystery that we will never figure out, maybe we should throw in the towel and call it quits. Why pursue what can never be understood? Just because we are unable to understand something doesn't mean that we cannot experience it. Why must understanding be the end goal? Why must it be a precondition to experiencing the divine? We are never asked to understand God, but we are invited to experience God. That is what intimacy is—relationship, closeness, and authenticity. Although we are not God, God is in us, and we are in God. That symbiotic relationship (abiding) is at work in our life, and it is the basis of divine intimacy.

God is like the wind that blows whenever, wherever, and however it wills. God is like a sacred presence that we deeply experience but cannot fully articulate. Unable to control or manipulate God in any way, we experience divine intimacy by walking into this cloud of mystery. Our deep yearning to commune with God arises from the very life of God within us—the *nephesh* God breathed into us at creation. It is a part of God's gracious invitation to intimacy. Dancing with the divine isn't something we command but something we simply experience. Where will God's invitation take us? We will experience peace, love, joy, communication, communion, and intimacy like never before, but the specific road we travel and the circumstances we encounter are not for us to say. It is a journey of faith—a journey into mystery.

In many ways, journeying with God is like an ocean so vast and deep that all we can do is float on our inner tube, relax, and allow the currents to take us where they will. We don't control the currents, make demands upon the currents, or set preconditions for the currents. As we move forward with courage and faith, the wind of God blows upon us, and nothing is more thrilling than feeling divine breezes upon our faith. Come and walk into the divine mystery and experience God afresh. Accept God's gracious invitation, and dance with the divine.

4

LIVING IN GOD

MY PERSPECTIVE OF GOD HAS CHANGED OVER THE years. As I grew older, gained valuable life experience, matured a bit, and gave serious consideration to the concept of God, my understanding and articulation of God morphed. This shift, of course, is positive and normal, for it means that my faith journey is progressing and changing me. I am growing, expanding, and ever moving forward. I started out on this road trip one way and now find myself at a totally different place. I haven't given up the faith. Heavens, no! Instead, my faith has deepened and is as solid as a rock. I only changed how I view God and articulate my faith. My God experiences have been a thrilling ride through life, for the journey itself causes our internal landscape to shift. If our faith journey doesn't change us from within, then what good is the journey? We might as well stay home.

Magic Eye

Spiritual journeys are about personal transformation—the discovery of new perspectives. It is a gift of sight that allows us to see things in a different light. I have personally experienced paradigm shifts on numerous occasions that not only gave me goosebumps, but also humbled me. Once you see from a new vantage point, you wonder how you ever missed it, for it all seems so evident now. That is growth. That is the maturing of faith. That is the transformational aspect of spiritual journeys.

I own a *Magic Eye* book that contains a gallery of 3D pictures that play tricks with the eye. Seeing the picture behind the picture requires a different way of looking at the image. Our initial outlook allows us to see one way, but when we adjust our focus, we see a three-dimensional picture rising forth that would have been missed had we not altered our perspective. It is a lesson to us that when our perspective changes, our view of what we see also changes. That is what happens in our quest for divine intimacy. Because the issue is one of awareness and sensitivity to God's sacred presence, we must adjust our sight if we want to see in 3D.

In a sense, God is like a *Magic Eye* book. We grow up viewing God one way, but our spiritual journey alters that perspective. This change is exactly what is supposed to happen. When we look beyond the physical realm, we see things in 3D. I am speaking not literally but figuratively. The *Magic Eye* illustration is helpful in getting across the point that when our perspective changes, everything is altered. We are meant to grow, change, and see things in new ways. We are meant to see in 3D.

A man was traveling home from work on a city commuter train. He used the time for quiet relaxation and decompression. On this particular occasion, the tranquility he sought was interrupted when a disheveled father and his small children entered the train. The father seemed out of sorts, while the rambunctious kids ran up and down the aisle. Clearly irritated by this lack of parental oversight, the passenger chastised the father for not being more attentive to his young children. They were, after all, interrupting his quiet time. The father apologized and revealed that he had just come from the hospital, where his wife had died. He was in deep thought as to how he would tell the children and care for them in light of the devastating loss.

In the twinkling of an eye, the passenger's perspective changed. The father who was once despised as an inept parent was now looked upon with understanding and compassion. We don't know what we don't know, and when our understanding moves to deeper levels of awareness, we can look at the same situation and see things in a totally different light. That is the *Magic Eye* effect of intimacy and the kind of God experience I seek.

Rethinking God

I grew up in a church that viewed God as a deity in the heavens, a totally separate being who resides outside the universe. In fact, most Christians understand God in this manner. In this traditional theistic notion, God sits upon a heavenly throne while executing his duties as CEO of the universe. God can handle such important responsibilities because God is big and powerful. God is portrayed as a male father who possesses a will, a mind, a body, and emotions, and who rewards and punishes according to perfect justice. Humans are finite, but God is infinite. Humans are lowly sinners, but God is sinless. Humans are limited in knowledge and power, but God is all-powerful and all-knowing. God, it seems, is a great big one of us, without the flaws and limitations intrinsic to humanity. Funny, isn't it, that we were created by God in God's image and turned right around and created God in our own image. In essence, we have envisioned God after our own likeness.

This view served me well in my younger days, when I was a novice in the faith, but it was unable to sustain me in the higher altitudes, where excess baggage is a hindrance. There came a time when I realized just how limiting this perspective really was. It dawned on me that my God was too small. I was merely ascribing human characteristics to God and articulating a particular religious view that brought me comfort and certainty, not expressing how God actually is. There is a difference between the reality of God and our explanation of that reality. These are merely human images applied to something we personally experience but don't understand. This realization changed my perspective and freed me to see the picture behind the picture. In my case, I had a great deal of unlearning to do, for the view out my spiritual windshield was obstructed by religious grime and spiritual bug guts. As is often the case, unlearning is the highest form of learning.

I originally viewed God as a separate being in the sky whom I tried hard to please. I wanted to *do things for* God, and far be it from me to be a disappointment. I sought to avoid sin and live a righteous life so that God would be pleased and proud of me. Obedience was viewed as the proper response of love, and if I obeyed, God would answer my prayers, reward me in heaven, and bless me with divine favor. You obey, you get blessed. You disobey, you receive divine chastisement.

You see, I saw God as outside this world, outside me. My role was to do things for God. The problem with that view is that I could never do enough, do it right, do it long enough, or do it with the sincerity God deserved. I was always playing catch up, living in deficit mode, and engaging in a never-ending cycle of trying to please the big guy upstairs. This perspective is shared by millions of Christians today, and it says a lot about their view of intimacy and the kind of God they serve. I no longer see God this way. Thank goodness, my perspective has changed!

Here and Near

This chapter presents a perspective that requires a bit more processing power to get our mind around, but this view enlarges our concept of God and frees us to more readily experience the divine dance. When God is viewed as an entity in heaven, separate from this planet, the only way God interacts with this world is to intervene in its affairs from the outside. God isn't "here and near" but "out there and up there." Through prayer, good behavior, and a host of other religious acts designed to appease the heavenly deity, we plead for this distant God to intervene on our behalf.

All too often, Christianity has been about getting God to do things for us, such as healing our diseases, blessing us with expensive new toys, allowing our children to get into prestigious colleges, or securing for us our dream job. This attitude produces a roller coaster of emotions. We praise God for the moments when we get what we want, wonder why God doesn't attend to our other desires, and ask why difficult circumstances befall us even though we prayed so hard for a different outcome. Apparently, we didn't exhibit enough faith, perform enough religious acts, or implement them in the correct manner.

I don't know about you, but this up-and-down stuff gives me motion sickness. Growing up, I was the kid in the back seat of the car with his head out the window, sucking in air while trying to keep the contents of my stomach in my stomach. This roller coaster ride to experiencing God is untenable, and it isn't at all what I promote or envision when it comes to divine intimacy. In fact, it is nothing more than a works-oriented, appeasement-driven, quid pro quo approach to a bipolar deity whose street address happens to be outside the universe, much like the "obedience" approach to experiencing God espoused by the author I mention in the previous chapter. If you obey, you gain intimacy. If you don't, too bad, so sad. There is nothing appealing about that at all.

God, however, is not an "out there and up there" kind of God. Instead, God is right here, right now, and always near us. God is inside us, outside us, over us, under us, beside us, through us, and beyond us. Although we are not God, we have the life of God within us, for we are partakers of the divine nature (2 Pet. 1:4). We have the Spirit of God, the power of God, the presence of God, and the love of God within us. In essence, this experience of God is exactly what Jesus possessed—not a far-away, disconnected God but a sacred power and presence that flowed from within. Jesus taught us what life could be like when plugged into this divine presence. We don't have to beg God for what we already possess. We don't have to earn what is already ours. We don't have to work hard at appeasing this deity in the sky by believing all the right doctrines and doing all the right things. God isn't a "thing" sitting in the heavens waiting on lowly humans to grovel in appeasement. God is a sacred presence that permeates all of life.

Indeed, God is a mystery beyond us in so many ways (transcendent), but God is also so close as to be within us (immanent). If we say that God is a being in the heavens, then we have taken transcendence to mean physical distance and have ignored the immanence of God. That perspective will never allow us to see God in 3D. God is most certainly transcendent, but not in a physically distanced sort of way, as if God's throne were a gazillion miles from Earth. By *transcendent*, we mean that God is a mystery beyond our ability to comprehend. The traditional theistic understanding of God is a dying view and one that hinders intimacy rather than enhancing it.

Panentheism

There is a biblical view of God that balances the beyondness of God with the closeness of God. It is often referred to in our day as "panentheism"—not "pantheism" but *"panentheism."* Pantheism means that everything *is God,* and that is not at all what I am referring to. *Panentheism,* on the other hand, breaks down like this: Everything (*pan*) is in (*en*) God (*theism*). This perspective isn't some New Age out-of-bounds philosophy but a concept grounded in Scripture. It might be illustrated this way:

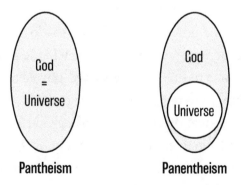

Pantheism   Panentheism

Paul's sermon to the Athenians declared the nearness of God, for "in him we live and move and have our being" (Acts 17:28, NRSVue). Do you catch the gravity of this statement? God isn't "out there and up there" but is something we live in, move in, and exist in. Mindboggling, isn't it? How can we be *in God* if God is a separate being living somewhere outside the universe? Panentheism is trying to say exactly what Paul is saying. The universe exists within God just as our diagram depicts, and yet God is much more than the universe. This concept addresses the transcendence of God and the immanence of God at the same time. The existence of all things is held together by an ultimate reality that is beyond us and close to us (Col. 1:15–17; Rom. 11:36; 2 Chron. 2:6; Job 38; Ps. 19:1–2; Jer. 23:24; John 1:2–5; Eph. 4:6).

God is said to be a living presence that fills the entire Earth. In Isaiah's vision, Seraphs declared that "the whole earth is full of his glory" (Isa. 6:3, NRSVue), and Ezekiel saw a similar vision (Ezek. 43:1–2). Psalm 19 notes that even the night sky announces the glory of God. Psalm 139: 7–10 asserts that there is no place where God's sacred presence is absent. God's presence is even seen in a storm, according to Psalm 29:3–9. Plenty of Scriptures point to the fact that God is not "out there and up there" but right here with us now, in this life. The "out there and up there" God is really a "here and near" God—a sacred presence that permeates all that exists, even us.

Wow, that is a deep concept, but the point is powerful, for how we view God affects our experience of God. If God is a distant deity who must be coerced into acting on our behalf, then the intimacy we seek is only experienced when the "out there and up there" holy curmudgeon decides to positively intervene on our behalf. This view produces an unstable roller coaster ride that lends itself to spiritual motion sickness, quite the opposite of the intimacy we seek.

However, when God is viewed as a sacred presence that permeates all of life, then God is perceived as being within us, beside us, over us, under us, outside us, through us, and beyond us. No longer do we plead for God's presence; instead, we recognize it in all things—even ourselves. We live in it and do not exist apart from it. No more spiritual roller coasters! We are in God, and God is in us. We already possess God's life, peace, power, and presence.

Fish that swim about looking for water don't realize that they are already swimming in it and breathing it in. Water is all around them, whether they recognize it or not. Similarly, God is like the air we breathe and the rays of sunshine that constantly bombard us. We live, move, and have our existence in God. Unfortunately, we look for an experience outside ourselves and miss the fact that we are already living in God. Experiencing God is all about recognizing and connecting with what is already within us. That is what it means to see in 3D, to see the picture behind the picture, the *Magic Eye* of God. When I talk about divine intimacy, I am referring to connecting with the sacred presence within, not begging a deity in the sky for an experience outside ourselves.

Compartmentalization

Humans have a tendency to compartmentalize life. We have the family compartment, the work compartment, the recreation compartment, the sports compartment, the spiritual compartment, and a host of other compartments. God is often viewed as an "add-on" to our busy lives. It is akin to fish looking for water when they are already swimming in it.

Placing God on a shelf all week long only to take God down on Sunday morning while driving to church isn't my view or experience of divine intimacy. That is compartmentalization, a foreign concept to Jesus, who experienced God as a sacred presence that influenced every fiber of his being. The hub and spokes of a bicycle wheel are a good way to illustrate this concept. If the wheel represents our life, God is the hub from which all the spokes attach and extend out to influence every area of our life. Jesus's connection to God wasn't separate from the rest of his life.

Instead, God became the source and power of his life, the sacred presence in which he moved, lived, and existed. God was the hub.

Living with awareness and sensitivity to this divine presence is not a series of isolated events, each assigned to its own compartment, but an interconnected way of living. It is the symbiotic vine-and-branch (abiding) relationship Scripture speaks of that is so empowering and life-giving.

Recognizing that we live, move, and exist in God's presence is freeing. God is the water, and we are the fish. We swim, breath, and exist in God. This awareness becomes a way of life, a way of living, and a way of seeing and being. Life is no longer lived in compartments, for the sacred power and presence of God touch every aspect of our lives. Are you ready and willing to walk in intimacy with God as a way of living life? Are you ready and willing to see the picture beyond the picture—the *Magic Eye* of God?

5

WELCOMING RESISTANCE

ANY JOURNEY OF WORTHWHILE PURSUIT INVOLVES obstacles and intentionality. Whether playing an instrument, taking up martial arts, speaking a foreign language, learning computer programming, earning a degree, improving parenting skills, overcoming bad habits, or increasing awareness and sensitivity to God, achieving the desired outcome entails plenty of roadblocks and heavy doses of intentionality. You don't just go to bed one night, wishing for your dream to come true, and wake up in the morning having achieved it. Life doesn't work that way. The goal is in front of you, obstacles lie in your path, and intentionality spurs you toward success.

Because divine intimacy is an issue of awareness and sensitivity to the sacred presence of God, our task is to become intentional about the journey and overcome resistance along the way. You can experience divine intimacy without earning a degree, securing permission from ecclesiastical bodies, learning a new religious system, or jumping on another hamster-wheel approach to earning God's favor. The last thing we need is another system that overpromises and underdelivers, where we get caught up in chasing rabbit trails that distract us from our quest. Increasing our spiritual sensitivity is a pursuit worthy of the effort, and that effort requires a willingness to confront pesky obstacles along the way. It is called a "journey" for a reason.

Can you imagine going through life without direction or intentionality? It would be like hopping into your car, putting it in drive, pushing the pedal to the metal, and zigzagging around like a drunk driver, spinning in circles, ramming into other cars, and driving on and off the road until the car is so damaged that it can go no farther. Traveling the path of least resistance is like driving a car without direction—you wind up going nowhere. Something is always competing for our time and attention, seeking to derail us from our best intentions. That's just how it is. But when intentionality gets behind the wheel, the vehicle can be steered to its proper destination.

For years, I felt guilty for not being a mighty prayer warrior. As a pastor, I was expected to be good at spending time in prayer. In reality, I failed miserably at it. I would get on my knees and fold my hands to pray, and my mind would wonder to and fro; my eyes would notice my rough hands, wrinkles, and hangnails; and I would find myself going through the motions and saying formulaic prayers filled with Christian jargon. My sweet hour of prayer was more like five minutes of hell. Had my parishioners known the truth, I would quickly have been labeled a bad Christian and an even worse pastor. I failed to be God's mighty prayer warrior, something they expected of me but not of themselves. How in the world was I supposed to pray without ceasing, as Paul instructed in 1 Thessalonians 5:17, when I couldn't even handle a few minutes?

I viewed prayer as one more item on my "good Christian soldier" checklist. It was my solemn duty to inform God of all the things I needed and wanted, even though God was supposed to already know this. I was, in essence, trying to move the hand of God, or, as I've said, treating God as a celestial vending machine who dispensed scrumptious goodies when the proper coins of prayer were inserted. No wonder prayer was so uninspiring for me. Even then, the Spirit may have been trying to tell me something, had I been listening.

I have journeyed beyond that infantile view of prayer. No longer do I see it as something I do; rather, prayer is something I live. Prayer means being in constant communion with the peace, power, and presence of God. The only way I know how to pray without ceasing is to be plugged into the presence of God as Jesus was. Prayer is a way of being, and in that sense, I pray without ceasing. It is the approach of *living in* God rather than *doing things for* God.

Obstacles will always seek to throw us off track, especially when divine intimacy is viewed as doing things for God. When our perspective of intimacy is focused on *living in* God rather than on *doing things for* God, the resistance we struggle to overcome is more internal than external, for we have to deal with such issues as fear, control, spiritual exhaustion, and the like. The way we overcome these internal obstacles is by welcoming them and meeting them head on. Unlike the subject of Monty Python's "Ballad of Brave Sir Robin," who "turned his tail and fled" when "danger reared its ugly head," we simply invite internal resistance to the table, and by doing so, we face the stiff winds head on.

What Are You Teaching Me?

At first glance, the thought of welcoming that which holds us back seems like the very last thing we should be doing. Instead of facing the stiff winds of resistance, shouldn't we find some sort of buffer to protect ourselves? The problem with hiding behind a wall is that nothing ever gets resolved, for that which is in the way *is* the way. We overcome by *welcoming resistance*, a phrase I need to explain.

Here is a typical scenario that plays out the moment you decide to be intentional about divine intimacy. You purposefully set aside a time and place to be quiet before the Lord. You are excited because you finally did it—you finally carved out time to quiet your heart, focus on God, and listen to the Spirit's voice within. This is a meaningful moment in your life, but instead of experiencing God, you experience fear as it wells up within and threatens to ruin your holy intention. What do you do?

You could abandon your quest, saying, "What am I doing? This quieting the heart stuff just doesn't work. I gave it my best shot, and it isn't for me." You could give up, grab your choice of beverage, hightail it to your personal comfort zone in the garage, get idiotized in front of the TV, or busy yourself doing things—anything. You could run to wherever you run to when things get uncomfortable. Instead of facing the stiff winds of resistance, you take the path of least resistance by scrambling off to your favorite bunker to escape the blistering winds.

It is far easier to hide behind a buffering wall where the winds are not as severe. But fleeing to momentary safety produces no long-term resolution and only serves to reinforce the path of least resistance. Rarely does anything get resolved in the buffer zone. Although we make no forward progress, we do *feel* safer in calmer winds until, of course, the next time we attempt to move forward in our faith. I readily understand this impulse to hide behind self-created buffer zones that offer comfort and familiarity. I once heard someone say, "There is no comfort in the growth zone and no growth in the comfort zone." That statement holds a lot of truth, and although we understand it intellectually, moving into discomfort is an act of courage. You'll never get out of a rut if you don't turn the wheel a bit and steer the car over the bumps. That's intentionality.

How do we grow, move forward, and get out of our rut when it comes to internal resistance? We simply welcome it as part of the intimacy process. Instead of sprinting to our bunker of comfort, we stay and face the resistance. It is a time for us to say, "Welcome, Fear, to my quiet time with God. I seek to learn from your presence in my life today and I invite the Spirit within to enlighten me." That is welcoming resistance. Simply acknowledge its presence, name it, invite it to the table, and learn from it. Most often, the fear subsides or the Spirit uses it to teach us. As psychiatrist Carl Jung once said, "Where your fear is, there is your task."

As we initiate our quest for divine intimacy, many forms of resistance seek to crash the party. About the time we have welcomed one uninvited guest, another one comes knocking at our door. Invite them all in with open arms and ask why they have crashed the party. Learn from their presence as you sit quietly with God. Internal resistance is merely a teacher of something within us that needs to be addressed. When resistance is allowed to sit at the table, then you, God, and resistance can have a holy conversation. Welcoming resistance simply means sitting instead of running, inviting instead of pushing away, and moving forward instead of hiding out in the bunker. See resistance as a teacher instead of a disrupter, and invite it to sit with you and God.

Welcome Fear

Fear is either a motivator or an immobilizer. At times, fear motivates us to act; at other times, it causes us to shrink. I once owned a house with a real wood fireplace in the living room. Drinking hot chocolate with the kids next to a warm, crackling fire is a wonderful memory.

One cold day, I asked my son to get the fire going for us. He was trained on how to do it, but this time, he forgot to open the flue. As smoke began to roll out of the fireplace, I realized that time was of the essence and asked him to open the flue quickly and release the smoke up the chimney. He froze. Although fear had immobilized him, my fear of a smoke-filled house motivated me to act quickly. I sprinted from my comfortable recliner, reached my arm into the fireplace, opened the flue, and saved the day. My son learned a valuable lesson about lighting a fire, and I realized that fear can be a motivator or an immobilizer.

We must welcome the immobilizing kind of fear—the kind that freezes us in a state of inaction and prevents us from boldly moving forward. When immobilizing fear strikes, we can't think, we can't move, we can't speak, and we often feel an inward sense of panic. This fear is the type many experience when asked to engage in public speaking. Their heart beats faster, they sweat, and they would rather die than publicly stand in front of others. Fear is an emotion meant to protect us, and although various intensities and phobias are associated with it, when it immobilizes our quest for divine intimacy, we must identify it, name it, welcome it, and face it head on.

Have you ever asked yourself why you are fearful—why the great immobilizer prevents you from experiencing something that you truly desire? Have you ever confronted fear by naming it, welcoming it, and asking what it is doing in your life? When fear raises its ugly head, our tendency is to flee. But welcoming its presence helps expose the lies that hold us hostage.

Because we already possess the life, Spirit, love, peace, power, presence, and acceptance of God, we can invite fear to sit with the life, Spirit, love, peace, power, presence, and acceptance within: "Come, Fear, sit with me and God for a while and let's see what you have to say in light of God's powerful presence in my life." Allow the Spirit to speak directly to fear, to speak directly to you about your fear, and to help you overcome its immobilizing effects. Don't flee. Don't run for cover. Instead, sit with it in the presence of God, and allow all that you are and all that God is to speak to your soul about it.

When the three of you (God, fear, and you) sit together for an internal conversation, the Spirit will whisper. You will sense an easing of tension, lies will be exposed, and fear's immobilizing grip will subside. You will learn a great deal about yourself and why fear is there to begin with. We can never get to that point if we don't face things head on, and we can face fear head on only by welcoming it into our conversation with God.

Welcome Control

Not only does fear seek to make a show-stopping entrance when we get serious about divine intimacy; our thirst for control also seeks to jump on stage and play a leading role. We often get a picture in our mind of what intimacy with God should look like. As long as the journey stays within the white lines we have established in our mind, we are good to go. When the Spirit steers us in a different direction, moves us off road, takes us on a deserted highway, or leads us into congested areas, we sense that our control is waning, and we slam on the brakes.

Have you ever known control freaks? Are you one of them? They are not easy to be around because everything must meet their approval. If they aren't happy, then nobody's happy! They make sure of that. In the end, they know best and see themselves as always being right. Calling them out on their controlling tendencies doesn't go over well, but everyone knows how tightly they grip the scepter of power.

Control freaks may struggle with divine intimacy because they are asked to walk into mystery and experience something they are unable to control. Controlling God, commandeering the spiritual journey, and directing Spirit winds simply can't be done. Yet at every juncture, control freaks face the urge to dominate, dictate, manipulate, and delegate. Needless to say, their experience of intimacy is hindered by their constant urge to take the reins.

It reminds me of the first wedding rehearsal I performed as a young minister. It became very clear that the mother of the bride didn't agree with how I approached my task. I brought everyone up front for introductions and prayer, provided clear instructions, and ensured that everyone knew where they were to stand on the stage. That is why they were up front to begin with. This approach ticked her off, for she wanted me to start at the back with the bride entering. She didn't get her way and sought to control me and the rehearsal. I made certain that the wedding party knew where they were to stand before practicing their walks down the aisle. After the rehearsal, this controlling mother said to me, "I have never seen it done this way before. It was organized and easy. You did an excellent job!" She was forced to surrender her controlling tendencies and, in the end, experienced a pleasant and unexpected outcome. Well, at least one of us did!

There is a difference between discipline and control. *Discipline* is the ability to avoid distractions and keep on track. We all need discipline in our lives in order to regulate ourselves toward reaching goals and living in alignment with our values. It is positive and enhances our ability to experience divine intimacy. *Control*, on the other hand, is the desire to dictate things outside ourselves toward a preferred outcome. It reeks of manipulative qualities and negatively affects our quest for divine intimacy.

This devious tendency rises up within each of us—some more than others. When it seeks to play a leading role in our experience of God, we can simply welcome its presence and say, "Welcome, Control. What are you trying to teach me today by your presence? Come, sit at the table with God and me, and let the Spirit speak to us." We identify it, name it, welcome it, and allow the Spirit to enlighten us.

Welcome Exhaustion

Another barrier we face in quieting our hearts is the sheer exhaustion we experience from our frenzied pace of life. About the time we sit down to be still, our eyelids become heavy as lead, and we find ourselves nodding off. We don't intend to conk out, but we are so run-down that we become like a car on its last leg. Any time we slow down to approach a stop sign, our engine sputters and dies.

If our bodies sputter when approaching the stop signs of life, we would do well to assess how our life is lived. Reconsidering our priorities and discovering what consumes our time and attention is a good first step. Often, the tyranny of the urgent takes precedence. How many plates can a person juggle before they all come crashing down? As the hamster wheel of life spins faster and faster, we do our best to adjust, but sometimes it is all we can do just to hang on and not get thrown off.

Think of the mother with three little kids who yearns for intimacy with God. The children are tugging at her heart for time and attention as she is changing diapers, running to soccer practice, keeping house, buying groceries, being a good wife, trying to maintain her own sanity, paying the bills, putting gas in the car, keeping up with technology, being a daughter and a sister within her own family of origin, and on and on and on. If you are a single mother, multiply all of this by a factor of five, and you get the picture. Progress was intended to make life less stressful, but instead of slowing down, we simply spin faster and faster on the merry-go-round of life.

Waving a magic wand doesn't work, but we can bring our exhaustion before the Lord? "Welcome, Exhaustion. What are you trying to teach me today?" When exhaustion presents itself, invite it into the conversation with you and God. Allow the Spirit to minister to your weary soul. You will know deep inside what changes are needed in your life. That's how the Spirit works. There is no audible voice, no blinking neon sign in the window—just a gentle nudging from within, a sense that your heart knows what to do. In the meantime, if you fall asleep while trying to quiet yourself, then you probably need to sleep. Your body is telling you something. Self-care is an essential element of being healthy in body, mind, and spirit. Listen and make necessary changes, but don't let exhaustion become a barrier that prevents you from dancing with the divine.

I am struck by how the sacred presence of God always enlightens us about those items we welcome to the table of three-way conversation. If you are tired, I get it. Been there, done that. But I have never let it stop me from my pursuit of divine intimacy. I don't feel guilty when resistance rises up, for that is a part of being human. There is no such thing as a perfect human, for we all carry scars from our travels. So, I simply welcome resistance, ask what it is trying to teach me, and allow a three-way conversation to occur between me, God, and the resisting element. God has a way of illuminating my heart and helping me know what adjustments are needed.

Welcome Discomfort

Ever notice how comforting the familiar is to us? We put the toothpaste back in the same spot, we sleep on our preferred side of the bed, we sit in the same seat in church, we eat comforting foods that make us feel good, or we grab a hot cup of coffee in the morning to wake us up. Years ago, when my father first took us to church, a long-time member informed my mother that she was sitting in her spot. How dare my mother sit in this woman's familiar and comforting pew! My mom had accidently invaded this woman's comfort zone. The parishioner would rather offend newcomers with her self-centered rudeness than lose her familiar nesting ground. There is something to be said about routine and familiarity, for nesting in the familiar is, indeed, comfortable. But there is a danger to this mentality.

Although our nesting tendencies can bring a sense of comfort, the dark side occurs when we are unable or unwilling to explore unfamiliar territories at the Spirit's leading. The comfort of the familiar can become a leash around our neck that prevents us from leaving the yard. We always want to bring God down into our yard so we can play within the safety of our own turf. But exploring the mystery of God always takes us down unfamiliar paths and across terrain that we have never seen before. Sometimes, they are roads we would never travel if left to our own devices, and at other times, the sights are breathtaking. When the comfort of the familiar becomes a roadblock to new horizons of faith, we impede the movement of God in our life. Intimacy with God requires a willingness to explore new territories beyond base camp.

This book challenges us to explore unfamiliar terrain and to think of things differently. It will be a real test for some who demand spiritual guardrails, safety nets, and welfare harnesses around their torso. We like the security of being able to opt out when things don't work like we think they should. If the Spirit leads us down a path we don't want to travel, we jump off the train, give up too soon, or make flimsy excuses for why we didn't fully follow. That is the dark side of the comfort zone, but make no mistake about it: If we desire intimacy with God, we must allow the Spirit-winds to blow as they will. We must risk moving outside the guardrails and safety features we have built around our life.

What do we do with discomfort when the Spirit leads us to places we have never been before? We do what we always do—we invite discomfort to the table. "Welcome, Discomfort. Why are you here? What have you to teach me today?" We allow discomfort to sit at the table. We allow the Spirit of God to commune with our soul and enlighten us. We allow the peace, power, and presence of God to do their good work, but we don't allow discomfort to derail our intimate journey with God.

I admire your quest for divine intimacy. It is a good and godly desire, a pursuit worthy of the effort, even though obstacles of resistance cry out for the path of least resistance. Intimacy with God is experienced when we identify the resistance within, name it, welcome it, and look for its teaching as we bring it into a three-way conversation with God, the obstacle, and ourselves. The Spirit has an uncanny ability to speak to our heart and help us move forward.

One must be intentional about welcoming resistance. Without the courage to invite fear, control, exhaustion, and discomfort to the table for a three-way conversation, we continue to wallow in a frozen state. Life, however, is a journey. Divine intimacy is always prompting us toward forward movement rather than a static state of nesting. Resting on our spiritual laurels isn't helpful for reaching the level of intimacy we seek. We experience God as we journey and move forward. It takes courage to face the many obstacles seeking to maintain the status quo. You have the courage within you to be intentional, for within you is God, and God can overcome any resistance that comes along.

6

MEANS & ENDS

A DISTINCTION BETWEEN THE MEANS TO DIVINE intimacy and *the end* of divine intimacy is of paramount importance and cannot be overstated. People easily confuse the two and often mistake the means to intimacy for intimacy itself. The two are entirely different. One is simply an avenue of travel, while the other is the actual destination.

Some examples may help clarify this distinction. When you turn on the faucet for a thirst-quenching glass of water, you are experiencing the difference between the means and the end. The faucet and the water line are merely the means for obtaining water, and yet we are after the water, not the water line. The pipes only transport the water; they are not the water. We turn on the faucet (the means) to experience refreshing water (the end). Don't confuse the means of transport with the water itself.

A map functions the same way. The lines represent roads and become a tool for helping us arrive at our intended destination. Actually arriving at our destination is the end, whereas the map is merely a means for helping us get there. The same could be said of a car. The vehicle isn't the destination but a means of transport. We don't confuse the map or car with the actual destination itself.

If I told you that Scripture or self-surrender, for example, was merely a tool or avenue for experiencing divine intimacy, it would be a mistake to think of it as the actual intimacy itself, for we would be confusing the tool with the outcome, the means with the end, the pipes with the water, and the map with the destination. Unfortunately, many fall into this trap. They believe that experiencing God is all about the means, when it is actually about the end. This confusion is prevalent within the church, and the church does little to distinguish between the two.

Christianity is a religion filled with symbols, such as the cross. Symbolism is present in the liturgical colors of the Christian calendar, in the placement of the pulpit, and in water baptism and communion. Fire and flame represent the Holy Spirit, as does a dove. White robes are worn during baptism to symbolize cleansing. We light Advent candles to symbolize hope, love, joy, peace, and the light of Christ. Everywhere you look, there are symbols.

There is nothing inherently wrong with symbols, for their role is to merely point to something beyond themselves, like a yellow road sign alerting us to a dangerous bend in the road ahead. The wedding ring on our finger symbolizes love. The graveyard marker reminds us of a deceased loved one. A steeple symbolizes a church building. Rock piles in the Old Testament symbolize events where God's presence was especially felt. Judaism, the birthplace of Christianity, is filled with symbolism. Life is filled with symbols. They are everywhere.

Symbols are merely road signs that point us toward something beyond themselves. If you point to the beauty of a full moon, you don't focus on the finger doing the pointing, and you certainly don't confuse your finger with that which it is pointing to. In a sense, that is exactly what happens in the church. We exchange the reality we seek for the symbol itself. This misconception is dangerous, disillusioning, and deceiving. Christianity talks an awful lot about the moon, but its people and practices focus on the pointing finger. The essence of intimacy (the end) has been replaced by the symbols of intimacy (the means).

This problem has existed throughout church history. Israel had an abysmal record of veering off into ditches, so prophets rose up as the reminding voice of God. The sacrificial system veered off into becoming a substitute for divine intimacy. The religious leaders of Jesus's day replaced divine intimacy with legalism. The replacement of God is nothing more than idolatry all wrapped in glittery religious attire. Anything that replaces the reality of God in our lives, no matter how religious it may be, is nothing but idolatry all dressed up for a night on the town.

Understanding the difference between the means of intimacy and the end of intimacy is essential. This distinction is akin to the difference between the water and the water pipes, the destination and the map, the reality and the symbol, the moon and the finger pointing to it. This distinction is vital because the second half of this book presents various avenues for experiencing divine intimacy. They are nothing more than helpful tools, not intimacy itself.

By elevating various means to the level of an end, we make the mistake so many before us have made: We equate a system, a symbol, a ritual, a belief, or a practice with divine intimacy. No wonder so many are spiritually exhausted! They have been pursuing pointing fingers, all the while thinking they were pursuing God. What a colossal disappointment to realize that you have been climbing the wrong mountain.

When life with God becomes more about pointing fingers than it does about the moon, we become hardened, rigid, unloving, and judgmental. Instead of nurturing the abundant life of God flowing in and through us, we have simply created a ranking system that allows us to feel superior to others. I follow the system better than you do. I give more money than you do. I attend church more often than you do. I serve more than you do. I know more about religious symbols than you do, and on and on and on it goes. It becomes a nauseating game of one-upmanship and is nothing more than mistaking the means for the end. It is devastating to our faith.

The beauty and wonder of the moon inspire us, not the pointing finger. Although we engage in a lot of pious moon talk, the way we live and practice our faith is all about pointing fingers that have little to do with the wonder of the moon. Moon talk, it seems, merely becomes the accepted jargon for finger-living. We miss out on moon inspiration because of our finger focus. We want to be at the top of Mt. Everest, but we have climbed the dirt mound in the backyard.

Jesus had to contend with this mentality in his own day when the religious leaders focused on the wrong things. For them, intimacy with God was all about doing things for God, about strict obedience to rules and regulations, about rituals, about religious minutia, and about external showmanship. Although they engaged in moon talk, they lived a finger-pointing life. They replaced the end with the means and missed out on the wonder and inspiration of the full moon.

I am so grateful for the example of Jesus. He knew the difference between the two. He experienced the wonder of the moon—intimacy with God. He was not enslaved to a system, a ritual, or a practice. Instead, he focused on experiencing the abundant life of God within. He was plugged into the peace, power, and presence of God. This connection to the Spirit became his way of living and being. It was divine awareness and sensitivity at their best. Jesus marveled at the moon!

This book presents various tools for increasing our awareness and sensitivity to the divine, but we dare not confuse them with intimacy itself. Life is far too short and the experience of God far too important to waste our time and energy climbing the wrong mountain or focusing on pointing fingers.

Remember this distinction: We are after intimacy itself, not the means of getting there. We dare not confuse the two.

7

A WAY OF LIFE

ALL TOO OFTEN, WE CONFUSE THE CHURCH, its symbols, its doctrines, and its practices with God. In doing so, we make an unwise exchange that is nothing more than idolatry—substituting the lesser in place of God the greater. The means replaces the end.

We not only mistake the church for God but also confuse heaven with God. God is either localized in the church on Earth below or in heaven above. Both views fall short because God's presence is not confined to a place, a thing, or a practice, no matter where it is located, for the sacred presence is everywhere—within us, beside us, above us, below us, and beyond us. We dare not confuse the *means to intimacy* with *intimacy itself*. Instead, we seek to know the sacred presence of God, for that is what divine intimacy is all about—becoming aware of and sensitive to the peace, power, and presence of God.

This goal implies that divine intimacy is a perspective—an internal awareness that changes our seeing, being, and living. It is about connecting with God in this life, in the present now, not outside it in some future place called "heaven." Our quest is to live each moment in this dynamic awareness. That is the end we are after; all else is merely a means.

Divine intimacy is not a fleeting moment we work hard to achieve. It is not some earned trophy we proudly display along with all of our other polished accomplishments. It is not an addition to our life but a *way of life* that is lived *within this life*. The call of the gospel is to live differently—to live in a vine-branch relationship whereby we connect with the abundant life flowing into us and out from us. It is a way of living, a way of being, and a way of seeing through the clear lens of a new perspective. It is an outlook that changes everything.

Living from the Center

When I speak of intimacy with God, I am not referring to transitory moments of inspiration or foggy feelings of religious fervor, for this implies that God's presence is far away or something we must capture before it fades, like dissipating steam from boiling water. We become storm chasers trying to lasso a tornado with the hope of intersecting with the thrill of God.

In this mountaintop mentality, we are religious junkies, desperately seeking our next spiritual high. Deficient in so many ways, this view sees intimacy as outside ourselves—something that occurs occasionally but isn't the norm. It turns us into spiritual thrill seekers instead of possessors of God's presence. The emphasis is on working hard to obtain intimacy rather than on opening ourselves up to what we already possess. It is a "try-harder" approach that always results in failure and exhaustion. Like a dog chasing its own tail, we never seem to catch what we are after. Divine intimacy, on the other hand, entails living from the center, from the core of who we are, and that is internal, not external. Many search high and low for this intimacy but fail to realize that the sacred presence is already within their possession.

Living according to our values is often mistaken for living from the center. Balance, we are told, is reached when our external actions align with our internal values. Apparently we can be "balanced" without ever scrutinizing the quality and nature of the values themselves, no matter how contorted they may be. It is possible to hold perverted values, live according to their twisted nature, and be considered "balanced." But we must account for the quality and nature of our values.

Living from the center is a much deeper concept. Values are merely a spoke in the wheel that is influenced by a whole host of things, including circumstances, family of origin, religion, geographical location, and so forth. Divine intimacy means being in communion with the peace, power, and presence of God in such a way that its life-altering power changes us from the inside. Our perspectives, actions, values, thoughts, passions, and every fiber of our being are connected to the abundant life of the Spirit—that which forms and changes who we are at the center.

In other words, we are back to the hub-and-spoke illustration. Divine intimacy means allowing the presence of God to permeate every aspect of our lives—even our values. Aligning internal values with external behavior is a positive act, but I would suggest that our actions may already be aligned with our values; they just may not be aligned with the *verbalization* of our values. There is a difference, for we do what we truly value, no matter what we verbalize. We can speak of our value of generosity and be so stingy as to "squeeze the crap out of a buffalo nickel," as my uncle used to say. In reality, what may need alignment is the *verbalization* of our values with the way we *actually* live.

My point isn't even about values, other than to say that living from the center goes deeper than our values, for divine intimacy means living from the hub, not the spoke. Center living means drawing from the deep reservoir of the Spirit. The hub is the presence of God, while values are a spoke. As the hub flows through us and radiates out from us, its powerful presence influences every spoke of the wheel.

The Authentic Self

Another important aspect of living from the center is becoming reacquainted with our authentic self. I am convinced that Christians don't know themselves very well. They live in the shadow of expectation. They believe the lies of a media-rich, computer-enhanced advertising world. They listen to what others tell them they are in light of the cacophony of voices vying for their attention. Thousands of mixed messages bombard them on a daily basis.

This confusion adds layers to our identity crisis and impedes the discovery of our authentic self. Living from the center means living authentically with who we are and how we are made, doing and being what we were designed to be and do. I once thought that the issue was confusing "who we are" with "what we do," but I am now convinced that we are more confused than ever regarding the "who we are" part. In essence, we identify ourselves by all the wrong metrics. It is as though we have blinged out our identity with all sorts of glittery decorations that distract from the natural beauty endowed upon us by the creator.

Divine intimacy is always about authenticity, and as we grow in awareness and sensitivity to the peace, power, and presence of God within us, we become acquainted with our authentic self, for the concealing layers are peeled back like an onion. The only thing we bring to divine intimacy is ourselves. Our ego, our false self, and all of our shiny bling and glittery decorations fail to secure intimacy. We don't barter for it, buy it, control it, or manipulate it. No, we come before the divine naked, open, exposed, and unashamed. We simply connect to it like a vine connects to a branch. Living from the center involves the discovery of our authentic self, our passion, our worth, our gifts, and all that we are created to be. It means coming to terms with ourselves, loving ourselves, and becoming our best selves because we are in God and God is in us. Divine intimacy allows us to see ourselves clearly, to live with ourselves dearly, and to be ourselves wholly.

Alive in the Spirit

Divine intimacy is about transformation, and even Paul recognized the Spirit's role in this internal reconstructive work. For Paul, the Spirit brings life to our deadness, wholeness to our brokenness, and freedom to our bondage. Whatever prevents us from living from the center is addressed by walking in the Spirit. Once again, we are back to the hub-and-spoke illustration. The hub is the peace, power, and presence of God, while the spokes represent various aspects of our life. In Galatians 5, we are encouraged to walk in step with the Spirit (the hub), which, in turn, produces the fruit of the Spirit—love, joy, peace, patience, kindness, generosity, and faithfulness. Paul commented further, "If we live by the Spirit, let us also be guided by the Spirit" (Gal. 5:25, NRSVue).

Paul understood the power of this sacred presence to transform us. Divine intimacy means walking in step with this sacred presence, communing with the abundant life offered through the vine-branch relationship, and living in the anointing power as Jesus did. It is a way of living, being, and seeing—a continuous connection with the divine whereby we are alive in the Spirit and to the Spirit.

Example of Jesus

Scripture presents numerous individuals who lived in this anointing power, such as Moses, Joshua, Abraham, Elijah, Elisha, Isaiah, and others. However, no one stands out like Jesus, who is said to be "the image of the invisible God" (Col. 1:15, NRSVue). The life Jesus lived caused others to see him as a mystic—a spirit-person who could perceive, interact with, and relate to a dimension of reality beyond the physical one right in front of us. However we say it—whether Jesus was plugged into the divine, filled with the Spirit, or connected to God in vine-branch fashion—we understand that it was the life of God flowing through him and out from him that touched so many lives.

Not only did others notice his heightened spiritual awareness; Jesus seemed to be quite aware of it himself. The Gospel of Mark, for instance, includes an appearance of the Spirit at Jesus's baptism and temptation experience in the wilderness. We also find Jesus rising early, withdrawing to a quiet place, and spending long hours communing with God in prayer. In Mark 6:4, Jesus compares himself to the prophets—mouthpieces for God who were in touch with the Spirit. According to the Gospel of John, Jesus moved, acted, and spoke at the moving of

God, "for I have not spoken on my own, but the Father who sent me has himself given me a commandment about what to say and what to speak" (John 12:49, NRSVue). It is reminiscent of Acts 17:28, NRSVue: "In him we live and move and have our being." Divine intimacy means living, moving, and having our being in God, just as Jesus moved, lived, and had his being in God.

The sacred dimension of life that Jesus experienced wasn't something outside this world or outside himself. Rather, the power and presence that flowed within him and out from him were experienced in the here and now. His level of spiritual awareness allowed him to live the way he did, and this divine intimacy conferred upon him the power to love and inspire others—so much so that the authors of the New Testament portrayed him as the Messiah, the anointed one, the Son of God, the Immanuel, the very image of God.

Christians have a tendency to discount the life of Jesus as an anomaly. After all, he was Jesus, and so we often think of him in superhuman terms—a combination of God and human, an amalgamation of sorts that would actually make him neither God nor human. No, Jesus was in all ways like us except that he lived in the anointing of God to a greater degree. That life is why he was called "the Christ." In other words, his connection and communion to the divine presence gave him the power to live life differently. It wasn't that he was born that way or was a one-of-a-kind spiritual freak. He was in all ways like us but connected to the Spirit, and that's what made the difference. Jesus was called "the Christ" because his communion with the divine allowed him to see the world through a new set of lenses. It allowed him to personally experience the abundant life he offered to others. When divine intimacy touches our life, as Jesus exemplified, we can, in turn, positively influence others. Life begets life.

Seeing Jesus as an anomaly misses the point of his communion and connection with the Spirit. All that we admire about him was due to his sensitivity to the divine presence. The same sacred presence Jesus experienced continues to be inside us, above us, under us, around us, and beyond us, for wherever we go, God is. Paul echoed a similar thought in Galatians 2:20, (NRSVue): "It is no longer I who live, but it is Christ who lives in me." The Christ power, the anointing, that sacred presence of God wasn't available only to Jesus way back in the day. That divine presence is accessible in the here and now, and it is this divine intimacy that Jesus calls us to experience.

Brother Lawrence

I was introduced to Brother Lawrence during my Bible college days many years ago. I still possess the thin little paperback about him that we read in class, even though its pages are highlighted, faded, and falling apart. I have kept it all these years because of its impact upon me, for Brother Lawrence practiced the presence of God in daily life. He spent most of his time washing pots and pans in service to his monastic brothers. He understood that God is experienced in the ordinary course of our lives.

Growing up in seventeenth-century France, where the Thirty Years' War had ravaged central Europe, Brother Lawrence was forced by poverty to join the army, where food and a small stipend were assured. His wartime experiences set him on a powerful spiritual journey. Having been injured, he left the army and found his way to a Carmelite monastery in Paris, where he served as a lay brother in the kitchen and also repaired sandals. These simple duties were performed by a simple man in simple service to God and others.

The amazing thing about Brother Lawrence that has stuck with me all of these years was his humble awareness of God's presence. He wasn't interested in wealth or status and was assigned menial duties, yet he sensed the presence of God in powerful ways. It matters little what our status is in life, for divine intimacy is available to all, no matter who we are or where we are on life's journey.

Brother Lawrence experienced this intimacy whether he was in the kitchen cleaning pots and pans for his Carmelite brothers or kneeling before the holy Eucharist. For Brother Lawrence, God was always near, and he was sensitive to this presence. He lived in it, rejoiced in it, and was enveloped by it. The life and joy of God flowed out from him. He practiced the presence of God in his life—in this life. In the highs and the lows, in the common and mundane aspects of the journey—from dirty pots and pans to the holy Eucharist—God was present.

Brother Lawrence serves as a wonderful reminder that divine intimacy is experienced in the ordinary here and now. Countless others throughout history and in our present age have lived in daily communion with God. Although they have come from all denominations, all faiths, and all walks of life, they have had one thing in common: a deep awareness of and sensitivity to the peace, power, and presence of God. If you know someone of whom you would say, "They know God. The sacred presence flows through them in a way that inspires me," you are, indeed, blessed.

Life Is the Journey

Too much energy is expended looking for God outside life—outside this world. Yet God is in the here and now—in the present moment. Mistakenly, many believe that God is only experienced on the mountaintops of life, so they scramble from peak to peak, forgetting that God is with them in the plain, in the valley, in the ascent, in the descent, at the top of the mountain, at the base of the mountain, and around the side of the mountain. God is found in this life, and how we journey is paramount to our experience of God. We shouldn't hide in a secluded cave or bury our head in the sand to escape from this world, for it is in our journey through life that we encounter the Christ. Experiencing God as a way of life, a way of being, and a way of seeing during this journey is what it means to practice the presence of God.

If all you are looking for is another mountaintop experience to add to your collection of thrilling religious encounters, then you don't understand what divine intimacy is all about. Experiencing the abundant life of God encompasses sitting and walking, climbing and descending, living in the plains, and trekking across mountains, ravines, and rivers. Intimacy with God is a way of life while living your life—in this life. It is not a moment *of* time or a moment *in* time but *time itself*.

Perspective: A Summary

This chapter is the last of the foundational concepts in our pursuit of divine intimacy. These foundational chapters are intentionally placed at the beginning of this book because our view of God and our expectations of divine intimacy affect our experience of God. It is my attempt to set the train on the right track so that misunderstandings and false expectations won't derail God's work in our life. It is my way of helping you let go and allow the winds of God to blow as they will in your life. The next section describes various avenues for experiencing God, but before we head in that direction, here is a brief summary of the crucial concepts that have been presented so far:

1. We sense an internal yearning for divine intimacy that comes from God.

2. God graciously invites us to intimacy.

3. Divine intimacy is a journey into mystery that we do not control or understand.

4. Instead of doing things for God, intimacy is about living in God.

5. The quest for divine intimacy always involves resistance, which we welcome into a three-way conversation (you, God, and the resisting element).

6. There is a difference between the means to intimacy and intimacy itself. Don't confuse the two.

7. Divine intimacy is a way of seeing, being, and living in our journey through life. It is not something we do but something we are.

The Pathway

8. Solitude & Silence   75

9. Simplicity & Surrender   95

10. Prayer & Scripture   121

11. Pain & Pleasure   141

12. Margin & Challenge   171

13. Odds & Ends   195

14. The Primacy of Love   225

8

SOLITUDE & SILENCE

Solitude and silence are time-tested avenues for experiencing God. The psalmists declared, "Be still, and know that I am God!" (Ps. 46:10b, NRSVue). In the vernacular of our day, we might say it like this: "Calm down, slow down, quiet down, sit down, shut down, and listen to God." It is good to get away from the distracting hustle and bustle of life and to quiet our hearts, minds, bodies, and pace, so we can listen with our souls instead of our ears. Practicing solitude and silence is a worthwhile endeavor that enhances our experience of divine intimacy.

To seek out silence and solitude is no easy task, and yet it is the part in our divine relationship where we take charge of our actions. We all have the same twenty-four hours in a day. We work. We raise a family. We have obligations and responsibilities. We are entangled in a web of relationships. We relax, seek pleasure, and so forth. Although we are pressed from all sides into good, better, best decisions, the choices are ours to make, along with their ensuing consequences. Where do our priorities lie? Although we yearn to know God, we often hold priorities that hinder our desire from becoming a reality. Solitude and silence are the "best" choices in our pursuit of divine intimacy.

Like you, I struggle with good, better, best decisions every day. Intellectually, I *know* what is important, but I struggle to carve out the appropriate time for what is best. Although the length of my day is the same as yours, I am keenly aware that my choices lead to the reality of my experiences. The single most important thing we can do in our quest for divine intimacy is to carve out time for solitude and silence.

Extroversion & Introversion

The solitude part is easy for me, for I am an introvert. My very nature gathers energy from being alone and engaging in the quieter world of inner thought. It is the silence part that gets me, for although I appear serene on the outside, my mind is racing the Indy 500. A lot goes on upstairs in that head of mine, which someone once described as a mental interstate with no speed limit and heavy traffic. I'm always thinking, strategizing, planning, and analyzing. Mentally, I put the pedal to the metal, and it is difficult for me to slow down!

I am a list person and can't imagine having a day without a goal to accomplish. For me, each day begins at zero, and I feel like a failure if I don't manage to accomplish something worthwhile. I do my best thinking, writing, planning, and mental work while I am alone, usually in the middle of the night. Even though I am all by myself and quiet as a church mouse, the internal noise from the mental interstate is so loud at times that divine whispers are drowned out.

Solitude and silence can be even more difficult for extroverts, whose natural lifeblood is to seek interaction with the outside world. These "water fountain" folks need to be externally invigorated. Interaction is their world, their life, and the very core of their being. To them, solitude and silence can feel like standing in the corner for a time-out while their internal battery quickly drains.

Whether introverted or extroverted, we all have our personalities, preferences, and idiosyncrasies that interfere with this avenue of hearing from God, and yet sitting in solitude and silence is a time-tested path for discerning divine whispers. Although it may be harder for some and easier for others, it is a positive path worth the investment of time. It is a best choice.

Back-Pocket God

Sometimes, we stick God in our back pocket and feel good about having God go with us wherever we go. After all, God is close by, and if we ever need anything, we just whip God out of our pocket, present our need, and then put God back in our pocket. That's not much of a spiritual relationship with the divine. How would you feel if your son or daughter did that to you? What if they liked having you around only when they needed you, not because they valued you, loved you, yearned to be with you, or desired deep relationship? If you are a back-pocket parent, and the sole reason for your existence is to provide things for your children, then that's not much of a relationship. Who wants to be relegated to a back-pocket status?

Is our relationship with God of such importance that we are willing to give it the serious time and attention that it deserves? Do we seek communion, intimacy, togetherness, and communication with the divine, or do we seek a back-pocket God we strategically manipulate as the need arises? The way we get to know others is by spending time with them in relationship. It is the same with God, except communion with the divine often occurs through solitude and silence. This idea is difficult for us to grasp because with all other relationships in life, we engage our physical senses in tangible ways. Because God is a sacred presence that we cannot see, touch, taste, smell, or hear in the traditional sense, the relationship is from Spirit to spirit—wordless soul conversations. In essence, we are connecting to the life of God within us, which is internal, not external, and it often takes solitude and silence to recognize and experience divine whispers.

The Silent Scream

Have you ever tried to sit in silence? It is more difficult than you might imagine. I often offer a moment of silence during church services, and I can tell that for many, those twenty seconds are excruciatingly painful. Other than sleeping in their bed at night, many don't know what to do with twenty seconds of silence, let alone twenty minutes. Even when space is carved out for such endeavors, many are so exhausted from the whirlwind of life that they simply fall asleep. Their bodies seek to catch up from a lifestyle of continuous sleep deprivation. It is the unintentional consequence of living without margin.

Silence can be challenging simply because we are not physically conditioned for it or because we have never intentionally engaged in the practice and don't know what to do. We feel as though we are not accomplishing something when so many items fill our to-do list. It is like driving through western Nebraska—long, dull, boring, and devoid of much interest or beauty. We can't wait to get through the state as our insides scream, "When will we ever get through this Godforsaken land?" Let me be quick to say that Nebraska is a wonderful state with wonderful people, but if you are not used to its natural beauty, the drive can be tortuous for weary travelers who view it only as a barren wasteland to be endured.

I often joke that I would be a missionary to the far ends of the world if I felt the call of God to go—but I could hear God more clearly if that far-away land were in the Virgin Islands and I were staying at the Marriott. But Nebraska? A desert? A wilderness? Solitude? Silence? How boring is that? Give me island sun and sand! I am sure that I could commune with God while lying on the beach in my Speedo. Even I cringe at that mental picture!

Solitude and silence can feel more like Nebraska than the Virgin Islands, for they require that we still our heart, focus our attention, and deal with ourselves. That is hard work, and our souls silently scream, "How quickly can I get out of this Godforsaken land?" until we recognize that our journey isn't about the Virgin Islands *or* Nebraska. It is about being in the presence of God on the most intimate level, where there is only you and God, and that kind of experience is frightening and refreshing. It takes time, practice, and patience to learn the value of solitude and silence, for we initiate the quest while screaming on the inside, only to find ourselves longing for the replenishment this Spirit connection provides. We start the journey in Nebraska and wind up in the Virgin Islands. It may be uncomfortable in the beginning, but we soon find ourselves aching for it.

Naked Before God

In solitude and silence, there is just you and God, for we bring nothing to our quest for divine intimacy other than ourselves. We leave our to-do list behind—there is nothing to accomplish, no people to converse with, and nothing that will impress God. We are powerless and lack control. We are not telling but listening—being still and knowing within our soul. We are the student, not the teacher. In silence, we bring before God our naked selves with all of our flaws and blemishes, all of our needs and desires, and all of the good, bad, and ugly. We sit in God's presence with nothing to hide and nothing to hide behind. We simply put ourselves out there and say, "Here I am, God. Speak to my heart," and then we listen for the whispers to nudge our soul. In vulnerability and nakedness, we are exposed to the pure light of God's presence.

Many of us function in life as a Martha when we are asked to sit at the feet of our teacher like Mary (Luke 10). Martha kindly opened her home to the itinerant Jesus, but instead of sitting in the presence of the wise sage, she was distracted by all of her preparations for the visit, so much so that she complained to Jesus that her sister, Mary, wasn't helping. Mary, however, ignored the distractions and chose to sit at the feet of Jesus while soaking up his teaching like a sponge. Martha was far too busy *doing things* for the teacher than *actually listening* to the teacher. Which is better, distraction or listening? Mary was commended for making the better decision. Sitting in solitude and silence is one way we can emulate Mary in a Martha world. It is a best choice.

Sediment Settles

I grew up in a blue-collar river town in Iowa. Unlike the crystal-clear mountain streams of Colorado, the Des Moines River that meanders through my hometown is anything but refreshing and inviting, for it is nothing more than a continuous flow of brown liquid filled with who knows what. But if you collect a jarful of this murky stuff and let it sit undisturbed for a while, an interesting phenomenon occurs: Soon, the sediment settles. The contents at the bottom of the jar turn brown, while the water above becomes clear. Solitude and silence produce a similar effect in our life.

We seek to know the peace, power, and presence of God within us, but, like the brown water of the Des Moines River, our life is filled with distraction, debris, trash, junk fish, and a whole lot of things we would rather not think about. We long for crystal-clear water flowing true and pure, but we park our camper along the Des Moines River instead of the Colorado mountain streams. Solitude and silence allow internal sediment to settle so we can see clearly, listen intently, and become alive to the life of God within us.

As long as the sediment and debris remain stirred up in our life, we experience the brown river of a Martha world. Solitude and silence help us separate the sediment from the water. Why make time for solitude and silence when so much is already on our plate? Because the "so much on our plate" muddies the river of life flowing through us. In solitude and silence, soul conversations can occur without the overwhelming distractions that so easily drown out the Spirit's voice.

Self-Knowledge

As the sediment settles and our ability to spiritually discern becomes clearer, there we are, just us and God. No filters, no log jams, no distractions, and no sediment to cloud our vision. We are merely open books and empty vessels inclining our heart toward a whispering God. All that we have gathered about us in this life and all the baggage we travel with is nothing but clutter, sediment, and Martha preparations. Listening to God in silence is a grand release, for we simply sit at the feet of our teacher and allow the Spirit of God to communicate with our spirit.

We learn a great deal about ourselves through solitude and silence, for in the stilled waters of the soul, we get a sense of what really matters and what divine promptings are all about. You see, when the sediment settles, we encounter the pure presence of God, and in an environment of honesty and authenticity, we can be real before the creator. When all the clutter we once gripped so tightly is cast aside, we realize that we are enough. We are worthy all by ourselves—just as we are—the best of us and the worst of us all entwined. All those things we relied on to prop us up are nothing but clutter. The Lord says to us what Jesus said to Martha: "You are worried and distracted by many things, but few things are needed—indeed only one" (Luke 10:41–42, NRSVue).

For most of us, life is chaotic. We are a raging brown river that churns from within. Solitude and silence provide a place of safety where all that we have stuffed deep inside, such as control, hurt, emptiness, depression, brokenness, anger, and the like, is allowed to rise to the surface. Divine whispers have a way of peeling back the onion so self-acceptance becomes real and our vine-branch connection to the peace, power, and presence of God becomes essential.

We can live in the grip of this world's clutter, or we can live in the abundant life Jesus spoke of and experienced himself. The clutter of this world is temporary and bogus, whereas life in the Spirit is true and eternal, for we are connecting to an infinite God. One is easy and worthless, for it is the path of least resistance and requires nothing of us. The greater outcome, however, involves a different approach where we intentionally choose the best path, not the easiest one. Solitude and silence don't always come easily, and traveling deeper into self-understanding often takes us through difficult terrain. Yet what good is a path that only gathers more clutter and prevents us from being our best selves? It is worth absolutely nothing, for it is merely a snowball rolling downhill and collecting more snow. We just keep building bigger and bigger snowballs when what we need is warm weather and sunshine to melt the ice encasing our heart.

Solitude and silence are places where divine soul conversations occur. These conversations lead to transformation, and once we get a taste of the Spirit's work in our hearts, we long for more. Intimate dialogues of the soul go beyond words as the finite communes with the infinite. We meet God on the base level of existence—our naked selves encounter the powerful presence of that which has always existed. The light of God's Spirit brings comfort, peace, and direction. It also exposes those things that prevent us from discovering our worth and being our authentic selves. As the divine presence draws us in, we begin to see ourselves, others, God, and life itself with new eyes.

Intimacy with God is ultimately about transformation—changing, shedding, and casting aside the old and choosing to walk in the new. In essence, it is a process of divine re-creation, for once our eyes have been opened, we cannot *not* see. As we allow the Spirit access to levels of our being that we are unable to enter on our own, transformation occurs— the result of divine soul conversations. We don't transform unless we are aware, and this sensitivity to God changes us. It is one way we know that we have communed with the divine.

This sort of transformation occurs not by walking the path of least resistance but by consciously choosing the best—intentionally leaving the Martha preparations behind to sit at the feet of Jesus, as Mary did. Intimacy with God doesn't come through incessant talk, constantly doing things for God, or mastering the doctrines and rituals of the church. Divine intimacy comes through awareness of and sensitivity to the Spirit. Solitude and silence help us become more alive to divine soul talk.

The Spirit's Voice

An audible voice from God? I've never heard one. Ever! Audible words are for the ears, whereas communication with the divine occurs through wordless soul talk. If you happen to hear an audible voice, then good for you, but most of us relate to God through faith and sensing the Spirit's moving upon our soul—what I call "whispers."

I knew a woman who would constantly say, "God told me" this or that, as though God were audibly relaying directions into her left ear. I have no doubt that people sense the moving of God in their life, but I don't go around arrogantly proclaiming, "God told me" this or that in nearly every sentence. This woman had a friend who also heard from God in the same way, and it was an interesting dynamic to watch them compete with one another over who actually heard God the most. It was spiritual jealousy and another irritating way Christians can act superior to all others. They loved to make "God told me" pronouncements. After all, they were the ones who heard from God, whereas others weren't nearly as spiritual. It was nauseating.

To top it off, most of the things God told them were flat-out wrong. One of the women announced that God had told her to move to a specific city and accept a specific job. When that didn't happen, I inquired whether God had made a mistake or whether she had misheard God's voice. A cogent response was not forthcoming. Although this type of incident happened countless times in her life, it was of no concern to her, for she was able to proudly declare, "God told me," even if her on-base percentage was low.

The movement of God in my life isn't like that at all, and to be honest, I think that this "God told me" shtick is just another game of religious one-upmanship that I am unwilling to play. I relate to the divine internally, not externally, and religious showmanship has nothing to do with it. In other words, I sense movings, nudges, stirrings, impressions, and a sense of deeply knowing. No audible words are spoken to me, and yet my soul senses the Spirit moving. That is soul talk, or how the whispering Spirit communicates with our spirit. Does God speak to me? Not in an audible, one-upmanship sort of way. Instead, the whisper of God is more of an internal sensing that rises from within. I just *know*, and the reason I know is because I have made myself spiritually available—silent enough to notice the stirring within my soul.

A Long Tradition

Rather than being new phenomena of recent discovery, solitude and silence are steeped in a rich history. In other words, people have been performing these behaviors for a very long time. It was the way of the prophets in the Old Testament. In solitude and silence, the word of the Lord came to them and brought clarity, direction, vision, and guidance. They didn't enter big cities, crowded venues, or local pubs for inspiration; instead, they sought the whisper of God in solitude and silence.

John the Baptist, the forerunner of Jesus, also sought solitude and silence. Like his Old Testament predecessors, he entered the wilderness of silence. The prophets had been quiet for four hundred years, and Israel was anxious to hear from God. Then, along came John the Baptist.

We think of John as the fiery preacher who confronted hypocrisy within the religious elite, but we often forget how he got to that point. His path led through the wilderness of Judea, where he discerned his mission, message, and method. There is not much to eat in the desert, and so John feasted upon locusts and wild honey, not ribeye, champagne, and caviar. There is not much to do in the desert except be by yourself in solitude and silence. It was the perfect place to be still and listen for divine whispers. John heard them, and from this wilderness experience arose a remarkable ministry of baptism and proclamation.

Jesus experienced his own wilderness journey. After being baptized by John, the Spirit led him into the desert for forty days and forty nights. Once again, we see how solitude and silence can become a pathway for divine intimacy. When distraction is at a minimum, intimacy with God is at a maximum. Through solitude and silence, Jesus affirmed his identity, calling, mission, and ministry. He emerged from the desert knowing who he was, what he should do, and how he should go about it. Immediately, he began to fulfill his purpose. This wasn't a one-time occurrence in his life but an ongoing aspect of his experience of God, and he often rose early to connect with the sanctity of solitude and silence.

Solitude and silence are also a huge part of monastic tradition. Around the year 270 CE, Anthony the Great moved into the Egyptian desert to become a hermit for God. He became known as the founder of desert monasticism. By the time of his death in 356 CE, thousands had followed his example. He became a model for the monastic practices we see today, whereby many pursue a life of tranquility, solitude, and devotion to God. I am not suggesting that we become monks or literally move to a desert, but it goes to show that people connected solitude and silence with divine intimacy. I often engage in personal retreats at monasteries. I love the surroundings, the quietness, and the life of simplicity. The sparse guest rooms and the joyful sound of silence provide the ambiance I need for realigning my heart.

Not only is there a long tradition of solitude and silence within Christianity, as demonstrated by the prophets, John the Baptist, Jesus, the desert fathers, and monasticism; the practice is highly prized in other religions as well. Solitude and silence seem to be universally recognized as pathways for experiencing God.

Elijah the Prophet

Perhaps the prophet Elijah, in 1 Kings 19:1–13 (NRSVue), demonstrated the value of solitude and silence in a most relevant way:

> Ahab told Jezebel all that Elijah had done and how he had killed
> all the prophets with the sword. Then Jezebel sent a messenger
> to Elijah, saying, "So may the gods do to me and more also, if I
> do not make your life like the life of one of them by this time

tomorrow." Then he was afraid; he got up and fled for his life and came to Beer-sheba, which belongs to Judah; he left his servant there.

But he himself went a day's journey into the wilderness and came and sat down under a solitary broom tree. He asked that he might die, "It is enough; now, O LORD, take away my life, for I am no better than my ancestors." Then he lay down under the broom tree and fell asleep. Suddenly an angel touched him and said to him, "Get up and eat." He looked, and there at his head was a cake baked on hot stones and a jar of water. He ate and drank and lay down again. The angel of the LORD came a second time, touched him, and said, "Get up and eat, or the journey will be too much for you." He got up and ate and drank; then he went in the strength of that food forty days and forty nights to Horeb the mount of God. At that place he came to a cave and spent the night there.

Then the word of the LORD came to him, saying, "What are you doing here, Elijah?" He answered, "I have been very zealous for the LORD, the God of hosts, for the Israelites have forsaken your covenant, thrown down your altars, and killed your prophets with the sword. I alone am left, and they are seeking my life, to take it away."

He said, "Go out and stand on the mountain before the LORD, for the LORD is about to pass by." Now there was a great wind, so strong that it was splitting mountains and breaking rocks in pieces before the LORD, but the LORD was not in the wind, and after the wind an earthquake, but the LORD was not in the earthquake, and after the earthquake a fire, but the LORD was not in the fire, and after the fire a sound of sheer silence. When Elijah heard it, he wrapped his face in his mantle and went out and stood at the entrance of the cave. Then there came a voice to him that said, "What are you doing here, Elijah?"

This section of Scripture follows Elijah's Mt. Carmel challenge to the prophets of Baal. It was his way of urging the oscillating Israelites to make a decision about which God they would follow. The God of Israel answered Elijah's call in an extraordinary manner, whereas the prophets of Baal were unable to summon their god to action. With victory in hand, Elijah captured and killed the false prophets of Baal.

King Ahab informed his wife, Jezebel, of Elijah's actions, and she became furious. She was a dominant voice in Ahab's ear and had persuaded him to abandon the worship of Yahweh. In fact, she had many of Israel's prophets killed in her quest to replace Yahweh with Baal. Upon learning of the demise of her prophets and realizing that her plans were now frustrated, she threatened the life of Elijah, and in fear, he fled for his life into the wilderness.

There he was, alone, physically exhausted, and emotionally spent from the Mt. Carmel incident. After serving so faithfully, he was now hunted like an animal, and his very life was in danger. He was angry, down in the dumps, and self-loathing, and he desperately needed to hear from God. He entered the wilderness not of his own accord—out of love or intentionality—but out of necessity and crisis. He was at a breaking point. Like Elijah, we are often forced into the wilderness by painful life circumstances, and sometimes we voluntarily seek God's voice out of love and intentionality.

In silence, Elijah sat under a solitary broom tree and quickly fell asleep out of sheer exhaustion. Sometimes, we do the same thing when our bodies are depleted and we are in need of rest. It is difficult to engage in soul conversations when exhaustion overtakes us. Fatigue is often a matter of lifestyle, and sometimes it is a matter of crisis. Either way, our ability to spiritually discern is enhanced when we are physically and emotionally healthy.

After some much-needed rest, an angel awakened Elijah and offered him food for the journey. A journey? What journey? Elijah simply wanted to pout in self-pity, but God had other plans for him at Mt. Horeb. Hearing from God always involves a journey, and most often that journey leads through a wilderness of the soul. For Elijah, it lasted forty days and forty nights, and this journey of solitude and silence prepared him for the soul conversations he would encounter.

The passage specifically informs us that God was not heard in the mighty wind that could split rocks, nor was God heard in the consuming fire or the forceful earthquake. After these noisy and formidable events arose, sheer silence followed, and that is when the word of the Lord came to Elijah. That is when deep soul conversations occur and when God sets us back on the right path. Elijah didn't ask for guidance or direction; instead, it arose from within. That's how soul conversations work. Our own voyage into solitude and silence is an inward journey, and when the sediment settles—when the winds, fires, and earthquakes in our life dissipate—we are faced with sheer silence, and that is when we are able to discern the whispers of God.

Practicing Solitude and Silence

We like the thought of solitude and silence, for they sound so spiritual. We grasp their value, but we often don't know *how to do it* or even *how to carve out time* for them in our busy schedules. The "how to do it" part is pretty simple, for the issue isn't so much doing it the right way as it is simply doing it. The point is to dance with the divine, not to waste time perfecting our dance moves. As Scripture notes, "When you search for me, you will find me; if you seek me with all your heart" (Jer. 29:13, NRSVue). Sincerity of the heart is essential, but some additional pointers may also prove useful.

Set aside a time and place for this practice. The time can be whatever works best for you. In my case, the middle of the night or early morning hours are when I am most alert. I find my way to a comfortable chair, where I can remain undisturbed. The place and time can be anywhere, as long as you are comfortable and undisturbed.

To elevate its importance in my life, I establish a routine or ritual that helps mark this time as sacred. Some people sit with legs crossed, arms on their knees, and hands open to signal their readiness to receive. However, this position is uncomfortable for me, for my legs fall asleep and my lower-back problems are exacerbated. I prefer to sit in a comfortable chair. I don't lie down; otherwise, I am tempted to sleep, and I want to remain alert.

I often begin by making pleasant sounds on my kalimba, an instrument of African origins. It is my way of initiating the period of solitude and silence. In essence, I am declaring, "My time of solitude and silence before God begins now." I know a woman who lays a circular rug on the floor, sits in the middle of it, and begins her sacred time by playing a Native American flute before the Lord. It is her way of creating sacred space and initiating her time of listening. Others ring a bell, strike a meditation gong, burn incense, or recite a meaningful Scripture. The issue is not only to create a sacred place and time that bring consistency to your practice but also to establish a routine way of initiating the moment.

I take in several deep breaths as a way of relieving stress and providing oxygen to my body. I bow my head and say a simple phrase that invites the Spirit to speak to me, such as "Here I am Lord," "I am listening," or "Come Lord." Find a short phrase that is meaningful to you and reflects your open invitation to the Spirit's voice, your readiness to listen, and your expectancy to hear. Then, listen.

It takes time and practice to quiet the mind. All kinds of extraneous thoughts rise up, from to-do lists, to sporting activities, to our children, to whatever. This quiet time isn't for planning your day, rearranging and prioritizing all the things you have to do, or doing anything else of the sort. Those thoughts are not helpful, and I let my mind know that I will not be focusing on them. I am trying to remove the clutter, not focus on the clutter. I want to go deeper into myself rather than continually skimming the surface. I am completely focused on being an open, empty vessel, ready to receive. If I am having trouble doing this, I simply invite the Spirit to help me. When extraneous thoughts arise, as they often do, I let them pass through rather than giving them my time and attention.

The point is that I am lowering the level of mental clutter. I want to focus sharply on catching the impressions, nudges, movings, and knowings of the Spirit. Emptying myself doesn't mean landing in some unconscious, catatonic, hypnotic state. It means that I move from cluttered and scattered thinking to quiet and calm mindfulness. I do not hold on to thoughts that distract me from listening. When my mind is occupied with surface noise, my soul is unable to hear the whisper of God, for divine intimacy is a wordless soul conversation.

Not only do I dismiss cluttered thinking; I actually receive items of resistance, such as fear, anxiety, anger, and the like, as they arise and linger. I invite them into a three-way conversation (me, God, and the resisting item). Resistance often alerts me to issues that need to be addressed in my life, and I invite the Spirit to speak to me about them. This becomes one way the sacred presence of God restores us, heals us, and allows us to deal with significant internal issues that prevent us from fully experiencing divine intimacy.

Dismissing cluttered thinking and inviting resistance to sit in the light of God's presence are profitable, but how do you know when you have heard from God? Wouldn't it be nice if some sort of tangible indication helped us out, such as a ringing bell, a flashing neon light, or an audible voice? It doesn't work that way. Instead, this connection to the divine involves subtle, wordless soul whispers that cause us to go deep within ourselves. Listening with our soul instead of our ears takes us far below the surface to the level of our raw, naked existence before God. When no clutter is competing for our attention, soul conversations can occur.

Soul talk is qualitatively different from surface talk. Soul whispers emanate in peace, love, strength, and humility. It is the Spirit bearing witness to our spirit (Rom. 8:16). You learn to recognize the Spirit's voice as you would recognize the voice of a treasured friend. Sometimes, the voice comes in the form of a question, a direction, a prompting, a nudging, an impression, or a soul knowing. It is an inner dynamic that we learn to recognize.

I was pastoring a church in northern Minnesota when I first discovered the inner dynamic of solitude and silence. I didn't possess the maturity or knowledge that I have today, but even then, I could tell that there was something to this solitude and silence stuff. As I spent time in this spiritual practice, I sensed the promptings of God, from big things, like new discoveries about myself, to small things, like sensing the need to seek forgiveness from those I had wounded. It was a special time in my ministry. Unfortunately, over the years, I allowed the clutter of life to drown out the whisper of God. I lived in my own strength and was led by my own feeble mind until I woke up from my spiritual slumber and once again recognized the importance of soul conversations. It is never too late for divine intimacy, and solitude and silence can help us discern God's presence.

Carving Out Time

We may have answered our *how to practice* solitude and silence question, but we still must address *how to carve out time* for such an endeavor. No one disputes how busy life can get, and yet we seem to find time for the things that matter to us, such as hunting, fishing, family, football, woodworking, writing, baking, church, eating, crocheting, and so forth. All too often, however, we allow the tyranny of the urgent to reign as we struggle to organize our time and see our way through the chaos and disarray.

I hate to be so crass about things, but hey, we seem to find the time for what matters. For most of us, it is really a matter of priority and commitment rather than actually fitting it into our day. It is like me and my guitar playing. I would love nothing more than to be proficient on this beautiful instrument, but I don't make time to practice, learn, and improve. The issue isn't that I don't *have* time for it; the issue is that I don't *make* time for it. It simply isn't a priority in my life. So, I dabble here and there, enjoy a few licks and cool chords, but I don't experience the full wonder of the instrument.

I often search for those moments when I can pause in solitude and silence, and although that helps me be mindful of God's presence throughout the day, I can't rely on that to carry me for the long haul. That is a good practice, but it is not the best practice. It is akin to dabbling here and there with a guitar, armed only with a few chords, rather than being proficient in the craft. Why settle for a few scattered minutes throughout the day when you can experience the full thrill of divine intimacy? Whether we are forced into this practice out of a crisis of necessity or we engage in it out of love and intentionality, our experience of divine intimacy will be nothing but a few chords on the guitar until we take it seriously. We must choose between good, better, and best. We can't continue doing the same old thing day after day and expect a different result. Setting the sails for the direction we want to go involves intentionality and commitment.

I am not trying to make you feel guilty—heavens, no. I struggle with carving out time just as much as you do. I am just trying to be honest with you and with myself. If communing with God doesn't rise to any level of significance in our life, then, well, what can I say? Until it becomes a priority, it won't become much of a reality. Give it a try and see whether it doesn't bring you spiritual refreshment.

If you have the blessed responsibility of raising children, I understand the enormous amount of energy it takes to be a good parent. Been there, done that. This is a spiritual discipline where spouses and significant others can help one another in their quest for divine intimacy. Thinking of soul conversations as an essential part of life instead of a spiritual add-on will help you become a better parent and spouse. Spending time with God is a wonderful way to calm yourself, recognize God's presence, increase your capacity to love, and become a better, more fulfilled you.

It is the difference between dieting and making a lifestyle change. If you think of solitude and silence as another unpleasant diet that must be strictly adhered to, one that restricts you from the more important things you want to do, then your outcome has already been deter-mined—failure. But when you embrace solitude and silence as a way of living, they become ingrained in you as indispensable elements of life.

Begin with a few minutes each day and increase the time as you become adjusted to it. You don't have to practice the schedule of the monks who rise in the early hours and maintain specific times of prayer throughout the day. I actually tried the monastic schedule for a while and failed miserably at it. No, start slowly and work your way up to five, ten, or fifteen minutes. If this practice becomes one more thing on your to-do list for pleasing God, then you have missed its intent and spirit. See its value. See God's value. Make time to cultivate this divine rela-tionship so that soul conversations become a part of your daily living. This practice will become so precious that you won't be able to imagine a day without it. In fact, you will long for personal retreats where you can spend even more time in solitude and silence—an hour, a half day, or an entire weekend.

This practice isn't the only way to commune with God, but it is a pathway that mystics throughout the ages have found helpful. Solitude and silence become profound means to experiencing God—paths that grate against the grain of modern culture, where thinking small, follow-ing the herd, and accepting the path of least resistance are the order of the day. Through solitude and silence, we are challenged to give our undivided attention to God's presence. We are challenged to deeper self-knowledge so that we can feel comfortable in our own skin, sense the love of God, and value our own intrinsic worth. We are challenged to live with intentionality and experience the divine intimacy for which we have longed. Start today, even if it is only for a few minutes. Choose a place, a time, and a routine that mark this time as holy, and protect it as a sacred space. God is inviting you to soul conversations through solitude and silence. It is time to dance with the divine.

9

SIMPLICITY & SURRENDER

Simplicity! Now there's a refreshing concept! It resonates deep within because we are so stressed out, so busy, and so preoccupied with the insignificant that we feel empty inside. As complex as life can be, we frequently yearn for a return to simpler times.

For some, simplicity means cleaning house and decluttering one's life from surplus possessions. How many knickknacks can a person own? Neat freaks absolutely abhor clutter, and local nonprofit organizations become a yearly mechanism for disposing of excess goods. Christmas gifts given in December often wind up in the spring garage sale. After all, one person's junk is another person's treasure.

My mother is one of these neat freaks, and, to her credit, she keeps a very clean house. Our garage was spotless—no clutter, no tools, no garbage cans, no workbench, no storage items whatsoever. It is a wonder Dad was allowed to park the family car in there. The only tools we seemed to own were a hammer, a screwdriver, and a saw. Cleanliness didn't allow for more. A garage was meant to be clean, and we could have eaten off the floor had we chosen to do so.

As the ultimate cleaner, my mother diligently cleans her floors on a daily basis, and most often there is no dirt on the cleaning pads, for the floor was in pristine condition before she began. Once, when I was lying on my back, fixing the plumbing underneath her kitchen sink, I laid one tool down to work with another. When I reached for the tool I had laid aside, I couldn't find it. She had already seized it, dashed downstairs, and put it away. Is simplicity the same as cleanliness?

Although my mother views simplicity in terms of less physical clutter, I have a tendency to simplify complexity. Over the years, I have exercised my mind to the detriment of my body. Now that I am older, it is a constant struggle to keep myself physically fit. For instance, what should I eat? What food is healthy? What is my approach to eating? Views strongly advocated by one doctor are quickly disputed by another medical expert. Such contradictions are annoying. What in the world are we to believe? It amounts to information overload, which is constantly shifting—like trying to shoot a 3-pointer into a moving basketball goal. Hard to do, and very frustrating.

Information overload doesn't cut it for me. I need something much easier to comprehend and follow. So, I simplify complex data into understandable principles that facilitate my quest for health. When it comes to healthy eating, I simplify it to eating as many vegetables as I want, lots of salads, real rather than processed foods, lean meats, and so forth. Simple approaches work for me, but is that what we mean by simplicity—moving from complex to simple?

For others, simplicity is akin to being a simpleton—that is, someone who is naïve and spouts off shallow answers to the difficult issues of life. I've come to think of some church folks as "bumper-sticker Christians" because they reduce everything to slick slogans rather than drinking from the well of deep mystery. Is this what simplicity means—being unaware of profound realities?

Each of these perspectives holds some truth. If we are being honest, we possess far more than we need, and decluttering can be liberating. From a spiritual perspective, we do well to unburden our soul from those items that prevent us from experiencing the joy of God. Cleaning our spiritual house is a worthwhile endeavor. Moving from complex to simple also has its benefits. Life is indeed complex, and data overload is real. We are not computers crunching numbers all day long but emotion-laden beings interacting with the shifting facets of life. It is true that we can get so far into the weeds that we miss the sunshine from above. The main thing, however, is to keep the main thing the main thing. We dare not avoid life's difficult issues, but there is something to be said for focusing on simple, powerful truths.

Although each of these perspectives has its upside and downside, the simplicity I refer to in this book is one of the heart—an internal simplicity that brings joy and helps us experience the abundant life of Christ. It is an uncluttering of the soul. It is living life from the center. It is a perspective, not a place. It allows the peace, power, and presence of God to flow through us. It is an internal unencumbering that frees us to pursue God to the fullest. It is living in such a way that our life, thought, conduct, and speech move at the impulse of God. Simplicity is not so much something we do as it is something we are.

Simplicity of Heart

Internal simplicity stems from the heart, and its freedom leads us toward practicing the presence of God. In fact, the heart seems to be what God is most interested in, for it is the wellspring of everything else. Proverbs 4:23, (NRSVue) notes: "Keep your heart with all vigilance, for from it flow the springs of life." When a compass aligns itself with true north, every other direction is easily discerned. Similarly, simplicity of heart clears a pathway for experiencing God as our true north.

That God is interested first and foremost with the heart shouldn't come as a surprise. It has always been that way, and yet we are tempted to focus our attention on everything but that. It is entirely possible and far too easy to perform religious acts and speak in pious terms without inclining our heart toward God. We see plenty of examples of this in the Old and New Testaments.

When King Saul failed to obey the Lord's command, the prophet Samuel stated, "Has the LORD as great delight in burnt offerings and sacrifices as in obedience to the voice of the LORD? Surely, to obey is better than sacrifice and to heed than the fat of rams" (1 Sam. 15:22, NRSVue). In other words, outward sacrifices without the requisite inward posture don't compare to a heart bent toward the divine. We focus on the outward while God meets us at an internal heart level. This same principle is well stated in God's choosing of David to replace Saul as king: "For the LORD does not see as mortals see; they look on the outward appearance, but the LORD looks on the heart" (1 Sam. 16:7b, NRSVue).

In Hosea 6:6 (NRSVue), the prophet spoke against Ephraim and Judah: "For I desire steadfast love and not sacrifice, the knowledge of God rather than burnt offerings." Again, God delights in the heart, not outward religious acts disconnected from a purity of motivation. This position couldn't be any clearer than in Micah 6:6–8 (NRSVue):

> With what shall I come before the LORD, and bow myself before God on high? Shall I come before him with burnt offerings, with calves a year old? Will the LORD be pleased with thousands of rams, with ten thousands of rivers of oil? Shall I give my firstborn for my transgression, the fruit of my body for the sin of my soul? He has told you, O mortal, what is good and what does the LORD require of you but to do justice and to love kindness and to walk humbly with your God?

It seems pretty clear in the New Testament as well that God is interested in the heart. One day, Jesus ate a meal with despised tax collectors and unworthy sinners—at least, that is how the Pharisees perceived the event. As religious perfectionists, they were disgusted by such a scene and sought to discredit Jesus. Who in their right mind would eat a meal with dreadful tax collectors, whose sole purpose was to seize money from oppressed Jews and hand it over to the filthy Romans wrongfully occupying their land? What holy man of God would dare sit for a meal with those who failed so miserably at keeping pace with the pious standards of the religious elite? To this arrogance and misplaced zeal, Jesus responded, "Go and learn what this means, 'I desire mercy, not sacrifice.' For I have not come to call the righteous but sinners" (Matt. 9:13, NRSVue).

Countless examples within Scripture reveal God's concern for our internal welfare. As things would have it, much of life boils down to the health and well-being of one's heart. You would think that we would get the point by now. The last thing we need is another religious hoop to jump through to experience the life of God flowing through us. Rules, regulations, and rituals can encumber the heart with great burden, and when that burden becomes too heavy for our heart to bear, we are in danger of breaking. We don't need heavy hearts—we need freed hearts, hearts that are light, happy, unburdened, and joyous. Simplicity and surrender unshackle the heart and allow the life of God to flow freely from the inside out. As if being released from a huge debt, we find the heavy burden lifted from our shoulders. The weight is gone. We can breathe again. There is life in our bones!

The Joy of St. Francis

St. Francis of Assisi knew the joy of simplicity. Born of wealthy parents in the town of Assisi, Italy, he experienced the benefits of aristocracy. Sometimes, however, life has a way of sensitizing us to the calling of God, and Francis experienced this. At one point, Francis's father brought him before the bishop to have his inheritance taken from him. Francis responded by stripping naked and walking away from it all to serve God in poverty. Not even the clothes on his body would come from his father's wealth. He left everything behind to pursue the Spirit's leading.

His newfound joy attracted others who also sought the happiness and simplicity of heart he was experiencing. Spiritual joy became his calling card—the hallmark of an unshackled heart. His joy spread to a love of all creation, to the poor, to lepers, and to all who desired to liberate their soul.

St. Francis and his band of followers set into motion a movement of Catholic monasticism that survives to this day—the Franciscans. Francis's decision to live a life of simplicity brought unimaginable joy to his heart. He discovered newfound happiness, the pleasure of God's presence, and the unencumbering of his heart. His focus on internal well-being led to the transformation of himself and others.

Internal Flows to External

Internal simplicity flows to outward practice, which merely reflects the biblical principle that what is treasured in the heart manifests itself outwardly. The Pharisees meticulously focused upon external religious rules and rituals which, according to Jesus, placed heavy burdens upon the backs of those truly seeking the Lord. Their fixation on the external revealed their internal heart posture, and it was nothing but white-washed-tomb living, not at all the kind of divine relationship Jesus experienced, demonstrated, and offered to us.

When the heart is simple—that is, connected to Christ's power and free from encumbrances—our flowering tree blooms with pleasant aromas, and its fruit bursts forth with succulent taste. Internal harmony, unity, and simplicity flow outward to a life that is attractive and winsome. We function outwardly in harmony with our inward condition.

Simplicity of heart allows us to "Draw near to God, and he will draw near to you" (James 4:8, NRSVue). Internal simplicity prevents us from becoming "double-minded and unstable in every way" (James 1:8, NRSVue), for when we choose internal simplicity, we are making a choice on how we will live. Doubt subsides, our compass is aligned with true north, and internal peace and harmony allow us to live without the variance and tension that often occur between internal status and outward action. Internal simplicity of heart affects us positively in so many ways, for we have chosen to center our life on that which flows outward to all things.

What enslaves your heart? What burdens does it carry? What double-mindedness exists to fracture your internal tranquility? On your dashboard of life, what flashing red lights indicate internal heart issues in need of attention? Simplicity of heart creates internal freedom—freedom to sail our ship without the resistance of an anchor dragging along the ocean floor and slowing us down.

It's about Surrender

At its core, simplicity is about surrender. In fact, virtually everything about divine intimacy has something to do with surrender—getting ourselves out of the way and clearing a path for divine movement. It is difficult to recognize the whispers of God with a heart full of clutter. Simplicity is about freeing the heart to live in the awareness of God's presence.

In an attempt to find our place in this great big scary world, we grab on to all sorts of things to assuage our fears and assure ourselves that we are okay. Our energy is given toward gathering things, not giving them away—holding on, not surrendering. We collect power, prestige, titles, degrees, money, possessions, and anything that makes us feel better about ourselves. We always seem to look for something outside ourselves, but any short-term fix is never enough, for nothing outside ourselves can bring us the abundant life our soul desperately seeks.

Virtually all religions speak of letting go as a pathway to experiencing God. The teaching of Jesus spotlights self-surrender and the embrace of spiritual paradoxes. We get when we give. We become first when we are last. The powerless become powerful. The seed must die before it sprouts into a healthy harvest. Jesus turned the world upside down with his life-transforming spiritual insight. The disciples didn't grasp much of it at the time, for they were busy arguing over which one of them was the greatest and who would sit next to Jesus in the new kingdom.

When Jesus informed his disciples that he must go to Jerusalem to suffer and die, they would have no part of it. This talk of suffering and dying didn't fit their narrative of power, fame, and influence. Jesus's rebuke was swift: "Get behind me, Satan! For you are setting your mind not on divine things but on human things" (Mark 8:33, NRSVue). Immediately afterward, Jesus began teaching the crowds about denying oneself.

His strong rebuke indicates that his disciples didn't understand what he was all about, which prompted his teaching on self-surrender and getting ourselves out of the way. Internal surrender is a sign not of weakness but of spiritual power—an indication that we are being awakened into deeper intimacy with the divine. Experiencing the sacred presence of God isn't so much something we do as it is something that is done to us when we surrender to the Spirit.

Living from the Center

Even Jesus experienced the power of surrender. Immediately following his baptism, he scurried into the wilderness to hear the voice of God in his life. It was a time of self-surrender, of simplifying the heart, of removing clutter and letting go—a way of ensuring that nothing would interfere with his perpetual connection to the power and presence of God.

All this teaching about losing to gain, seeking last place to gain first place, walking in step with the Spirit, and becoming a dying seed that produces a harvest, wasn't just fancy spiritual talk from someone who ate the best food, drank the best wine, wore the best clothes, and sat in an ivory tower looking down upon others. This teaching flowed from the very heart of Jesus, who lived it and experienced it. It was this simplicity of heart—this living from the center—that allowed him to do the things he did, to teach the way he taught, and to be the kind of person who could win the hearts of millions. He lived from the center—from an internal perspective and awareness that enabled constant communion with the divine. He was a living example of how this internal connection could flow to the outer world.

How in the world do we suppose that Jesus was able to endure betrayal, arrest, beating, mocking, humiliation, a sham trial, and crucifixion without resistance, bitterness, or revenge? His life was a living example of the truths he taught. He didn't desperately cling to life, for he understood that his identity, calling, and power came from within. The very life of God was flowing through him and could not be taken from him in life or in death.

When I say that Jesus lived from the center, I am saying that his life was tethered to the Spirit. He simplified his heart and maintained an uncluttered spiritual pathway for expressing constant communion with the peace, power, and presence of God. This is what simplicity and surrender do for us: They help us practice the presence of God through thick and thin. Jesus was willing to give his life away because he wasn't self-centered and didn't rely on external things to ensure his place in this world. With that kind of divine connection, nothing can separate us from the love of God—not even death.

Compartmentalizing Life

Simplicity of heart leads us toward the center, where the wellspring of abundant life bubbles forth. Unfortunately, it is a reality most never experience, even though they long to drink from its refreshing waters. The problem isn't one of unavailability, for the well isn't dry; the problem is that living from the center isn't understood or intentionalized. Instead, we compartmentalize life into various pieces without seeing its unified whole. When life is lived from the center, all things are united and connected. Simplicity of heart isn't a place but a way of seeing—a perspective that allows us to live life in all of its many dimensions while experiencing the life-giving presence of God flowing through us.

We go to the office compartment and do our work thing. We come home and ready ourselves for the next compartmentalized task, whether it be gardening, surfing the Internet, spending time with the kids, or traipsing off to some church function. They are examples of how we compartmentalize life into individual sections, all sealed off from one another. The God compartment becomes just another segmentation of life that is disconnected from all other life compartments.

Rather than existing as a series of sealed-off submarine compartments, living from the center allows the power and presence of God to touch every aspect of our life, not just the religious or church compartment. We go to work with an awareness of God's indwelling presence. We see co-workers in the light of Christ and in the image of God. Empathy and compassion well up within, and we are safe, satisfied, and secure because, like Jesus, we are intimately connected to divine power flowing within us.

Simplicity and surrender allow us to maintain constant communion with the Spirit so that nothing disrupts our peace. Our commute home from work isn't just another compartment but an opportunity to live in the moment—to be present, to notice our surroundings, and to experience the awe of God's indwelling presence. Living from the center isn't about achieving a goal, earning a prize, or arriving at a destination; it is a way of being and of seeing life with new awareness. It doesn't get any better than that.

No circumstance, person, or event can shake our foundational connection to God, for we no longer rely on external things to validate us, assuage our fears, or impart worth. Now, we walk in step with the Spirit, and all of life is seen through a new lens, for all is connected and intertwined. We become internally aware and spiritually awake because we have uncluttered our soul. We have room for the Spirit to freely move to and fro. Now, we are in tune with God, and our internal ears are carefully listening to the most important thing—the whisper of God unto our soul.

The negative result of compartmentalized thinking is that we rank segmented areas by priority and pleasure. In my experience, many who compartmentalize life verbally affirm God's priority when everything about their life screams otherwise. If God is the ultimate compartment, then no other compartments are worth occupying, for the supreme compartment takes precedence over all others. It is, however, quite unspiritual to admit that God is actually way down on our real-world priority list. We lie to ourselves about which priority is number one. Our predicament is nothing short of a juggling act between various compartments.

When we live from the center, we experience no compartmentalizing, no ranking, no juggling, and no guilt. For all of life, every dimension of it, is lived in the fullness of God's presence. What matters is the Christ connection that helps us view every aspect of life as sacred. Rather than sealing God off into a disconnected compartment called "religion" or "church," we allow God to become the hub that touches and influences all the spokes in the wheel of life.

Contentment

One liberating effect of simplicity and surrender is the joy of contentment. Unfortunately, contentment is often viewed as a huge burden placed upon our shoulders—another one of those crosses we must bear in serving the Lord. With this perspective, contentment is merely a euphemism for all the things we give up to please the great deity above, and it becomes another notch on our spiritual gun belt displaying just how dedicated we truly are. God sure is lucky to have us as followers— people so dedicated to the cause that we are willing to be content with so little.

What a great misunderstanding this is! Rather than being a begrudging display of compelled obedience, contentment is a blessing that brings untold freedom from the trappings of the heart. What wondrous freedom caused the Apostle Paul to write from his prison cell that he was rejoicing, content, and able to do all things through Christ who strengthened him? What wondrous freedom allowed Jesus to bear the brunt of constant criticism, betrayal, and death, yet maintain a sense of contentment that all was well? What caused countless others to experience the peace, power, and presence of God in spite of dire circumstances?

Paul and Jesus lived life from the center—from a core identity and deep connection with the divine. When the heart is free from clutter and we surrender ourselves to the Spirit, it matters little what our life circumstances may be, for only one thing ultimately matters, and we are deeply connected to it. All else pales in comparison. All else is insignificant. That divine connection we experience through simplicity and surrender ensures that nothing can upend our internal tranquility. Contentment is not a burden we must endure but a blessed state of being that many search for their entire lives.

How can we be content when we constantly face the onslaught of "just one more thing"? The world's marketing machine works hard to convince us that we need everything it is trying to sell. By purchasing various products, we would most certainly be happier, for they would patch up the internal deficiencies we perceive in ourselves. In reality, the marketing machine keeps us in a never-ending cycle of addiction, making it seem there is always one more thing we lack.

As a list person, I write down all the things I want to accomplish in any given day, and I feel a great sense of relief and self-satisfaction every time I cross an item off that precious list of mine. The downside of being a list person is that the list is never completed. As I cross one item off, I simply replace it with another. I am captive to the vicious cycle of "just one more thing." I get a great deal accomplished, but I am never finished, and as far as my list goes, I never reach a state of contentment.

This vicious cycle of "just one more thing" describes life for many of us. Our current vehicle isn't good enough, and we feel discontented until we acquire the newest model. It wasn't even on our "wants" list until the slick marketing machine showed us how a newer version of what we already possessed would satisfy our internal deficiency. How can we be content when there is "just one more thing" we are lacking? This cycle is destructive and produces constant restlessness in our attempt to soothe the soul with "things." Because we have not experienced the contentment that simplicity of heart and self-surrender bring, what we have is never enough. Not even God is enough.

Whenever we attempt to fill the longing of our soul with anything other than God, internal restlessness is sure to raise its ugly head. It is like trying to satisfy our thirst by purchasing a new cup, when what we need is water. Outside God, there will always be "one more thing." But when we unclutter the heart and surrender the soul, we live in constant communion with the divine, and contentment is our joy, for we are connected to life itself—the same life that sustained Jesus. There is no need for anything else.

We must be careful when speaking of a restlessness of soul, for the internal uneasiness that comes from God has nothing to do with filling a void, assuaging anxiety, or seeking identity and worth. Instead, it is a stirring of the Spirit to move, act, and engage. This kind of restlessness is good and prompted by the Spirit.

Paul was moved to preach the gospel, even though doing so often placed him in danger and landed him in prison. Jesus was moved to gather disciples and teach others, even though doing so eventually cost him his life. Martin Luther King Jr. was moved to raise America's consciousness by becoming a leading voice in the Civil Rights Movement, even though doing so made him the target for an assassin's bullet. Although he was severely excoriated for his action, Martin Luther was compelled to speak out against corruption within the Catholic Church.

His restlessness led to the great Reformation. Countless examples of Spirit-led restlessness could be cited. When you are connected to Christ's power, you cannot do otherwise, for it is a divine prompting that compels action. This restlessness is the good kind—a Spirit-directed stirring of the soul.

Contentment is a blessed gift that comes from simplicity and surrender. When we have an uncluttered heart, there is room for the Spirit winds to blow, for we are not tethered to temporal things but to the source of abundant life. When we live from the center, nothing can disrupt our inner peace. We are content in whatever circumstances we find ourselves. What a gift!

Possessions versus Real Wealth

A friend used to tell me of all the items she bought for her children. After describing each item purchased, she would say, "Because I could." It went something like this: "I bought Mikey a brand-new car, because I could, and he really likes it." Her "because I could" statement always made me wonder whether we purchase things because we can or because we should. She cared deeply for her children, but her "because I could" phrase prompted me to think more deeply about possessions and my desire to be a good steward of the resources entrusted to me. One reason for the avalanche of cluttered hearts these days is due to the ease with which we are able to acquire things. It is a "because I could" mindset, whereas decluttering pursues a "whether I should" perspective.

Years ago, a funny commercial featured a man named Stanley Johnson bragging about his large four-bedroom home in a great neighborhood with a plush lawn, his new car, and his membership in the local golf club. He appeared to be living the American dream of personal success. As he was cleaning his swimming pool, he turned to the camera and said, "And how do I do it? I'm in debt up to my eyeballs. I can barely pay my finance charges. Someone, please help me!" The fictitious Stanley Johnson epitomized the price we pay for the illusion of success—entrapment. We accumulate because we can, not because we should.

Let me be clear: There is nothing inherently wrong with possessions. They are not intrinsically bad, for they are just things. I know plenty of smart, hard-working, industrious individuals who have put in the time and effort to move up the socioeconomic ladder. Good for them. They weren't handfed from a silver spoon but worked hard to get where they are. Many of them are caring and thoughtful—generous with their time, finances, possessions, and talents. The issue isn't with possessions themselves but with our attitude toward them.

I have lived with a sense of physical security, but I have also experienced precarious paycheck-to-paycheck living. I prefer the former. If I had my druthers, I would much rather drive a newer car as opposed to an older one. But I know that a new car, a used car, a status symbol, or an old, beat-up jalopy is merely a thing that transports me from one spot to another. Not all cars are equal in quality and value, and some are better designed than others, yet their primary function is the same—to transport us from one location to another. They are just things, that's all. Some are shiny, some are dull. Some are expensive, others less so, and although there is nothing intrinsically wrong with any "thing," the question is how we perceive and value our possessions.

The issue is internal, not external; a condition of the heart, not competition as to who owns the most toys. As Jesus put it, "But what comes out of the mouth proceeds from the heart, and this is what defiles" (Matt. 15:18, NRSVue). The issue isn't one of outer riches so much as it is of inner poverty—being poor in spirit.

The outward sign of God's covenant with Israel was circumcision (Gen. 17). Many Jews saw this covenant badge as a sign of divine favor. The Pharisees bragged to Jesus that they were sons of Abraham—sons of the covenant—and they had the outward sign to prove it. In their minds, all this talk about knowing the truth and being set free didn't apply to them, for they already possessed the sign of the covenant. The Apostle Paul discussed this very thing in Romans 2:25–29 (NRSVue):

> Circumcision indeed is of value if you obey the law, but if you are a transgressor of the law your circumcision has become uncircumcision. So, if the uncircumcised keep the requirements of the law, will not their uncircumcision be regarded as circumcision? Then the physically uncircumcised person who keeps the law will judge you who, though having the written code and circumcision, are a transgressor of the law. For a person is not a Jew who is one outwardly, nor is circumcision something external and physical. Rather, a person is a Jew who is one inwardly, and circumcision is a matter of the heart, by the Spirit, not the written code. Such a person receives praise not from humans but from God.

Once again, we see God's interest in the heart. Outward circumcision merely involves cutting away flesh, but circumcision of the heart removes all clutter blocking the Spirit's voice. Real circumcision is a matter of the heart.

Divergent Hearts

Contrasting a rich young ruler with blind Bartimaeus may help to illustrate my point. In Mark 10, a rich man approached Jesus to ask how he might inherit eternal life, and Jesus responded by listing several of the commandments. Noting that he had followed them since his youth, the rich young ruler was beginning to feel self-confident until Jesus exposed the real issue within his heart. Much to his chagrin, he was instructed to sell all of his possessions and follow Jesus. In response, the rich young ruler went away sad, for he had many possessions. It is easier to externally fulfill commandments than it is to simplify the heart and surrender what encumbers our soul. As Jesus said, "For what will it profit them to gain the whole world and forfeit their life?" (Mark 8:36, NRSVue).

As Jesus began to list the commandments, we notice he threw one in that is not in the Ten Commandments as we know them: "You shall not defraud" (Mark 10:19, NRSVue). Why did Jesus do this? He slipped it in because he knew that it pinpointed the internal issue of the rich man, the one who sought to justify his status by implying that despite his wealth, he had kept all the commandments since his youth. In typical fashion, Jesus went straight to the heart of the matter and asked the young ruler to sell all that he had and come follow him.

I am not sure whether I would have reacted much differently had Jesus directed me to do the same. How about you? What treasure enslaves your heart? That is the real issue, isn't it—treasuring things over God? We treasure our possessions, our reputation, our prestige, our titles, our bank account, and so forth, above the peace, power, and presence of God. One is a temporal item, while the other is an eternal reality. We often go away sad, unwilling to give up that which prevents us from experiencing God because we cling to worthless idols like the rich man.

The rich young ruler wasn't a bad person—he was just caught up in a lie. He was involved in fraud because his life was built upon the lie that "things" are the sum of our value and worth. He was using the wrong measuring stick. Jesus knew that this man would never be free to experience the kingdom until he faced the internal challenge before him. His heart was encumbered with clutter that he was unwilling to surrender to the Lord. He owned possessions, but in reality, his possessions owned him. He was an owner rather than a steward—a protector of "things" rather than the guardian of a generous and free heart. He had substituted shiny objects for real wealth.

Contrast the rich man with blind Bartimaeus, described later in Mark 10. The rich ruler asked how he could receive eternal life, whereas

Bartimaeus simply pled for mercy, for he had nothing to brag about. The rich man approached Jesus, whereas Jesus went to Bartimaeus. When Jesus bid him to come, Bartimaeus jumped up and quickly obeyed without hesitation, whereas the rich man engaged in a cost-benefit analysis and walked away sad. When asked what he sought, the eager blind man simply said he wanted to see, for he was a beggar with nothing to show for his life—wholly dependent upon others. Jesus restored his sight, made him whole, and applauded his faith.

Do you see what is happening here? The one with untold possessions thought he was rich when, in reality, he was poor. Bartimaeus, on the other hand, was physically blind, yet he was the one who could spiritually see. You can be blind and still see or be rich and yet poor. This paradox causes us to consider the true nature of wealth: Does it lie in the accumulation of things, or is it something within us? From the perspective of Jesus, the real seeing comes when we let go of all that encumbers the heart, for only then will we find the internal freedom and peace we desire. The blind man was ready to receive because nothing enslaved his heart. The rich man, however, allowed the entanglements of possessions to hold him hostage, and that is the danger of "things"— they so easily deceive and entangle the heart.

Jesus calls us to see things differently and walk a contrary path. Rather than buying into a system built upon power, prestige, possessions, and false promises, we are asked to recognize that true wealth comes from within—from simplicity and surrender. Simplicity of heart and self-surrender are means of disentangling ourselves from such encumbrances. They help us dismantle barriers to experiencing God and set our sights on real wealth that leads to lasting peace and joy. We are beginning to see just how important the heart is to experiencing God and how things flow from the inside to the outside.

Poor in Spirit

In the famous Sermon on the Mount, Jesus spoke to the necessity of simplicity and surrender: "Blessed are the poor in spirit, for theirs is the kingdom of heaven" and "Blessed are the pure in heart, for they will see God" (Matt. 5:3; 5:8, NRSVue). The issue is one of internal magnitude, for it is poverty of spirit and purity of heart that allow us to experience the kingdom of heaven and to "see" God. What does it mean to be poor in spirit?

In answering this question, my mind moves to several biblical examples. The first example is found in the contrast between two Greek words for "poor": *penichros* and *ptochos*. In Mark 12, Jesus and his disciples observed a poor widow depositing two small copper coins into the temple treasury right alongside wealthier individuals giving a great deal more. Seizing this teaching moment, Jesus stated, "Truly I tell you, this poor widow has put in more than all those who are contributing to the treasury. For all of them have contributed out of their abundance; but she out of her poverty has put in everything she had, all she had to live on" (Mark 12:43–44, NRSVue). This widow was *penichros* poor, for although she didn't have much, she gave from her meager resources, even if it was only two small copper coins. Her action revealed the condition of her heart.

Another New Testament Greek word for "poor" is *ptochos*. This word refers to abject poverty. Those who were *ptochos* poor had absolutely nothing to give to the treasury, for they were reduced to begging and dependent upon the generosity of others for survival. The beggar's heart revealed absolute dependence upon God for sustenance. The widow and the beggar demonstrated what it means to be poor in spirit.

The second illustration comes from Luke 18, where Jesus contrasted those who elevated themselves with those who were humble before God. Two men went to the temple to pray. One, a Pharisee, prayed loudly in an attempt to impress God and others. He elevated his own goodness and looked down upon those who didn't measure up. The despised tax collector, on the other hand, stood at a distance, kept his head bowed low, and beat his breast while humbly asking God for mercy. Jesus concluded the story with these words: "I tell you, this man went down to his home justified rather than the other, for all who exalt themselves will be humbled, but all who humble themselves will be exalted" (Luke 18:14, NRSVue). The point is that those who experience God live with simplicity of heart and an internal posture of self-surrender.

In these scriptural examples, Jesus is addressing the inward condition of our heart because he knows that the divine flows from the inside to the outside. Jesus doesn't condemn anyone who gives generously, for giving is a good thing. These examples, however, teach us that real wealth emanates from within, for it is the attitude of our heart that is pleasing to the Lord. Those who go deep with God and experience the kingdom in unprecedented ways know the value of simplicity and surrender.

Slavery or Freedom

Surrender is a catalyst for freedom. In fact, the great religions of the world all seem to agree that spirituality is essentially about letting go, releasing, surrendering, and recognizing our own sense of powerlessness. All spirituality is filled with paradoxes, and Christianity is no exception. For instance, we discover fulfillment in giving, not in accumulating. We become powerful in our powerlessness. We are exalted in our humility. We become first by becoming last. We experience freedom by letting go of those things that enslave us, such as power, prestige, reputation, money, sex, drugs—you name it.

Even religion can enslave us with power trips down the highway of self-righteousness. Religion is a great place for bondage to go unnoticed. In typical self-serving fashion, the church often uses the precious truths of Scripture for its own end—as another mechanism for controlling the behavior of its adherents through guilt and subjugation. In other words, it promotes self-surrender while advancing its own power of control.

The reason the great religions and their mystics embrace these paradoxes is because experience proves them true. They are not pious platitudes uttered without basis, for in reality and in truth, simplicity of heart and self-surrender enhance our ability to experience the divine. Self-surrender is about letting go of our control. Only then will we realize our utter dependence upon God. This same concept is used in the twelve-step Alcoholics Anonymous program: The first step toward wholeness is acknowledging one's own powerlessness—a form of self-surrender.

In reality, we simply don't know as much as we think we do, and we don't control much of anything, yet we strut about as though we were kings and queens of an empire built with our own hands. This comment is not to denigrate hard work and human ingenuity, for that is admirable. But our addiction to control and our craving for power are deceptive forms of enslavement. In essence, we are caught up in the machine, the system being sold to us that causes us to accumulate and hoard things, to elevate ourselves, and to measure life according to a false value system. We think that we are free when we are enslaved and addicted.

Yet when we finally break free from our bondage, we feel like the Israelites wandering in the desert, all the while longing once again to eat leeks and onions by the Nile River. In their mind, it was far better to be enslaved and comfortable than to be free and uncomfortable! One reason why we are uncomfortable with the freedom surrender offers is that we become responsible. Spiritual enslavement means that there is always someone to blame, someone other than ourselves who is at fault, and we justify our stuck condition. Freedom, on the other hand, forces us to assume responsibility, for we are accountable for our own spiritual well-being and our own decisions—and that can be uncomfortable.

The point is that surrendering those things that enslave us leads to spiritual freedom—freedom to experience God the way we were designed to experience God, for according to John 8:36 (NRSVue): "So if the Son makes you free, you will be free indeed." Discerning between good, better, and best choices can be difficult, but it is our responsibility to decide. We cannot blame others for the decisions we make. To me, the choice is an easy one—freedom or enslavement. As for me and my household, we will serve the Lord. I choose freedom!

Less Is More

Our collection of spiritual clutter is detrimental because too many things compete for the attention of our heart. It is time to whittle things down to what really matters. We know that this principle works in the real world of possessions, but do we apply it to our experience of God? Rather than promoting an ego-driven life of self-indulgence, the call of Christ is to unclutter the heart and let go of those things that enslave our soul. The abundant life that Jesus experienced and promises to us is experienced by all who unclutter the heart. Less is more. Simplify the heart, and you are well on your way to experiencing the sacred presence of God.

Toward Simplicity and Surrender

To my knowledge, there is no fast and furious formula for quickly arriving at the doorstep of simplicity and surrender. That isn't how it works, at least not for me. Rather, my journey has often involved internal wrestling matches with God—the sort of internal sifting God uses to draw us closer.

Throughout the years, my work has taken me across the country and provided the perfect opportunity to whittle things down. With each move, I took less and less with me. Each relocation was a time of sorting, deciding, and letting go. It wasn't always easy. I surrendered my emotional attachment to certain items, and each time I decided to let go, I experienced a freeing effect. As in mountain climbing, what is required at base camp becomes an unnecessary burden at higher elevations of spiritual maturity.

Life is similar to mountain climbing. As we make our way up the mountain, we realize that extra burdens are useless, and we discard what maturity no longer needs. Rather than being a static, one-time event, achieving simplicity and surrender becomes a lifelong process of letting go at deeper levels of faith. I haven't met anyone who, in one fell swoop, cleaned and organized everything down to where they wanted to be. In our climb to higher elevations of faith, the Spirit provides the courage and the impetus for spiritual decluttering. It is all a part of dancing with the divine.

Taking Inventory

Checks and balances keep us honest and on track. Taking inventory helps us get our bearings so we know where we are and where we need to go. What internal thoughts prevent you from decluttering? What feelings hinder your willingness to let go? What lingering hurts are still tender and in need of healing? Pay close attention to what the Spirit reveals, such as fear, loss, bitterness, stress, anxiety, depression, people, possessions, coping mechanisms, and the like. It often helps to write things down, so list it, identify it, name it, surface it, and expose it. In this process of cleaning house, no "elephants" are allowed in the heart. Instead, they are named and escorted out.

Taking inventory exposes heart entanglements. It is a way of acknowledging our own powerlessness—a first step toward surrender. Inventory checks help raise our level of awareness, and with the Spirit's guidance, we release what shackles our heart.

Awareness is a great start, but it only gets us so far. If simplicity and surrender are to become a way of living, then certain perspectives offer valuable assistance in the decluttering process. The first helpful

perspective is to determine the center of our life, the second is to oblit-
erate the distinction between secular and sacred, and the third is to take
pleasure in God.

What Lies at the Center?

We build our lives around something that is important to us. What
is that "something" for you? Asking what lies at the center of our life
helps distinguish the clutter from the core. What does your life revolve
around? What is at your core? Who are you? What do you want to
become, and why? We are also asked in Scripture to guard our hearts:
"Keep your heart with all vigilance, for from it flow the springs of life"
(Prov. 4:23, NRSVue). It is the center of our life, that which we treasure
and guard over all else that is important, as Jesus noted in Matthew 6:33
(NRSVue): "But seek first the kingdom of God and his righteousness,
and all these things will be given to you as well." What is it that you
guard above all else? Is it your connection to the divine? Simplicity and
surrender begin there, for whatever lies at the center is that which you
treasure and guard. The path to decluttering the soul begins with identifying your center.

Sacred versus Secular Distinction

Drawing a line between the sacred and the secular is compartmentalization—a duality that we must scrap if we ever hope to experience divine
intimacy. When God is at the core of our life, going to work or painting
our house is just as holy as receiving communion or studying our Bible.
All is sacred. Everything about life is connected to the divine, for God is
everywhere. There is no place we can go and nothing we can do where
God is not present. Seeing all of life as an awareness and experience of
God makes every act, every situation, every moment of every day sacred.
It is a perspective that changes how we perceive life itself.

Taking Pleasure in God

Jesus said, "If any wish to come after me, let them deny themselves and take up their cross and follow me" (Matt. 16:24, NRSVue). The cross speaks of death—self-surrender. As we give all that we are to God, we receive all that God has for us. Without self-surrender, we merely go through religious motions that are disconnected from any life-giving union with the divine. In a sense, dying occurs before living—surrendering before receiving. It is when we let go, unclutter the heart, and live from the center that we treasure God, and when we treasure God, we experience deep joy and pleasure. It is not a burden to walk with God but the very joy of our heart.

There is no test or formula for simplicity and surrender—there is just doing it, living it, and being it. Begin by determining what your life is centered around. What is it you treasure most? If it isn't God, then there isn't much else I can do for you, for everything begins with the core of your being. When God becomes the treasured center, everything is lived in connection to and under the influence of the divine. Getting rid of distractions, deceptions of the heart, worries, and all sorts of extraneous clutter has to do with what lies at your center. When life is lived with simplicity and surrender, there is no distinction between the secular and the sacred, for God is present everywhere. All is sacred. As we practice the presence of God, we take pleasure in dancing with the divine.

10

PRAYER & SCRIPTURE

PRAYER AND SCRIPTURE, TWO WELL-WORN PATHS FOR discovering newfound intimacy with God, have brought comfort and direction to Christians throughout the centuries. Although many find these tools to be useful in their spiritual journey, others see them as irritating obstacles, and the difference, it seems, stems from one's understanding of prayer and Scripture. One perspective enhances divine intimacy, while the other leads to spiritual exhaustion. Let me explain.

The typical view of prayer is one of activity. In other words, prayer is a religious obligation in which good Christians are expected to engage fervently. It is something "we do" rather than something "we are" or "we live." Often pulpit-shamed for not being mighty prayer warriors, we feel guilt creeping in when we don't clock enough time on our knees. If we only prayed harder, longer, better, and with greater sincerity, then surely we would discover the divine intimacy we so desperately seek. Let me be quick to challenge this debilitating perspective that has led to the disillusionment of so many. With bubble-bursting effect, this traditional view of prayer is losing all meaning in the modern world. No wonder so many are frustrated by an activity that promises so much but produces so little in the way of intimacy.

I grew up in a denomination that held Wednesday-night prayer services. We sang a song or two, listened to some teaching, and then broke into small groups for prayer. A list of needs was set before us that seemed to be the same week after week. There were big-ticket items, such as significant health issues, and petty issues that seemed trivial and unworthy of our time. In reality, little progress was made regarding any of the requests on the list. We prayed for the same things in the same manner over and over again, to no avail.

We prayed for healing, for instance, but it never came. Yet on those occasions when things went our preferred way, we gave God glory, and when it didn't, we attributed our lack of success to God's will being done. God could never lose, and we were always left wondering whether we had done enough to secure divine favor. Was our ineffectiveness due to a lack of faith on our part, or were we somehow misunderstanding what prayer was all about? Those who attended the Wednesday prayer meeting were deemed to be faithful Christians dedicated to the cause of Christ. Surely, God would be impressed with such commitment and inclined to grant divine favor. Dedication, perseverance, and loyalty should be rewarded. Isn't that how it works?

Most books I have read on prayer treat it as a holy activity—something good Bible-believing Christians are expected to do. Their focus is upon the how of prayer—the mechanics of doing it properly, because, you know, God is interested in that! One book provides instructions for praying all kinds of prayers, such as the prayer of relinquishment, the prayer of adoration, the authoritative prayer, the covenant prayer, the meditative prayer, and on and on. My goodness, how many prayers can there be that must be prayed just right? This mechanical, ritualistic, external, and measured activity becomes another "essential" item on our list of things to impress God. Surely, there has to be more to prayer than learning the "how-to" steps of performing another religious obligation!

Years ago, at the invitation of a friend, I visited her tiny Baptist church. When it came time in the service for public prayer, an individual sitting behind me was given the honor. I could tell that calling upon him was not unusual and that he enjoyed the spotlight. He stood to pray, and everything was going along just fine until he messed up his well-rehearsed lines and lost his place. A sense of confused panic overtook him as he stumbled to find his way. Instead of simply praying from the heart and moving on, he went back to the beginning and started his memorized prayer all over again. This time, he made it through the formulaic ritual without incident. For him, prayer was a "performed-just-right" activity. It was nothing more than perfecting dance moves instead of dancing to the rhythm of the divine.

The problem isn't a lack of sincerity but an inadequate view of God and prayer. When prayer becomes another religious duty that earns us divine intimacy, we become spiritually exhausted. We end up praying to a Santa Claus God who doles out rewards (answered prayers) to good boys and girls while punishment (unanswered prayers) is the lot of those who misbehave. If God is viewed as the supernatural CEO of the universe who can be manipulated to our own end, what happens when the celestial slot machine doesn't dispense the goodies we desire, even though we inserted the right prayer tokens? This perspective of prayer simply cannot stand in the modern era, for it is nothing more than a *quid pro quo* exchange of activity. I do this for God, and in exchange, God does this for me.

In the ancient flat-Earth worldview, God was portrayed as a powerful deity who lived in the sky just beyond the clouds. Life happenings were explained as the will of this divine being who was either rewarding or punishing humans for their obedience or lack thereof. The ancients were clueless about germs, atoms, DNA, cholesterol, plate tectonics, the theory of relativity, and a host of other things that are commonplace these days. They would have scoffed at the idea of a spaceship escorting men to the moon or landing on Mars.

In this ancient milieu, sacrifices were made in an effort to appease this divine being and stay the consequences of God's displeasure and wrath. As Christians seek to influence the hand of God, most pray that good things will befall them and that evil will be kept at bay. It is nothing more than the work of appeasement. It is walking on eggshells so God's anger is not aroused. It is the lingering effects of an outdated and irrelevant worldview.

Our advanced knowledge and understanding of the universe means that the modern world can no longer embrace such archaic worldviews and flat-Earth perspectives. Earthquakes aren't caused by an angry deity. Cancer isn't the result of a vengeful God ensuring that sinful humans pay the price for disobedience, nor are tornados God's method of showing us who is boss. What kind of a God would do such things, especially one that is said to be benevolent? In light of the knowledge we now possess, that kind of a God is inconceivable and is nothing more than a museum relic from a less enlightened era.

An exuberant retail manager shared with me how God spared her store and her employees from an oncoming tornado after she prayed for God's intervention. God answered her prayer by turning the tornado toward another path of destruction. Instead, the twister created havoc for others by damaging their homes and businesses while sparing hers. Maybe *those* people should have prayed, and if they did, maybe they should have prayed harder, longer, better, or with greater sincerity. After all, it was merely a competition to see who could move the hand of God. For the store manager, God had been influenced to reroute the tornado toward others who weren't originally in the path, all because of her fervent prayers. Too bad, so sad for them. I guess they were "out-prayed," and their loving and kind deity chose others over them. Is that how prayer works? There is so much wrong with this perspective that an entire book could be written on this topic alone, and yet it is a mindset held by millions of Christians.

My point is this: When prayer is viewed as a religious activity designed to manipulate a supernatural being into acting on our behalf, it is an antiquated and inadequate view of prayer and God. This kind of praying and that kind of God have become obsolete in today's world. Rather than moving us toward divine intimacy, they move us toward constant disappointment and spiritual exhaustion.

What Is Prayer?

When prayer is looked upon as a perfunctory religious obligation, our experience of God becomes a roller-coaster ride of emotions. We experience guilt for not logging enough time on our knees and disillusionment when the divine outcome isn't in our favor, especially after pouring our heart out to a compassionate, all-powerful God. When things go our way, God is great, and when they don't, we are to blame. That kind of emotional rocket ride yields spiritual motion sickness. If prayer isn't petitioning God to protect us, cure us from disease, ensure that our children get into prestigious colleges, or cause the political party of our choice to win at the polls, then what is it? If we aren't asking God for things, then why pray at all?

First of all, we must jettison the notion that prayer is an activity that we do. The Apostle Paul instructed the church in Thessalonica to "pray without ceasing" (1 Thess. 5:17, NRSVue). Was Paul really asking that we engage in an activity without ceasing? If that were the case, we couldn't eat, take a bathroom break, sleep, or do anything else. We would be petitioning the heavenly CEO all day long for things we need and want. Maybe Paul was speaking of prayer not as an activity but as a way of life—an attitude that permeates our very being. In the same passage, Paul encouraged the Thessalonians to rejoice always and give thanks in all circumstances. That seems like an internal posture of the heart rather than a perpetual external activity.

If praying is a religious duty that determines our experience of the divine, then we are doomed to failure, for none of us can engage in a religious activity without ceasing. I have heard that the average American pastor prays less than five minutes a day and that most Christians spend even less time on their knees. We pray when there is a crisis—when we really need God to do something for us—but other than that, the activity is relegated to a religious afterthought. Prayer is spoken of with great importance but used only when the chips are down and the odds aren't in our favor. My point is this: If intimacy with God is dependent upon some religious activity, no matter what that activity is, then we are all in a heap of trouble.

Prayer or Praying?

I make a distinction between *prayer* and *praying*. Prayer is simply communing with God. Isn't that what we are after, discovering and relating to our creator? Prayer, then, becomes an integral aspect of how we live this present life. If we are going to dance with the divine, we must do it in the here and now.

If prayer is simply our attempt to commune with the sacred presence of God, then it becomes an *approach* to living rather than an *obligation* of religious activity. As an approach to life, prayer is opening ourselves up to the divine and meeting God in this life. We don't sequester ourselves away from the complexities, ambiguities, and hardships of this world. Instead, we take them in, face them head on, and discover God in and through them, not outside them or despite them. We live life fully, and we live it with gusto. We soak in the joys, pleasures, loving relationships, and beautiful scenery all about us.

God is not *separate* from life but found *in life*. God is not the "big guy upstairs" sitting on a heavenly throne, but a sacred presence that permeates all of life. As such, God is in us, around us, under us, over us, through us, beyond us, and everywhere present. Our life becomes one big prayer when we approach living in a way that allows us to enjoy God in this life with all of its ups and downs. Life is lived with the sacred presence dwelling within us and pouring out from us. Since God breathed life into us, we experience the divine as we live our life. So, take life in. Breathe it in deeply. Be aware of and sensitive to the indwelling divine presence and experience this life in the here and now. To do so is to experience God, and to experience God is to live prayerfully. In essence, prayer is nothing more than practicing the presence of God as we live life.

When prayer is viewed as an approach to life—that is, living in the constant awareness of God's sacred presence—we are able to pray without ceasing, for it is simply a way of being and living, rather than the performance of religious obligation. It is a living, dynamic, life-giving soul conversation with the divine—a constant connection to the source of life itself. St. Basil the Great sums it up pretty well, "This is how you pray continually, not by offering prayer in words, but by joining yourself to God through your whole way of life, so your life becomes a continuous and uninterrupted prayer."

If prayer is a way of life, then of what value is the act of praying? I am certainly not against verbalizing my heart's longings and deepest thoughts, but when I do, I am not petitioning a heavenly deity for a favorable outcome that advances my personal agenda. I don't play that silly game. Why would I pray for God's mercy when God is already merciful? Why would I pray for God to work for good in my life when God is already good and benevolent? Would a good and benevolent God act in a manner that was inconsistent with what is good and benevolent? To pray for such things assumes that God could do otherwise, and it assumes that God is a thing—an entity upon a throne in a faraway place who needs to be cajoled into correct action.

Loved ones, our nation's leaders, the infirmed, members of our military, and a host of other people and things that come to mind are uplifted in my thoughts. It is one way that I hold them in my heart and show love and concern. It helps me humanize individuals and their journey. It allows me to express love and compassion, and when I am praying for others and with others, it shows them that I care. I seek for them greater awareness of the sacred presence within and a sense of peace and joy. That is my high hope for them, and I express it as a gesture of love. Verbalizing these things increases my own sensitivity to the rhythm of God. As I hold others close to my heart and express my good will toward them, I am at the same time preparing the soil of my own life to receive the seed of the Spirit.

During the lockdown days of COVID-19, I took some time for a personal spiritual retreat in my own home. An Anglican prayer-bead kit was mailed to me, which I assembled during my spiritual respite. I had never heard of prayer beads for Protestant Christians, for they certainly weren't part of the religious tradition from which I came. I had thought that prayer beads were something Catholics and Orthodox Christians used in ritualistic fashion, but these were prayer beads designed for Protestant Christians. How cool is that? Much to my surprise, these treasured prayer beads have enhanced my quest for divine intimacy.

I am not ritualistic about it at all, and I have made up my own way of using them, but when I hold this helpful tool in my hand, recite Scripture, and express words of thanksgiving and loving thoughts of others, I sense a divine connection. When I find myself wide awake in the middle of the night, I often lay still, experience my own heartbeat, and sense the pace of my own breathing. I become acutely aware of my own consciousness and that the breath that I breathe is the life of God animating my body. With joy, I give thanks in my heart, for I realize that God is not only with me in the present moment but also within me. I am deeply moved and in tune with the divine life flowing from within.

Approach to Life

Prayer as an approach to life rather than a religious activity is a concept that many struggle to grasp. If I were to tell you to kneel, fold your hands together, bow your head, and recite specific words with a pious look on your face, you could understand that. These are checklist items—things to perform on a spiritual "to-do list" that showcases an external piety that keeps us in God's good graces.

To speak of prayer as an approach to life, however, is far too abstract for hearts that yearn for concrete religious activity. They want something to do, and they want to do it in the right way. They want something to track, score, and compare to others. In essence, they waste precious time perfecting their dance moves when God just wants them to dance to the beat of the Spirit. Let's talk a little more about this "approach-to-life" perspective.

The purpose of prayer is not to influence God but to change us from the inside out. As an *approach* to life, prayer is about *being* rather than *doing—living in God* rather than *doing things for God*. It has to do with connecting to the life of God within us, not getting things from God. When you journey through life in deep awareness of the Spirit, you share a bond with the divine that reaches indescribable depth. It is an experience, a feeling, a sense of unity and togetherness with the pulsating divinity within. That awareness influences every aspect of your being. It is living as Jesus lived—connected to the world of spirit.

As an approach to life, prayer is living out our union with the divine. We are, after all, partakers of the divine nature, according to 2 Peter 1:4. Even Jesus prayed that we would all be one, even as he and God were one—God in him and he in God (John 17:20–23). From the thrill of the mountaintop to the ghosted valley below, everything is filled with life when God is seen in all things. It is in the living of life—this life—that we experience divine intimacy, so how we approach our time on this planet either helps or hinders our ability to experience God.

Prayer is merely another term for practicing the presence of God—that is, experiencing a perpetual awareness of and communion with the Holy. As we dance to the rhythm of the divine, we are practicing what Paul refers to as walking in step with the Spirit. As Romans 8:14

(NRSVue) declares, "For all who are led by the Spirit of God are children of God." We experience divine intimacy when "it is no longer I who live, but it is Christ who lives in me" (Gal. 2:20a, NRSVue). Moving to the beat of the Spirit equates to constant communion with God, and that, my friend, is prayer as an approach to life.

Prayer is always relational, whereas praying often becomes mechanical and ritualistic. Prayer is moving and responding to divine life within, whereas praying is often about appeasing and manipulating a Santa Claus God. Prayer is the natural sense of belonging that deep relationships produce, whereas praying can become a mark of spiritual superiority. As a way of being, prayer is where the presence of God meets our human longing for divine intimacy. It is the crossroads of transformation. Simply put, prayer is nothing more than a living, loving relationship with God whereby our soul connects with and draws from the Spirit's life-giving presence. Mindful of this great mystery, we are ever ready to yield more and more of ourselves to God's self-communication and self-disclosure to us.

In my experience, divine intimacy rarely comes through adherence to outward religious rituals, for they are but symbols that point to God, never the essence of ultimate reality. As such, they can never produce the kind of intimacy we long for. All they can ever do is point to God, for they are merely a form of religious expression, not the substance of which we seek. Prayer is about the heart and is experienced when relational awareness of God's presence becomes a way of living, being, and seeing.

Scripture

Whereas prayer is a living, breathing, lifelong conversation with God that emanates from the heart, Scripture is a more tangible form of interaction. We physically hold it in our hands, read it with our eyes, hear it with our ears, and engage our mind and activate our heart when studying it. Yet how we approach Scripture is extremely important in our quest for divine intimacy. In the Western world, Scripture is often viewed as the literal words of God to humankind, as though God dictated each and every word found in the Bible. Every word mind you, even though we do not possess the original manuscripts that God supposedly dictated! The writers become passive human pens moved by the very hand of God. This view is fraught with serious problems (see my book *Leaving Religion Finding God: Rediscovering a Faith Worth Believing and a God Worth Following* for a serious discussion of the matter).

An approach to Scripture that interprets its content literally and sees every word as the divine expression of God leads to severe misunderstanding. It is the faulty application of a Western lens to sacred texts produced by Jewish writers in the Middle East. In reality, literalism is the lowest level of expression and interpretation possible because it minimizes the use of sacred storytelling and other equally valid literary methods.

For instance, Scripture speaks of God as a father. The Lord's Prayer, which Christians from around the globe recite every Sunday, begins with "Our Father." Is God a literal father who procreates with a human female, or is this merely a culturally conditioned view of God arising from the hierarchical, male-dominated culture of the day? According to Scripture, it was God's righteous right arm that saved Israel, but does God literally possess a right arm, and is it righteous, or is this a culturally conditioned way of attributing a specific outcome to a divine source?

We must be extremely careful with interpreting Scripture literally, for doing so means worshiping a God who commands genocide, despises homosexuals and seeks their death, promotes slavery, views females as second-class citizens, sends people to eternal damnation for temporal sins, murders his own son to appease a warped sense of justice, and seems to think that the sun revolves around Earth. That's literalism, and it leads to a ridiculous understanding of God.

Scripture contains a richness far beyond what literalism allows. If God is a spirit that is worshiped in spirit and in truth (John 4:24), then God is not limited by gender, for God transcends gender. God is mystery to us—something we simply can't get our arms around—and yet something that we personally experience. As mystery, God cannot be spoken of in definitive terms that authoritatively declare "God is," for the very nature of mystery is undefined, obscure, and uncontainable within human expression. No human words can do justice to the deep mystery of God. Instead, we can only state what "God is like" from an experiential and comparative standpoint.

Our understanding of God is influenced by our personal experiences, our reservoir of knowledge, and the culture of our day. We use metaphors and similies to help us express our God experiences. God is *like* a loving, protective father. God is *like* a strong mighty tower for protection. God is *like* a rock that is stable and secure. These are merely tools that help us articulate our *experience* of divine mystery; they are not definitive, literal statements about God.

All writings, whether Scripture or not, are directly related to and limited by the knowledge, experiences, and worldviews of the culture in which the writings arose. Scripture is but a collection of works from various individuals all trying to express their understanding and experience of God in the culturally conditioned language, worldview, and knowledge of their day. This explains many of the "hard-to-swallow" parts of Scripture that are so objectionable to the modern mind.

Scripture isn't the dictated words of a divine deity but rather the religious views of specific individuals writing about God from ancient perspectives. Some parts struggle to align with modern knowledge, but other parts remain inspiring and wholesome. The institutionalized church recognized value in these writings and, over time, established an official list of collected works it *declared* to be the official holy books of the church. As a "declared-by-the-church" collection of writings, the

Bible has helped many in their quest for divine intimacy, but it is not the dictated, literal, once-for-all-time words of God to humankind.

My intent is not to demean Scripture, for we shall soon see its usefulness in the pursuit of God; rather, my point is that once we move past a limited, literalistic understanding of the Bible, we free ourselves to discover a richer and deeper spirituality that enhances our relationship with the Holy. The God of literalism is far too small for the magnitude of divine intimacy we seek.

The Word of God

If Scripture isn't the once-for-all-time literal words of God to humankind, as many believe, and instead contains human words locked into cultural, time-bound language and perspectives, then why is Scripture even in the equation for divine intimacy? This is an excellent question, and the answer is found in how we approach Scripture.

Over the centuries, Scripture has been referred to as "the Word of God." For many, this phrase is simply another way of saying "the very words of God," which allows them to elevate the value of Scripture. In reality, however, quite the opposite is occurring. Literalism does nothing but *restrain* God's ability to speak to us in the present. A once-for-all-time understanding of God's communication with humankind looks back to what God *once* did when God *once* spoke *once* in time past. Boundaries are forced upon us, and we are locked into an ancient worldview that no longer exists. Divine intimacy, however, dances to the rhythm of God in the present now, with a God that is still speaking, freed from the time-bound, culture-bound, ancient-bound shackles of a "has-been" God.

When we use the phrase "Word of God" appropriately and understand what it really means, Scripture comes alive and is filled with depth and riches that literalism can never provide. The distinction between "Word of God" and "words of God" is essential, for it makes all the difference in the world. If God has spoken in the past and is done speaking in the present, then divine intimacy is about learning to correctly interpret ancient dictated words. Faced with such a task, we throw up our hands in despair, trying to interpret literally what was never meant to be taken literally. Intimacy now centers around education, learning, interpretation, and correct doctrine. Look at all the denominations in the world today, all with their own "correct" interpretation of Scripture. If this is what divine intimacy is all about, then our boat has already capsized!

Fortunately, Scripture as the Word of God isn't about literal interpretation, correct doctrine, education, and orthodox belief but about opening a doorway into greater communion with the divine. Did you catch the "opening a doorway" part? In a metaphorical sense, Scripture is an open doorway that invites us into divine intimacy. In other words, Scripture has a sacramental or revealing nature. It is this revealing nature, this "opening-a-doorway" aspect, or this "God-is-still-speaking" element of Scripture that has helped so many over the years. That's what a sacrament is—a revealing, a doorway. There are all kinds of revealing moments and open doorways in life, and although Scripture isn't the only doorway into intimacy, it is certainly one that has influenced the lives of many throughout the centuries. In fact, life itself is one big sacramental doorway into experiencing the divine.

Jesus was called the Word of God. That doesn't mean that he was a literal word on a page but that his life and teaching become a doorway to divine intimacy. He reflects for us what God must be like, which, in turn, helps us experience God like Jesus did. In like manner, the Bible is called the Word of God, for it, too, acts sacramentally in our life. As we interact with its revealing nature, our experience of divine intimacy is enhanced.

I don't view God as having spoken once-for-all-time at a particular moment in past history. No, God is *still* speaking, *still* moving, *still* creating, and *still* influencing. It is this still-speaking sacred reality that I pursue, and Scripture becomes a sacramental vehicle that helps take me there.

Pathways for Intimacy

Because God is a mystery that I can neither explain nor understand, about all I can do is *experience* the sacred presence in my life. As a living, thinking, feeling individual, all I really know is that I have experiences I attribute to that which is real but unseen, experienced but unfathomable. There is something beyond me that I am connected to, and it moves my mind and my heart. I no longer spend time trying to figure God out, for that is an impossibility. Now, I simply relax and enjoy the show. I humbly float in the deep waters of mystery and enjoy the ride as I pursue greater awareness of the divine life deep within me. To that end, my time with Scripture involves three avenues. In other words, if Scripture were a cabin in the woods, I would use three paths to get there: mind, heart, and meditative pondering.

All too often, the mind is either elevated as the supreme element of humanity or diminished to an obstacle level. I find that neither extreme is the case. We seem to have rational, emotional, and spiritual components to our being, so to throw any one of them under the bus is to ignore the reality of our human makeup. Each has its limitations, but I engage all of my humanity in experiencing the divine, not just one aspect of it.

I have seen people cast dispersions upon their humanity as though they were entrapped in a suit of smelly garbage. Their humanness becomes something to run from and avoid at all costs. To experience God, they seek to rid themselves of who they are in order to rise above and beyond their humanity. From my perspective, nothing could be further from the truth, for this attitude diminishes the creation God sees as "good." I have never experienced God outside my humanness.

Instead, the only time I experience God is in this life and in my own humanity, not outside it. I have come to love this "smelly" garbage suit of mine. I embrace my humanness as the dwelling of God, for although God is beyond my humanity, God is also within my humanity. God is not "out there" but "in here."

To enhance my mind's connection with divine mystery, I actually study Scripture. "Studying" means that I do more than enjoy a cursory reading: I seek to learn, grow, dig deep, and increase my knowledge and understanding, for the more I know and learn, the more my mind is transformed and renewed. Oh, I will never understand God, I am fully aware of that, but I learn from the divine encounters of others as revealed in Scripture. Studying the Bible takes time and effort, for there is nothing sacred about ignorance. Why would ignorance ever be considered a prized spiritual quality? Through the study of Scripture, I have experienced greater appreciation for the divine, increased awareness and sensitivity to the great mystery, and a deeper understanding of what is important in my life.

Knowledge is powerful. If I seek to truly know someone or something, I get to know that person or learn as much as I can about the subject of interest. I become informed and aware. It helps me relate and interact. It also influences my life, the way I live, and the way I view and experience God. Increased knowledge is but one avenue of interaction with the divine. Countless times, the study of Scripture has revealed a new concept, truth, or perspective that opened me up to the Spirit's moving. Often, I find myself weeping with joy and wonder. It is a moment of divine connection for which I am deeply moved and eternally grateful.

In addition to the mind, my heart also finds itself traveling to the cabin in the woods. In other words, I also read the Bible devotionally. As I engage the more emotive side of my humanity, I am simply reading with a heart that is open to the Spirit's moving. Much like Samuel in the

Old Testament, my heart cries out, "Speak, Lord, for I am listening." It is a time when my brain is relaxed and my expectant heart extends an open invitation to the Spirit. As a sacramental doorway for the revealing of God, my senses are primed for divine nudges. I am reading, but in reality, I am listening. My heart is fixed upon the open doorway. What will come to me through this sacred portal? What is the still-speaking God whispering to my soul today?

Devotional reading isn't about parsing words, studying cultural backgrounds, or putting on the lens of Jewish thought. It simply focuses upon the present moment with Scripture as the spiritual prompt for the nudgings of God. These are precious moments, and whether through study or devotion, mind or soul, it is always helpful to remove distractions so the whispers of God can be heard.

My final path toward the cabin in the woods is what I refer to as "meditative pondering." It isn't full meditation, and it isn't a full-mind exercise. Instead, it is a pondering deep within my heart and mind—an active awareness of awe and wonder, much like Mary, who "treasured all these words and pondered them in her heart" (Luke 2:19, NRSVue).

Whether studying Scripture deeply or reading it devotionally, I engage in a further step that helps move printed words to an internal reality of the soul. I want what comes through the open doorway to get into my blood and bones. In other words, I desire that it take root in my life. I do this through meditative pondering—at least, that's what I call it. My mind is not disengaged or placed in neutral, and neither am I jacked up on emotionalism. Rather, I look for inner application, an inner witness, and an attitude of awareness and appreciation. Much like savoring every bite of a favorite meal, I seek to fully digest what comes through the sacramental portal as a means of nourishing my soul.

One summer, I visited San Francisco, and my eyes beheld the famous Golden Gate Bridge. A tour boat took me under the bridge, and I felt the tug of the water's currents while getting up close and personal with this massive wonder. I viewed this iconic structure from a distance, up close, under it, beside it, and even at night and from an airplane. Learning about its construction and history enhanced my appreciation and awe. At one point, I was able to stand on a high point and take in this panoramic visual feast. There I was, soaking in this magical scene like warm rays of sunshine on a brisk autumn day. It felt good. I sensed the bridge's beauty and grandeur. I experienced the wonder of human ingenuity. I realized my own smallness in comparison. I drank deeply from the well of amazement, and doing so moved me toward God. The same thing happened to me on Pikes Peak and the Royal Gorge in Colorado.

In a similar way, that is what is happening in my state of meditative pondering. I don't scrutinize, analyze, or criticize. I simply take it in and allow it to touch me, transform me, validate me, and move me toward intimacy. Like Mary, I treasure it all in my heart. As I stand in awe and wonder, I am drawn closer to God.

To such wonder, I often find myself bursting forth with such phrases as "yes, Lord," "I love you," "I hear you," "thank you," and "I stand in awe." They are merely impromptu responses to an inward treasuring. At other times, I am drawn to silence, as though the moment were filled with holiness in the same way Moses experienced the Shekinah glory of God's presence during his desert get-togethers with God at the tent of meeting. Meditative pondering allows me to experience God's presence through Scripture as I bring it close to home, wrap my arms around it, and take in the breathtaking views. It is but one way I experience divine intimacy.

Many Ways to Travel

Although my well-worn paths to the cabin in the woods involve study, devotional reading, and meditative pondering, divine dancing has many options. We are accustomed to using our eyes and reading printed words on a page, but have you ever listened to Scripture with your ears? Take turns reading Scripture out loud with a friend or significant other, or listen to recorded Scripture being read by a professional voice actor. In the days when I drove sixty-five miles one way to work each day, I often listened to Scripture being read aloud. It was an entirely different experience for me, and I picked up on things that my eyes would have easily missed.

Early in my ministry, I would sing Scripture as part of my daily routine. I made up my own creative melodies that allowed my heart to express gratitude. The act wasn't really about the melodies but about my heart dancing before God. The Psalms are amazing to sing. In fact, they were Israel's hymnbook.

I have used various versions of the Bible over the years, and each has touched my heart. I prefer a more literal translation while seriously studying the text and a simple paraphrase for devotional reading. Taking time to memorize key verses has also been helpful. For instance, as a youngster, I memorized Isaiah 26:3 in the King James Version of the Bible, and it has stuck with me ever since. Look it up and memorize it yourself in whatever version you prefer. It will be a comfort to you. As a teenager, I attended a Bible conference in Iowa, where I memorized Romans 8:1. Look it up and memorize it for yourself. It will bring you comfort and strength. Have you ever read Psalm 1 in *The Message*, a contemporary paraphrase of the Bible written in the vernacular of the modern age? Look it up and compare it to other versions. It will make Psalm 1 come alive.

Interaction and Connection

Interacting with Scripture is a good thing. After all, if the Holy Writings are a time-tested doorway to divine intimacy, it may be time to take them off the shelf, dust them off, and actually spend some quality time with them. Scripture's sacramental nature becomes one way we experience a connection with God.

Scripture has had a profound effect upon my life. It sparks desire and delight in my spiritual pursuit. I find immense value in its pages. It has assured me of God's presence through good times and bad. I find courage, comfort, and challenge as I read the stories of old and look for the underlying truth they are conveying. I see exhilarating and inspiring intimacy on display as the Psalmist pours his heart out to God, as the author of Ecclesiastes wrestles with the ambiguities of life, as Job seeks clarity in the midst of suffering, and as the love of God reaches far beyond my own limits in the story of Jonah. I am reminded that God is real and that people throughout the ages sought and experienced a connection with the divine. My spirit is uplifted, and my heart is filled with gratitude. I am in awe of the great mystery, and although I can't explain this mystery, I experience it. That is divine intimacy. Prayer and Scripture become two avenues that help me dance with the divine.

11

PAIN & PLEASURE

I FIRST HEARD ROBERT BROWNING HAMILTON'S poem "I Walked a Mile with Pleasure" while visiting a friend in England. We were discussing the topic of pain and pleasure when he shared it with me. It impressed me so much that I have committed this prized jewel to memory:

I walked a mile with Pleasure;
She chatted all the way;
But left me none the wiser
For all she had to say.

I walked a mile with Sorrow;
And ne'er a word said she;
But, oh! The things I learned from her,
When Sorrow walked with me.

This little poem reminds me of a memorable father/son moment back in the day when my son was much younger. Both of our bladders had reached their painful capacity. If we didn't locate a restroom within the next couple of minutes, we would publicly embarrass ourselves. Finally, we stumbled upon what we were desperately searching for, and at just the right time. What a relief—literally! No doubt, you have found yourself in a similar situation.

There we were, standing side by side for what seemed like forever, personally experiencing the difference between pain and pleasure. I can't say that it was a bonding experience, but I took it upon myself to use this extraordinary moment to teach my son a valuable lesson about pain and pleasure. I will have to ask him whether he remembers engaging in urinal theology while making application to the real world!

We have all experienced pain to varying degrees, some more than others. Although there are different levels, types, and responses to the challenges we encounter, we quickly realize that pain is a very real part of life, from little nicks and bruises to severe wounds that result in physical, spiritual, or psychological harm. Pain can even lead to death. To be human entails familiarity with pain and pleasure.

We prefer pleasure over pain, for pleasure stimulates joy, goodwill, and happiness. It brings a smile to our face and makes us feel good about ourselves and about life. Pain, on the other hand, often produces hostility, confusion, and bitterness. Which one would you rather experience? The answer is obvious. However, if God's sacred presence is experienced in this life, then it is experienced in the totality of life with all of its ups and downs, mountain tops and steep valleys. In other words, God is experienced in pain and pleasure, for God is not absent from any experience or situation we encounter.

Jesus knew the pleasure of crowds following him, the joy of teaching his disciples, and the power and presence of the Spirit throughout each day. His experience of the divine was just as real during seasons of pain as it was in times of pleasure. He experienced God in the Garden of Gethsemane, in the betrayal of Judas, in the scattering of his disciples, and in the public shame of his crucifixion. Jesus experienced the power, presence, and peace of God in all of life's circumstances because he lived every moment in divine connection. He lived in God's presence and died in God's presence. Divine whispers were known to him through it all.

The same could be said of the Apostle Paul, who bore the confinement of prison, the hate of detractors seeking to take his life, and the mistreatment of a Roman citizen, which he was. He also experienced the pleasure of planting new churches throughout the region, broadening the gospel's appeal to Gentiles, and receiving the encouraging dedication of colleagues in support of his ministry. Paul experienced the peace, power, and presence of God in pain and pleasure.

Intimacy with the divine is not dependent upon one's circumstances, for it is associated not only with pain or pleasure but with the totality of life—all the experiences of our journey. When we see God as a rewarder and punisher who doles out pleasure to those who appease and obey, while dispensing pain and tribulation to the faithless and disobedient, our view of God and our view of pain and pleasure are perverted. Pleasure becomes the blessing of God, while pain becomes divine punishment. If this situation were actually the case, divine intimacy would be unattainable for a good portion of life itself, at least the painful parts of the journey. In fact, God would be separate and distinct from the reality of our world and present only in the good times. But God is here now, experienced in our life circumstances, whether painful or pleasurable.

We tend to be selective in our evaluation of data and skew them toward our preferred interpretation. We look at a picturesque sunset, a majestic mountain, or a newborn baby and marvel at the reflection of God found in such beauty. God is experienced in the pure pleasure of the moment. But what about the other side of the coin, such as earthquakes, hurricanes, disease, war, child abuse, racism, injustice, genocide, the exploitation of women, and a host of other data staring us down but readily ignored? What does that say about life, about God, and about us? Can God make beauty from a stain, or is God only experienced in those data that best appeal to our senses?

To see the divine only in beauty and pleasure is to worship a God that is divorced from the reality of our world—a half-God, in a sense. For me, any God that is detached from our existential reality isn't a God worth following. But God isn't disconnected from our journey, for God is a sacred presence that permeates this life—our life and life in its totality. God is present in us, with us, and through us, no matter what circumstances befall us. There is no need to skew data to our liking, for whether we are viewing a thrilling mountaintop vista or stumbling through a deep, dark valley, God is there, and where God is, divine intimacy can be experienced. Now that is a God worth following!

The Gift of Pain

Let's begin with the pain side of the equation, for it is much more difficult to accept God's presence in adversity than it is in pleasure. Without diminishing pain's power to wound us—and believe me, it has the power to do that—it seems that pain may actually be a gift. When viewed in this light, we are able to learn from it, experience God in it, and redirect its power toward transforming our faith journey.

Pain has been envisioned as the enemy when it may actually be a friend. Maybe we need to rehabilitate its image and see it as another avenue for experiencing God in this life. If you have gone through a great deal of pain and are still raw and reeling from its debilitating effects, you may not be open and ready to receive this teaching. I understand how repulsive it can be to consider pain a friend, for I have walked this very road myself. Take in what you can at this time and be open to God's presence in all circumstances—even yours, even now. One of the best things I did in my pain was simply to be honest and open before God. I shared my heart, even when it spilled out as anger. Have an authentic conversation with the divine and then sit back and listen to what the Spirit whispers to your soul. Be real, but also be open to the God who whispers.

My first ten years in full-time pastoral ministry were filled with enormous pain, and what an eye-opener that was. I had the unpleasant distinction of pastoring two of the most difficult churches in the entire region in which I served. I can sure pick them! With two children in diapers, I lived on nothing but love and struggled to make ends meet.

When my young son was hospitalized, I wondered how in the world I was going to pay the mounting hospital bill. Discretionary funds? What in the world were those? I had no funds, and I had minor discretion over their use. I was the poster child for the church phrase "Lord, you keep him humble, and we'll keep him poor."

Although I had little to my name, owned no possessions to speak of, and could barely pay the bills, that wasn't what brought pain. I felt called to be a minister, and I intentionally chose a path of service over monetary gain. As difficult as it was sometimes, I was okay with not having much. It came with the territory.

The painful part wasn't the lack of funds or possessions but the way I was treated by these two churches. I didn't realize it at the time, but this abuse had been their modus operandi for years. I wasn't the first to endure such treatment. I could relate a plethora of stories that would bring tears to your eyes and cause your head to shake in disbelief, but rehashing the details serves no grand purpose. Immeasurable pain and internal destruction were occurring in my life at the hands of those who proclaimed Christ the loudest.

Unable to sleep because of the stress and chaos upending my life, I spent many nights learning to breathe again, trying to reduce disruptive anxiety, and scouring job openings for ways to make a living without the hassle. The cost-benefit analysis was no longer adding up for me. If this type of existence was what ministry was all about, I would be far better off waving the flag of surrender and moving on to something that wouldn't annihilate my soul. My point in telling you this story is to assure you that I have also experienced the devastating effects of pain in a tangible and personal way.

My district superintendent, a seasoned and wise minister who would go on to become a college president and a denominational president, said to me, "In all my years of ministry, I have never seen anyone go through as much as you have." I knew then that my mind wasn't playing tricks on me and that I had, indeed, endured a harsh brand of "love." Years later, when healing had performed its restorative work in my life, I would look upon these two churches in a new light. During those painful years, I learned so much about myself, ministry, relationships, life, leadership, and God. In a sense, I walked a mile with Sorrow, who never said a word, but I learned a great deal when she quietly walked beside me.

I now view pain very differently. Rather than being my enemy, it turned out to be a friend. I do not deny pain's power to wound, but I now redirect its might toward positive ends. Pain became the path for smoothing out the rough edges of my life. Pain softened my stiff resistance and readied the soil to receive the planting of divine whispers. Through pain, I deepened my ministry to others, reaffirmed my values, and enlarged my commitment to experience God in the totality of my life.

As painful as that ten-year period was for me, it was absolutely transformative. I learned to hear divine whispers in challenging circumstances and was forever changed from within. I feel a bit like Søren Kierkegaard, who once said, "With the help of the thorn in my foot, I spring higher than anyone with sound feet." Indeed, I discovered the whisper of God in the most unlikely of places, and I now spring higher than I ever imagined.

The Gift of Softening

One day, I heard a snap in my back that landed me in the emergency room. The pain was excruciating. I couldn't stand, I couldn't sit, and I couldn't lie down. I remember standing with one hand on a cane and the other on a chest of drawers, exhausted and unable to move. When it dawned on me that I couldn't remain in that position forever, I miraculously made it to the emergency room with the help of a friend. I had extended my body beyond my physical capabilities, and an MRI revealed significant issues with my lower back. Pain captures our attention and softens our underbelly unlike anything else.

Laying flooring was the straw that broke the camel's back, but the underlying issue had built up over time with unnoticed damage. When pain immobilizes us, it gets our attention, and it is then that we are willing to try something new. I am very careful now with how I bend, lift, and enter a car. I have made the necessary adjustments to improve the health of my back. I heard the voice of pain—how could I miss it screaming at me?—and it prompted me to change my ways. Sometimes that's just how it goes. Unwilling to listen to whispers, we finally hear the crystal-clear shout of pain.

Pain is unpleasant and has the capacity to wound deeply. I don't want to give the impression that it is in any way trivial. It is called *pain* for a reason. It is a friend not because it is pleasant but because of its refining effect upon us. James 1:2–4 (NRSVue) notes this very fact: "My brothers and sisters, whenever you face various trials, consider it all joy, because you know that the testing of your faith produces endurance. And let endurance complete its work, so that you may be complete and whole, lacking in nothing." Difficult circumstances are not easy to endure, but the refiner's fire burns up the dross while leaving behind valuable gold. Although nobody likes the pain associated with refining fire, the valuable gold it produces is priceless.

Isaiah 48:10 (NRSVue) also notes the refining furnace of adversity: "See, I have refined you but not like silver; I have tested you in the furnace of adversity." The heat of the fire produces pain *and* gold. Isaiah 43:2–3a (NRSVue) further reminds us that God is with us as we walk through the fires of adversity:

When you pass through the waters, I will be with you,
  and through the rivers, they shall not overwhelm you;
when you walk through fire you shall not be burned,
  and the flame shall not consume you.
For I am the LORD your God,
  the Holy One of Israel, your Savior.

Even Jesus acknowledged life's pain in John 16:33 (NRSVue): "I have said this to you so that in me you may have peace. In the world you face persecution, but take courage: I have conquered the world!" We all experience hardship in its many forms, and if it can't be avoided, we might as well use it to our advantage. One way we do that is by recognizing its value, and in doing so, we allow it to transform us.

The pain I experienced during my first ten years of full-time pastoral ministry was exceptional, and I can still feel its sting upon my life in so many ways. Yet it softened me and taught me valuable lessons. It gifted me with a deeper level of compassion that allowed me to identify with others in pain. It prompted me to sort through a myriad of issues and arrive at values that would become the bedrock of my life. It moved my anger to joy and permitted me to experience the breath of God upon my life.

In essence, pain was the perfecter of my faith, as noted in Hebrews 2:10 (NRSVue): "It was fitting that God, for whom and through whom all things exist, in bringing many children to glory, should make the pioneer of their salvation perfect through sufferings." This pain is the refiner's fire doing its good work in us. Pain doesn't make us perfect in the absolutely flawless sense—none of us will ever be that. *Perfect* is the Greek word *teleos*, which focuses on completeness and reaching one's purpose. The goal isn't to suffer but to experience completeness in trying times. Although his life was short-lived, Jesus experienced the very thing we seek—an intimacy with God that brings about a sense of completeness, calmness, purposefulness, fulfillment, and wholeness. That is the precious outcome of the refiner's fire.

Pain has a way of unmaking our lives. Things get messy, chaos ensues, and the trajectory of our world is altered. Within the field of change management, it is well known that before new outcomes can be achieved, the status quo must be destabilized. In other words, we can't keep doing the same things in the same way over and over again and expect different results. Change doesn't occur unless our current comfort zone is challenged.

The destabilizing nature of pain unmakes our world and undermines the status quo. This shift, of course, is necessary for the roots of change to grow deep and produce a harvest. The status quo is comfortable, but it is not the way of transformation, for it always seeks to maintain sameness, which only serves to filter out divine whispers. When our lives are unmade, we become softened and primed to move forward. This path toward transformation is challenging for sure, but it is an essential element in our quest for divine intimacy. Jesus noted in John 12:24 (NRSVue), "Very truly, I tell you, unless a grain of wheat falls into the earth and dies, it remains just a single grain, but if it dies it bears much fruit." It is the dying part that is difficult, for there is no fruit-bearing without it.

In many ways, people experience life in two major sections: the first half and the second half, with many chapters in each section. For me, the first half was about pain getting my attention, softening me up, and smoothing out my rough edges. It was stressful and often unbearable. The pain spawned all kinds of emotions and perspectives regarding life and God. In the second half of my life, I realized the transformative nature of pain—that it was a pathway to wholeness and that God was with me through those deep waters. Rather than drowning in my sorrow, I simply learned to float in the deep waters of mystery, with my feet unable to touch the bottom, and it was there that I learned what whispers were all about.

Today, I am a better version of myself than in the past—more patient, accepting, and kind. My values are better aligned with my actions. I like the transformed me and realize that I would never be who I am today without the gift of a painful yesterday. Pain was an invaluable teacher and became the path for embossing the maker's mark upon my soul. Through pain, I learned a great deal about divine intimacy. Although we may struggle in the heat of those moments to recognize divine whispers, as time passes and wounds begin to heal, we may be able to look back upon those experiences as times when God's best work occurred in us.

I never diminish the pain that was so real to me during those arduous days, and neither do I excuse the behavior of those intent on wounding me while flying the banner of love. Yet I have this strange sense that I was exactly where I was supposed to be—that "in the fullness of time," I had come to my time and place for meeting the Spirit and overhauling my heart. I was softened and sensitized to divine whispers.

The Gift of Protection

I read of a medical doctor who performed hand surgery upon lepers back when leprosy was not well understood. The disease produces severe nerve damage whereby lepers can no longer feel physical pain. Without the sensation of pain, they wind up injuring themselves unknowingly. Hands are cut and feet are damaged, and limbs can no longer be used, for without pain, greater damage befalls them. This doctor's surgical skills were deeply needed and appreciated.

If you have ever touched a hot pan, spilled coffee on yourself, or stubbed your toe, you know the protective nature of pain as it screams, "Don't do that again. It is bad for you." We learn that pans can be hot, beverages can burn, and the corners of furniture can be hazardous. Pain is an ingenious method of protection that alerts us to harm and signals that something is wrong.

Taken to the extreme, we could spend our whole life avoiding everything that brings pain. But this goal is impossible, for one would have to eschew life itself. Although my first ten years of ministry were pretty hard on me, I don't avoid ministry, people, or my calling because of it. That would be nothing more a trained incapacity—a knee-jerk reaction rather than an appropriate response.

It would be like a fish happily eating all the bugs in the water until a bright yellow one with a hook attached to a fisherman's line yanks him pretty good. Finally, with evasive maneuvers, the fish gets free. It was a close call, but now the fish avoids all food that is yellow. That is a trained incapacity—an overreaction that incapacitates our ability to learn and discern. We wind up throwing out the good with the bad. We avoid all yellow bugs even though most of them are fish-friendly and delicious.

Initially, the pain of those early ministry years created rash reactions in me. Over time, I realized that my pain actually protected me in that it showed me a great deal about myself, God, and others. I learned to protect myself from certain types of situations and certain types of people, but I didn't stop eating yellow bugs altogether. I just became more discerning in my food choices. As one regional minister once told me, "Terry, you are not a zookeeper. You don't have to shovel sh*t all day long." I couldn't agree more, but I had to learn to discern which situations were zoos to me as I continued in my calling without becoming a religious sh*t shoveler. These days, I am much wiser and more selective in where I go and what I do. I wouldn't have known such discernment without the pain of those early ministry years.

The Gift of Gratitude

It seems counterintuitive in our current culture of complaining to say that gratitude is a by-product of pain, but when viewed with new lenses, pain offers up the gift of gratitude, which helps us live in the present moment. When we are wounded, gratitude is the last thing on our mind, and yet that is exactly what Scripture calls for: "Rejoice always, pray without ceasing, give thanks in all circumstances, for this is the will of God in Christ Jesus for you" (1 Thess. 5: 16–18, NRSVue). To my knowledge, we are asked to give thanks not "for" all circumstances but "in" all circumstances—there is a difference. A spoonful of gratitude always helps the medicine go down.

When you get to the point where all circumstances, whether good or bad, become pathways for divine intimacy, you are primed to recognize whispers. When pain upends our idealism, we are more prepared than ever to hear from God. Viewing pain as devoid of God merely shuts the doorways through which divine whispers travel.

Gratitude is a response to life in general, not just to pain. That breath you just took in was from God. Be grateful for it. The person you just interacted with was the image of God in your life. Recognize it and rejoice in it. In pain or pleasure, an attitude of gratitude enhances our ability to see God in every aspect of our lives. It is just a little harder to do when times are tough, for instead of being grateful, we would rather lash out and blame somebody for our discomfort. Most often, God takes the hit.

It is similar to love, a good religious concept that we believe in, proclaim, and base our lives upon. When the rubber hits the road, however, our love seems to have limits, for loving people whom we don't like requires something of us that we may not be willing to give. It is easier to categorize them as enemies than to love them as divine image-bearers. The same thing could be said of gratitude: It is a good religious concept that we believe in, proclaim, and base our lives upon, but mustering up the courage to be grateful in adversity requires something of us that we may not be willing to give—intentionality. As we find the strength within for gratitude, we discover the precious gift of seeing beyond our pain and focusing our attention on God's presence.

The Gift of Community

God often whispers to us in our pain through the experience and encouragement of others. In painful circumstances the Christian community becomes invaluable. If pain is an ever-present reality of life, then it is a present reality for everyone. Others within the community have traveled similar paths and are able to offer valuable perspectives, for they have "been there, done that." A similar thought is offered in 1 Corinthians

12:26 (NRSVue): "If one member suffers, all suffer together with it; if one member is honored, all rejoice together with it."

Shared life within the community of faith means that we are all in this together. We are a family, one of Paul's images for the faith community. In essence, we are brothers and sisters united by the bond of Christ—a community of God followers who walk together toward wholeness. We care for one another, support one another, challenge one another, and uplift one another because of our common connection to the Holy One.

We are not alone in our journey, as we have the power of Christ within and the power of community without to share in our suffering and help shoulder the burden. When the church functions well, its members become the ministering hands, feet, and voice of the divine. God often whispers to our soul through the kindness of others. That is the community at its best, a group of people who relate to one another through love, compassion, and care.

The community of faith has a tremendous opportunity to become a healing balm in the life of others, but all too often it is nothing more than a cesspool of further pain—a finely tuned, judgmental juggernaut skilled at wounding the hearts of those who need healing the most. Yet when the community of faith chooses to live in loving relationship with one another, it becomes a powerful voice for healing.

The Power of Perspective

Ever hear someone say that perception is reality? I hear it all the time, but reality is reality, regardless of whether my perspective is aligned with it. I get the point, however, that in a practical way, the perception of the beholder becomes their perceived reality. Notice that I said *perceived* reality, not *actual* reality. If everything we perceived was *actual*, what would be the point of changing our perspective? To change a previous perspective is to acknowledge that what we originally perceived was incorrect. Whether perceived or actual, there is power in perspective.

How we view things influences their effect upon us. By *choosing* our perspective regarding any given topic or circumstance, we wind up changing our *perceived* reality, which, in turn, alters our actual experience. If we view pain in a negative light and something to be avoided at all costs, then we miss its positive attributes and become deaf to God's voice.

Unfortunately, we often focus upon our woundedness and the injustice we have suffered. But God prompts us to ask, "What should I do with what's been done to me?" What we give power to in the mind has the ability to control us, and that is why our view of pain is important. If our perspective becomes our perceived reality, then how we think of pain is paramount to our experience of God. What if we thought of pain as a friend rather than an enemy? What if we viewed pain as a teacher rather than a punisher? What if we saw pain as a tool of service instead of a cruel taskmaster? Imagine that—pain as the caboose, not the lead locomotive! What if pain became an avenue for hearing God's still, small voice? Would we then have the courage to say, "God, speak to me about me during these difficult days"?

In one sense, pain occurs in the mind. A physical wound sends signals to our brain that are interpreted as pain. While the cut is real and deep, our perception of that pain takes place in the mind. If we are the lead locomotive and pain is the caboose, could we choose to view these pain signals differently? Must pain always lead to suffering? In other words, there may be a difference between the pain we experience and the suffering that occurs in our mind. Could we respond with gratitude, openness, a listening heart, and a willingness to learn? Could we transform the pain in our mind—redeem it, reinterpret it, and learn from it—merely by changing our perspective about it? Will we suffer, cope, or conquer? Our experience depends upon how we view pain. When we view pain as a valuable conduit for divine whispers, we more readily see the light of God that radiates from adversity, and, in turn, we become light to others trying to find their own way through trials and tribulations.

Someone once commented to me that daily watering trees was not good for them because they are never required to grow their roots deep in search of water. When drought comes, they struggle to survive, for their root system is too shallow as a result of their dependence upon easy and pleasurable waterings. Drought, it seems, causes root systems to grow deeper in search of life-giving water. I don't know whether this is true, but it sure makes a good illustration.

No circumstance can separate us from divine whispers, not even pain. Our spiritual root system can grow deep, and when it does, we over-come seasons of drought, experience divine whispers, and become more than conquerors, as noted in Romans 8:35; 37–39 (NRSVue):

> Who will separate us from the love of Christ? Will affliction or distress or persecution or famine or nakedness or peril or sword? No, in all these things we are more than victorious through him who loved us. For I am convinced that neither death, nor life, nor angels, nor rulers, nor things present, nor things to come, nor powers, nor height, nor depth, nor anything else in all cre-ation will be able to separate us from the love of God in Christ Jesus our Lord.

Deep roots allowed Paul to sing while in prison. Deep roots allowed Jesus to travel the path of crucifixion without bitterness. Deep roots allow us to rejoice in painful circumstances and to see God in all situa-tions. Because suffering occurs in the mind, a renewed perspective of pain can open doorways to the whispers of God. It is possible to face life's tribulations with the peace, power, and presence of God, and that is divine intimacy.

Pleasure

Divine whispers are found not only in pain but also in pleasure. We have been taught that the good things that come our way are the result of divine blessing and favor. Adversity, on the other hand, arises from sin, disobedience, or our own stubbornness. Pain and trouble are sure evidence of God's displeasure or chastisement. In other words, God is lovingly present in the good times but nowhere to be found in the bad times. This belief results in a God that is separate and aloof from our real-world experiences—a God that is experienced as a divine punisher, a harsh disciplinarian, or simply nowhere to be found during the rough patches of life. If hard times are the chastisement of God, then Jesus, the Twelve, the early Christians, and followers of God throughout church history were being punished by an angry God who supposedly loved them. Unfathomable!

How can this be if God is everywhere present? It seems to me that *everywhere* actually means EVERYWHERE—that there is no place or circumstance where God cannot be found. God whispers to us throughout life in its totality. There is no divine favoritism, chastisement, or punishment from a capricious heavenly deity. These are merely human notions—ancient worldviews that people used to justify or explain their circumstances. They are not divine truths about God's essence or nature but rather human explanations of life events from prescientific mindsets that no longer find relevance in the modern world.

The point is that God is in the here and now of this life. According to Acts 17:28 (NRSVue), "In him we live and move and have our being." In other words, everything that is exists within God. Every situation we encounter is encountered in God. Mindboggling, isn't it? But it goes to show that there is nothing we do, nothing we go through, and no place in this universe where the divine cannot be found. So, let's not ensnare ourselves in a religious trap whereby pain is devoid of God while pleasure is bursting of God's presence, for God is found in both circumstances.

I use the term *pleasure* loosely and broadly. Some differentiate between *pleasure* and *happiness* and teach that pleasure is a fleeting, in-the-moment feeling, whereas happiness is a long-term lasting effect. I don't really buy that differentiation, for you could just as easily turn the terms around. However, I note the distinction between chasing after short-term addictive fixes and securing a grounded long-term perspective. When I speak of pleasure, I am referring to joy, happiness, smiling, contentment, and all those helpful terms associated with positive thoughts about God and life. I use the term broadly in referring to the many ways we joyfully experience God through pleasure.

Just as our view of pain can be warped, so can our view of pleasure. For instance, on the one hand, pleasure is seen as the blessing and favor of God. When things go our way, God is being good to us, and when we experience hardship, God is punishing us. This antiquated remnant from centuries ago still finds expression in the modern age.

On the other hand, another view is just as warped—where pleasure is seen as bad or sinful. In other words, God doesn't want us to be *too* happy, for we should be focusing on serious spiritual items rather than the pleasures of this world. To enjoy the pleasures of this world is to turn our back on the holiness God requires of us. Christians are to be sanctified, uncontaminated, and separate from the sinful pleasures of this world. So, which one is it? Are pleasure and joy the blessing of God, or are they ungodly involvement in worldly pleasures? Both views are warped perspectives of God and pleasure.

Much of my spiritual growth has entailed "unlearning" bad theology taught by the church. I have had to shed these archaic and nonsensical notions from a less enlightened era. Why can't we simply enjoy pleasure, happiness, joy, and all the great things about life with a smile on our face and in our heart? Why must it either be God's blessing upon us or sinful involvement in worldly pleasures? Why can't it just be the full enjoyment of life itself, in its entirety, which was given to us by God? Why can't pleasure simply be a part of the human experience—another avenue for experiencing divine whispers? We don't need to elevate pleasure to some super-spiritual state or demean it to an egregious sinful status. Pleasure is simply another element of life where God is present and experienced; the difference is that this experience brings joy rather than pain.

Just as suffering from pain occurs in the mind, so does the pleasure we experience, which means that our perspective is of critical importance. The simple point I am trying to make in this chapter is that God is present in pain and pleasure, and where God is present, whispers can be experienced. Because God is everywhere present in this life, God can be experienced in the totality of our experiences. Pretty simple, isn't it? We don't need to elevate one over the other or make one out to be sinful while the other is holy. Both are elements of our reality in which God is near.

What Is Your Pleasure?

I have learned to stop doing things for God in an attempt to earn divine approval. I am already approved by God, loved by God, and accepted by God just as I am. God doesn't need me to do anything. Instead, my life is about *experiencing* the divine mystery we call God and *connecting* to its peace, power, and presence in my life. To that end, I seek to practice the presence of God in the reality of pain and pleasure. I seek to accept each moment as it is, to live in the now, and to welcome each day, person, and circumstance that comes my way.

Let me share how simple pleasures become a conduit for experiencing God in my life. They are not religious acts, church activities, or something I do *for* God but simple pleasures associated with this life that I find enjoyable. I have no trouble experiencing divine intimacy in the things that bring me joy. Because we are individual, unique creations of God, the simple pleasures that whisper God's presence to me may be very different from the pleasures that speak to you. My list only serves to illustrate the larger truth: that divine whispers can be found in life's simple, ordinary pleasures.

The Pleasure of Music

The powerful pleasure of music has the capacity to move us from deep within. When I am up in the night—and I am up most nights—music is playing in the background. It soothes my soul and allows my thoughts to transcend the mundane. Often, I just close my eyes and take it in while its beauty and power sweep over me. I sense God in the pleasure that it brings me.

Sometimes, I lie on the floor with earbuds on and arms outstretched, lost in the world of music. Aware of God's presence, sometimes I well up with tears, break into a smile, or sense tremendous peace envelop me. It is pure bliss, and I sense God smiling, as if to say, "That's it, Terry. Relax, enjoy, and sense my pleasure in you." This divine connection comes to me through the simple sounds of notes, harmonies, instruments, and vocals.

I remember when I first recognized the pleasure I receive from music. I was in junior high school when I listened to an album owned by my older brother. (Yes, in those days, music was produced on vinyl albums and played on record players.) It was Paul McCartney's *Ram* album, released in 1971. The Beatles had disbanded, and Paul was now on his own.

I was mesmerized by this album and still listen to it today. I know nothing about Paul McCartney's character, theology, interests, or much of anything else about him. To me, that information is irrelevant. All I know is that his album took me to a place of peace and joy, a place that I associate with God's presence. That probably wasn't McCartney's intent, but it was the effect upon me. At that moment, I knew the power of music and the peace of God whispered to me through a vinyl record. Who would have guessed that such divine whispers would come through Paul McCartney?

The same thing happened to me with Elton John's 1975 album *Captain Fantastic and the Brown Dirt Cowboy*. Paul McCartney and

Elton John aren't religious people performing religious works but talented and creative artists sharing their love of music in a way that spiritually moved me. Why would these two albums remain with me as important connections to God? I am not sure I know or that I could explain it even if I did. I only know that through them, I sensed the power and pleasure of music as peace and joy flooded my heart. Really? Elton John and Paul McCartney? They were not producing religious, church-approved music, and that is exactly my point: God used a simple pleasure in the ordinary course of life to minister to my soul.

As I began attending church, I became familiar with church music, and at that time, the genre of contemporary Christian music was bursting upon the scene. I should point out that I don't believe that there is such a thing as "Christian" music any more than I believe that there are Christian cars, cafés, food, clothes, and so forth. *Christian* is just a label attached to a variety of music styles with religious content. Musical notes have no theology; they are merely tones played in various arrangements.

Christian music implies that there is a biblical, holy, and God-ordained arrangement of notes. Although lyrical content differs depending on the purpose of the song, a note has no religious affiliation, and what moves me is the music itself, those nonreligious notes and sounds. God is not locked into one genre, for God is the author of music itself, and as various individuals and groups share their musical talent, I receive pleasure.

Church hymns were prevalent during my impressionable years, and as a young Christian, I became familiar with this expression of faith. I still like them. As I traipsed off to Bible College, the music of contemporary Christian artists, such as Tim Sheppard, Leon Patillo, Keith Green, Larry Norman, The Imperials, and a host of others, moved my heart. To this day, I still listen to this music, and, as you might suspect, it still moves me.

A friend was driving me around England when a song came on the radio that moved me to tears. It was a moment I will never forget, and it served to remind me of the beauty of classical music. Recognizing its effect upon me, the driver purchased the CD and gifted it to me prior to my departure back to the States. It was Mozart's clarinet concerto, and it swept me off my feet. It reminded me of my younger days, when I fell asleep each night listening to classical music on a public radio program called *Starlight Concert*. I didn't know much about classical music back then, and I still don't, but Mozart's clarinet concerto, NPR's *Starlight Concert*, and many other classical selections drew me toward divine whispers.

During the years when I was working on my doctorates, I would rise at 3:00 A.M. each day to engage in my studies. I worked a full-time job and had two children and family responsibilities, so those quiet hours in the morning when others were sleeping was about the only time I had to pursue my education. Music was my constant companion during these precious morning hours. One song in particular brought the presence of God near, and I listened to it over and over again. It was "When the Snow Melts" by Phil Cunningham and Manus Lunny from Wyndham Hill Records *Sampler 96*. It still melts my heart as I remember its ministry to me. It wasn't "Christian" music but simply music from artists whose talent originated from the very creator of music! Their musical endeavors became a conduit for divine whispers.

I still listen to music. I can't stop. In fact, I listen to music pretty much all the time, for it touches my soul in ways that I cannot fully articulate. These days, I find myself drawn to blues guitar, instrumental piano, relaxing spa music, and the sound of choirs. I don't know what music tomorrow will bring, nor do I care, for music is merely notes on a page arranged in different ways that bring me pleasure, and through that pleasure, I experience divine intimacy.

I not only listen to music but write simple songs and play them on my guitar as an offering to the Lord—an audience of one. I am not an accomplished musician by any stretch of the imagination, but I take pleasure in creating beauty from the heart—my deepest self. Music is a powerful and pleasurable way to experience divine intimacy.

Your musical tastes may differ from my own, or music may not even be an avenue of pleasure in which you sense divine whispers. That is absolutely fine. You just be you. Many are surprised when I share such simple pleasures as avenues of divine intimacy. After all, my musical tastes don't appear to be very religious at all. When will we finally grasp that God is found in the ordinary, everyday elements of life? There is no distinction between secular and sacred. That is a false dichotomy— a system of compartmentalization designed to make us feel holy. In reality, all is sacred, for we live, move, and have our being in God. Everything is spiritual, for God is everywhere whispering to us, if we would but listen.

The Pleasure of Animals

I am a dog lover. I grew up with the small yappy ones, but as an adult, I owned a beautiful male golden retriever named Coaster and a rescued chocolate Labrador–golden retriever mix named Lottie. I often joke that if a dog isn't big enough to use as a pillow while I'm lying on the floor and watching television, then it isn't my kind of dog! I now own whippets named Finnian and ilo. All of these animals reflect back to me the pure pleasure of God in us. Caring for them, training them, building their trust, and showing them love have brought me immense joy. Their radiant loyalty, infectious joy, and unconditional love are good for the soul. As the saying goes, "The more I get to know dogs, the less I want to be around humans!" What a joy our pets bring to us.

There is not much more to be said about the joy of animals in our lives, for most of us clearly grasp this point and have personal experience in this regard. As the creation of God, their life emanates from the divine just as ours does. Although they are not self-conscious beings like we are, we are fortunate to experience divine whispers through them.

They are living, breathing God creations that seem to reflect the nature of God much better than we do. I miss Coaster, who passed away some years ago. Lottie recently crossed over the rainbow bridge herself, but my heart smiles when I think of them—conduits of God's love for me. Now, I have the blessed presence of Finnian and ilo. Music and pets? Nothing too deep or religious to be seen here, just me experiencing God through the joys of pets and the sounds of music.

The Pleasure of Nature

Although I am no wild wilderness man, I appreciate the way my soul is whispered to while I enjoy the beauty of nature. When I took a new job out of state, I lived in a basement while trying to save money until my house sold. The basement fulfilled its role, but it was a basement—dark, damp, and cold. I found myself going for drives in the Kansas country-side as a way to maintain my sanity and rediscover sunlight. The farther I got away from town, the freer my soul felt. I sensed peace and energy coming over me in waves. I soaked it up like a dry sponge. There I was, experiencing the whisper of God in the windy, wide open spaces of Kansas.

At one point in my life, I took a break from the religious scene so I could read, rethink my theology, awaken my heart, and reconnect to the God who whispers. On Sunday mornings, Lottie and I would head out to a local lake together. She enjoyed the intriguing sounds and sniffed the air like dogs do, while I strategically parked the car to enjoy the best view of the lake and catch a gentle breeze. I read, conversed with God, and let the whispers come to me while Lottie enjoyed her own tranquility. Words cannot describe the inner joy these excursions brought me. My time at the lake became a healing balm that worked its restorative magic upon my soul.

I enjoy walking outdoors. It is good for my physical health, but, more importantly, it is good for my spiritual health. I think, I ponder, I appreciate, I listen, and I love. I am enjoying the wonder of nature and the wonder of God at the same time. I have access to an acreage with nice living quarters, and there is nothing more inspiring than walking the land, listening to singing birds and hooting owls, observing all sorts of wildlife, and watching the changing seasons alter the look and feel of the place. I am a part of it all. In this secluded and quiet place, I can be alone with God and my innermost thoughts. Without the pollution of city noise and the annoyance of haloed city lights, I experience the magnificence of the nighttime sky. The pleasure of nature enhances my sensitivity to divine whispers.

The Pleasure of Relationships

As an introvert, you won't find me hanging around the water fountain at work. I understand expected social pleasantries, but I have little interest in small talk about the weather, the price of fuel, jabs at a political party, or poorly told jokes. In fact, I don't mind solitude, for it has become one of my best friends. I am wired to interact with the inner world of ideas. Extroverts, on the other hand, gravitate toward interaction with the world of people, events, and external stimulation. One is not better than the other. They just happen to be different. While I prefer introversion, I love extroverts who easily exhibit skills and abilities that I don't possess. We need each other. Our lives are enriched by our differences and the world is blessed by the beauty extroverts and introverts bring to the world.

You may never suspect that I am an introvert on Sunday mornings as I interact with others, but when I go home, I am nearly in a vegetative state. On Sunday afternoons, you might find me riding my Harley to clear out the cobwebs, regain a sense of balance, and recharge my internal batteries. Don't get me wrong—I am a lover of God and a lover of people, but I love best when I am being myself and using the gifts and skills bestowed upon me by my creator. When I function outside my internal wiring, I am no good for myself or others. I am into deep relationships, not water-fountain pleasantries that always leave me empty on the inside.

Extroverts have a way with people. They seem to be inviting, are easy to talk to, and possess a winsome warmth about them. Their gift to the world is potent, and I have been fortunate to see them in action throughout my years of ministry. They add a zest to life that flows from within their very being, for they are just being who they were meant to be. I feel good when others shine in the capacity for which they were made. On the other hand, I prefer in-depth discussions on topics of substance. In my mind, social gamesmanship is a colossal waste of time, and time is valuable to me.

Some find ministry success by skimming the surface waters, but I prefer deep dives under the water. I am not good at networking and rubbing shoulders with others, something that comes easy to extroverts. Instead, I help people think deeply, and I challenge their paradigms. People open up to me, not because I am extroverted but because I invite them to go below the waterline, to be authentic, to tell their stories, and to be real about their journey. I extend permission for them to share their deepest selves and whatever is on their heart, no matter what it is or how it is shared. In short time, we are having a conversation that extends far below the surface waters. We are not snapping pictures of the iceberg tip but exploring the large mass below the waterline that is rarely seen. Unfortunately, many have never engaged in that type of conversation before, for their entire life has been about iceberg tips. I would rather have three friends with whom I can be real than a hundred water-fountain acquaintances.

Both deep dives and surface-water interactions have their place. The pleasure of relationship is all about people being themselves and doing their thing, whether viewing iceberg tips or exploring the unseen world below the waterline. Without a doubt, people can be a mammoth pain in the backside, but I find immense pleasure in relationships that are vulnerable, genuine, and loving. In these relationships, I hear divine whispers.

Pleasurable relationships have challenged me to look at things with greater integrity. Through authentic relationships, I get a sense of my own value as grace, patience, kindness, and encouragement are extended my way. Extroverts have extended love to me, an introvert, and taught me that God is in all people and that all are valued, even when they are the same kind of different as me.

Relationships become the fertile environment for living, loving, learning, and experiencing the great mystery of God. There may be no greater power to heal, no greater power that prompts transformation, and no greater power to enliven the whispers of God in this life than through relationships with others. However, relationships can be a double-edged sword, both the bane of our existence and the deep joy of our heart. The people who have treated me the worst have been Christians, while those who have treated me the best have also been Christians. I have learned from both of them.

The Issue of Value

One aspect of relationship is extremely important to me because of its ability to either enhance or undermine our sensitivity to God's voice: the issue of value. I never cease to be amazed at the dysfunction that exists within families, work environments, religious organizations, and just about any other relational environment.

Within family dynamics, for instance, members seem to know their place—their value within the clan. I know of a family with three children where the firstborn male might as well have been a god. How do you overcome that kind of idolization and favoritism? The middle girl was next in value, for she was the first female, another prized offspring. The third child, a female, was of the unintentional, unexpected, "oops" variety, who maybe someday would grow up to emulate her older sister.

The firstborn god could do no wrong, the middle girl was the female to emulate, and the third child carried upon her shoulders the heavy load of knowing her lesser value within the family. This information, of course, negatively affected her self-talk, her self-esteem, and her ability to self-discern divine whispers, for how could someone as unworthy as her hope to hear from God?

I know of aged parents who expect and readily accept their child's offer to mow the lawn, roll new paint on the walls, and fix things around the house but refuse to offer a return value. When holidays roll around, they would rather be alone than spend Christmas and Thanksgiving with their child. What does that behavior communicate? The child is valuable enough when assistance is needed, but not valuable enough to spend time with on the holidays.

Many years ago, a friend of mine asked to attend a school basketball game on the south side of town. His father balked, for this excursion would entail driving to the venue twice, once to drop off and again to pick up, with each trip costing a whopping 25¢. Imagine how that young boy must have felt when he realized that he wasn't worth 50¢ to his father. It doesn't get any better in the church or at work. Similar dynamics exist, where people are ranked according to their perceived value and treated accordingly. It is hurtful rejection that can wound for a lifetime.

I bring up this subject because I see it happen over and over again in so many who are seeking divine intimacy, all the while wondering whether they are worthy enough to receive such whispers. My point in this little rabbit trail is that people are more open to God's voice when they feel loved and valued. When people are intrinsically treasured for who they are and not for what they can do for us, the healing whispers of God freely flow through the pleasure of relationship. I know firsthand what it feels like to be rejected and viewed as having little worth. A huge part of my relational pleasure is helping others see, feel, and value their own intrinsic worth. In doing so, I not only affirm their quest for divine intimacy but often become the very whisper of God in their life. How exciting is that? The whispering work of God often comes to us through the pleasure of relationship.

The Pleasure of Writing and Reading

When I am writing books, I sense God's pleasure in me, for I am doing the very thing I was meant to do—using my giftset to positively affect others. Writing not only extends my ministry reach but also becomes an avenue for me to hear divine whispers in my own life. Using our gifts and doing what we were called to do brings immense joy, and in that pleasure, God's presence can be felt. It happens to me with regularity. Sometimes, it causes me to break down, cry, shout praises, or get up and dance a jig in excitement. God whispers to me in my pleasure, and I am forever grateful.

Not only do I experience God while writing books; I experience divine intimacy as others extend their own gift of writing to me. I learn from their whisper reach, even though many of the authors have long since passed away. The writing they left behind continues its good work and becomes the hands and feet of God in my life. Authors mentor me. Their writings challenge me, encourage me, humble me, and inspire me. I have sensed God's presence through the pleasure of writing and reading.

The Pleasure of Being Me

The last example of pleasure in my life is the joy of being myself. When I was growing up, preachers told me that I must be like Jesus, Peter, Paul, David, Solomon, Joseph, and a host of other biblical figures, which amounted to another "gotta go do something for God" perspective. Comparing myself to everyone else is a fast track to depression and devaluing my own worth. Just think, if only I were more like Peter, maybe God would love me more. That's not how it works. God wants Peter to be Peter and me to be me. There are certainly many aspects of

Peter's life that I can learn from, but I can never be anyone other than myself, and I am enough. When you come to terms with who you are, it is freeing. When you accept yourself and love yourself just as you are, it is freeing. Absolutely!

Isn't that part of our deepest problem, measuring ourselves against someone else or measuring ourselves against some arbitrary standard set by the church, Wall Street, or some slick advertising company? I hear the clarion voice of God more clearly when I am simply loving God, loving others, and loving myself. Pretty simple, isn't it?

Most are quite aware of their shortcomings. Fortunately, perfection is not the standard by which we measure ourselves, for if it were, we would be nothing but never-ending failures. God created us to be human, and humanity comes with emotions, intellect, personality, imperfections, and all the ups and downs associated with being human. Christianity is about finding God among the ordinary and imperfect. It is a lifelong journey of transformation—a spiritual evolution. It is always about becoming and moving toward wholeness—never arriving at the front door of perfection—for God is found in the journey. Many long for heaven, their final destination, so they can finally enjoy God's presence. Yet they completely miss out on God's presence in this life. We experience the whispers of God in the here and now journey, in this imperfect and ordinary world of ours, and that is the way things were designed to be.

It took me a great deal of time to love myself and feel comfortable in my own skin. I like myself now, not in a narcissistic way but in a healthy way. I understand and embrace my intrinsic value, and I sense God's pleasure in me when I live within the boundaries of my authentic self. No more games, no more lies, no more pretending, and no more trying to measure up to someone else's standard. I no longer desire to be like anyone else. I simply seek to be the best version of myself I can be in my personal journey toward wholeness.

Experience God While Living Life

Could it really be as simple as experiencing God's sacred presence through every life circumstance we encounter—a divine presence that is with us, in us, around us, beside us, and beyond us? As our awareness of God's sacred presence grows, our sensitivity to divine whispers also grows.

What pain has come your way? Do you recognize God's presence in your woundedness? Do you experience the peace, power, and presence of God in adversity? Do you view pain as a friend or an adversary? When you can hear divine whispers in the most trying of circumstances, you are well on your way toward wholeness.

What about pleasure? Do you experience God in the simple and ordinary moments of life, or is God found only in serious spiritual endeavors and devout religious activities? Learn what makes your heart smile and what brings you inner pleasure, for there you will find God whispering to your soul. Life is filled with God because life comes from God. In fact, we live, move, and have our being in God. Listen for divine whispers in pain and pleasure, for God can be found in both.

12

MARGIN & CHALLENGE

LIFE HAS A WAY OF UPENDING OUR BEST INTENTIONS, and according to many, the main obstacle to divine intimacy is life itself. This is a fundamental error that puts them on the road to disappointment, for God is not in the "oughtness" of our world but in what I call the "*is*ness" of life. In other words, the long shadow of disillusionment sets in when we erect parameters regarding how the world ought to be, how God ought to operate, and how our divine experience ought to unfold. We get stuck in an "oughtness" mindset, when God functions in the reality of what actually is. This distinction, of course, is difficult for many to swallow.

From my personal experience, the obstacles I encounter have nothing to do with life itself but everything to do with my orientation toward it. In other words, obstacles to divine intimacy reside within me and my approach to life. Life is what life is, and God doesn't bow down to my idea of what life "ought" to be. This reality produces a gap in my perspective that I must wrestle with—an obstacle within myself.

Have you ever daydreamed about living on a secluded island in the South Pacific as a way to get away from the rat race? Finally, you could live a stress-free, coconut-filled life complete with God, a white powdery beach, and a piña colada in each hand. Now that I think about it, that *does* sound kind of refreshing! Oh, I might enjoy that tranquil landscape for a month or so—just enough time to rest up and charge my internal battery—but isolation, even if it is in the South Pacific, is not a long-term solution to much of anything, except maybe a contagious outbreak of some deadly disease!

In vain, religious seekers of old tried this very approach—living in dark and out-of-the-way caves to avoid a world of sinful contamination. Because the real problem is an internal one, all they did was face the same issues inside the cave that they would have faced outside it. As for me, I think that I would prefer island living over cave dwelling, but neither one will work, because God isn't hiding in a cave or tucked away on a secluded island. God is found in the real world of life itself.

This idea isn't some generalized statement with no real-world grounding, for it is particularized to each individual life. Let me be very specific and ground this for you: God comes to you as *your* life during *your* lifetime and in the full circumstances in which *you* live. Whatever your life situation happens to be at this very moment, and in every moment, God is with you, within you, beside you, and beyond you. God comes to you disguised as life—*your* life. Running from life is akin to running from God. Searching for God outside your "isness" is a colossal waste of time and leads to bitter disappointment.

That doesn't mean that we cannot better ourselves, educate ourselves, advance from one socioeconomic rung to another, or leave an unhealthy situation for a better one. That is all part of life. What I am saying is that the solution to the problems we encounter in our quest for divine intimacy isn't moving to a new geographical location, isolating ourselves in a cave, hating life, or enjoying sand between our toes on a beautiful secluded island. Internal problems demand internal solutions that create internal margin, which, in turn, allows space for God. Margin helps us experience God in this life—in our particular and specific life circumstances, no matter what they may be.

Progress

Who could deny that our world has progressed in innumerable ways? Computers, copy machines, cell phones, jet airplanes, space exploration, medical advances, renewable energy, artificial intelligence, self-driving cars, and so forth. We know more about our universe today than at any other time in history. The advancements are astounding, and they keep growing. I, for one, am grateful for the curiosity and ingenuity of humanity that leads to new knowledge. In many ways, life has become easier. Those antiquated mimeograph machines sure were messy and time-consuming to use! Who wants to go back to those days? We even see a progression of thought in our thinking about God—the move from believing in a hateful, punishing, tribal God to a universal God of love for all people.

On the other hand, progress may not be all it is cracked up to be. As technology advances, it seems that interpersonal relationships, the ability to actually communicate and to live in community, have deteriorated to the limits of a 160-character text message. Has technology created an impersonal virtual reality? Is this result of progress positive?

As with most things, good and bad, positive and negative exist in our progression as a species. Progress continues and advances are made, but at what cost? Does the hectic pace of the modern world destabilize any sense of inner balance we might have possessed? Does our penchant for rugged individualism impinge upon community and interpersonal relationships? Are we now addicted to social media, where the real world is exchanged for glamorous filters and a false reality? Have our increased accumulation and consumption of things upended the value of people to the point where they are manipulated as pawns for personal gain rather than seen as divine image-bearers worthy of love and dignity?

We have certainly progressed in many ways for which I am thankful, but the downside of progress is that some important things get left behind—things that hold us together and give shape and meaning to our lives. Some believe that we have taken three steps forward and two steps backward in a way that leaves our soul as dry as kindling. Humanity will continue to advance as long as curiosity and ingenuity exist, but going backward and living in yesterday's world isn't a viable option, although some try. Both positive and negative side effects accompany progress, and that's just the way it is. With every step forward, some things get left behind (such as mimeograph machines), and when progress makes life better for us (such as the development of new medicine), we are happy. The opposite is also true. When things that matter to us get left behind (such as relationships and human dignity), we wonder whether the progress was worth it, no matter how much easier day-to-day life has become.

Because we don't control the pace or nature of progress, the real issue is how we choose to live in this ever-changing, fast-paced world of ours, where the voices of distraction and sleight-of-hand cry out for our attention. We have a tendency simply to give up and give in, to go with the flow, ride the tide, and do what everyone else does without giving much thought to living with purpose and intentionality. When the masses are herded like cattle, life becomes chaotic and unmanageable—trapped on a fast-spinning hamster wheel of our own making. Many have little hope of ever getting off the treadmill.

I have been so internally fragmented with hamster-wheel living that I went to a local movie theater and bought a ticket to a film I had just seen the week before. I have called my own phone and left a message on my own answering machine after hearing my own voice asking me to leave a message. How is that for fragmentation? I didn't realize what I had done until I got home and heard it myself. And yes, a long, long time ago in a galaxy far, far away, we had answering machines that connected to landline phones by a cord! No cell phones. No wireless communications. Imagine that! How did we ever survive?

My hamster wheel had me spinning so fast that sometimes I just stood still, frozen with overload while staring at the wall. Unable to move, I felt as though I were rebooting my mental hard drive just to gather my scattered thoughts and physically move forward. When you are spinning that fast, all you can do is hang on for dear life. I struggled to sense God's presence in my life, for I was in survival mode.

I had no time for God, and even if I did, I was so dizzy as to be nonfunctioning. I was consumed with overload. My internal processing unit was fried, giving off smoke, and emitting a foul odor, like something was melting down. That something was me! I was more concerned with not flying off the spinning wheel and injuring myself than with thinking about my spiritual well-being. When I began to slow down, I also began to experience God, for I could finally pause, breathe, reflect, and perceive a reality beyond my own striving. I gave myself the gift of margin. I needed a different approach to life that didn't require hopping on the hamster wheel day after day like some apocalyptic zombie.

It doesn't help that we try to cram a week's worth of activity into a twenty-four-hour day. It is like trying to fit your entire wardrobe into a carry-on suitcase. We are meant to drink water, but not from a fire hydrant! All that does is damage your face and cause fillings and false teeth to come flying right out of your mouth. It is anything but refreshing. What we desire and need is to drink from the refreshing waters of God—slowly, deeply, and fully, without the force of fire-hydrant living.

Without margin in our life, we become a bunch of overloaded, burned-out, mentally exhausted, spiritually drained, depressed, charred, frustrated, angry, rudderless, disconnected people who play "church" and call it victorious living. Who are we kidding? We are saturated with noises, distractions, and a plethora of choices. We can barely function on a day-to-day basis while our energies are spent trying not to fly off the hamster wheel that keeps spinning faster and faster. Did I get it right? Does that seem like living to you?

You see, life is going to be life, and progress is going to progress, whether we like it or not. We are not in control of any of it. Furthermore, we don't control God either. Who in this world can get their arms around such a grand mystery? Because we don't control God, don't control life, and don't control progress, the only other variable is within us—the way we decide to live this life. That is the one thing we can control! In fact, that is what this chapter is all about—choosing and safeguarding margin in your life so you can discern divine whispers. If God comes to us in this life—in our specific life circumstances—then how we choose to live is paramount to our God experience. Something else will always compete for our time and attention, and so learning to choose between good, better, and best options is necessary when instituting the boundaries of margin.

Margin

It is time for me to explain what I mean by *margin* because I have used the term several times and believe that it helps us hear the still, small whispers of God. *Margin* is the gap between what we possess and what we need, the gap between the energy available and the load required. We understand this principle in other areas of life. If you drive to Grandma's house with a full gas tank and use half of it to get there, you still have a half tank of gas remaining. You had plenty of energy (gas) available for the load (trip) required. If you make $70,000 dollars a year and your annual expenses amount to $45,000, you have a margin of $25,000. If you have $1,200 dollars in your checking account and spend $400 on unexpected furnace repairs, you still have a reserve of cash in your account. You get the concept.

Margin acts as a contingency fund—the amount you have in reserve for when you need it. It is the difference between always living at your limit and having space to breathe. It is the ability to rest between loads—gaps and buffer zones of energy. If life is a car, too many of us are driving on fumes. Our internal tank is always on empty, and we wonder how we will get through the day. If we live this way for too long, all sorts of physical, emotional, and spiritual problems pop up. Who wants to live with that kind of pressure and overload? It is simply unhealthy.

When I speak of *margin*, I am contrasting the amount of spiritual, physical, and emotional energy you need with the amount of energy you have available. When what you need is more than what you have, overload occurs, and you run out of gas. Margin, then, is the necessary gap between what is needed and what is available. To get back to a point of margin in your life, you must either reduce the amount of gas you use, increase the amount of gas in your tank, or do a little of both. Without spiritual, physical, and emotional reserves, you have no margin from which to draw upon when the load is heavy. Lack of margin is simply another symptom of hamster-wheel living and a huge obstacle to hearing divine whispers.

When margin is absent, we have little time or energy for pondering, being amazed, sitting in awe, being inspired, listening, and wondering as we wander. Instead, we are imprisoned by the limits of available energy. We lack time to relax, to let our guard down, to enjoy the moment, to be present and aware, to experience joy and pleasure, and to make ourselves available to others. Instead, we experience brokenness and pain as spiritual, emotional, and physical lethargy looms large in our life. Spiritually speaking, we live from paycheck to paycheck, barely scraping by, like machines on autopilot. No joy is felt in that kind of living, nor is it a life that inspires the soul.

In my experience, deep awareness of the divine arises out of margin, not overload. If this is true, which I believe it is, then creating margin in your life provides the space needed for intimacy with God. Without it, we are preoccupied with a cacophony of noisy, distracting, and competing interests.

Prioritizing Margin

Creating space in your life is what margin is all about. It generates deep reservoirs of emotional, spiritual, and physical energy for you to draw upon as needed. It provides power for the journey and inspiration for the soul. When the well is dry and your energy stores are depleted, you are stuck with no place to go, and that is unhealthy in so many ways. That is why I promote simplicity, resting, loving, living within your means, and assessing your approach to life: These practices establish deep reservoirs of life and energy for the blossoming of divine awareness.

Fundamentally, margin begins with a firm mindset regarding how you choose to live life. Although we readily grasp the need for margin, we continue living in a way that disallows it. Speeding through life at 100 miles per hour, without slowing down for curves and stoplights, congested traffic and unexpected hazards, is a deadly accident waiting to happen. Our speed prevents us from properly navigating the road. You only get one go around at this life, so decide wisely how you will live it.

Essentially, you have to decide what role and priority margin will take in your life. Will it take precedence over the accumulation of possessions, over money, over status, over your job? I can't say it enough: This life constantly presents us with choices from which we must distinguish between good, better, and best options. By intentionally choosing to live at a pace that allows you to store energy reserves, you have made a conscious decision to undergird and enhance your desire for divine intimacy, for it is the best choice.

I have resolved in my mind and my heart to live with margin, which allows me to pursue what I most value in life. I want to live according to *my* values and *my* priorities, not someone else's. It has made all the difference in the world to me. In a sense, it acts as a directional stake driven deep into bedrock. It anchors me. This resolve provides the initial bearing from which I navigate my existence, and I no longer cruise through life as though I am the lone driver on the Autobahn. Margin allows me to pace myself appropriately.

I realize that life situations are different, from the stay-at-home mother inundated with the boundless energy of little children to the older son caring for a beloved parent with dementia. I get it, and I am not suggesting that life is ever easy, for I am well acquainted with its many bumps and bruises. I am not asking you to quit your job and spend the rest of your life sitting on a log pondering God. I am a realist, and that isn't real. What *is* real is finding, securing, and valuing margin in whatever ways you can.

I am sensitive to those whose lives are lived on the edge, not by choice but by necessity—single-parent households, those working multiple jobs to make ends meet, those living with chronic disease or pain, or those wondering where their next meal will come from. A life of butlers, champagne, yachts, and jetting across the globe with nothing but time on our hands just isn't how most people live. Nevertheless, even in the most trying of circumstances, margin can be found—in little acts of recognition, like pausing to admire a sunset, closing your eyes for twenty seconds to sense God's pleasure and presence in you, or receiving the day when your eyes open in the morning. No matter what the situation, creating gaps between the energy needed and the energy available will be one of the best decisions you can make when it comes to awakening your heart to God's presence.

Take Time for Yourself

Are you overloaded with obligation and taxed with responsibility? Are you driven to succeed—striving to secure a prized possession? Are you working yourself to death? About the only margin some people allocate for self-care is eating pizza and drinking beer while watching a football game. It provides a temporary reprieve from the daily grind, but it isn't deep enough, long enough, or meaningful enough to last for the long haul. When the beer runs out, the pizza is gone, and football season is over, then what? There is nothing left but the crying!

Certainly, there are narcissists in this world whose primary concern is for themselves, but most people I know really struggle in the realm of self-care. They are far better at, and much more comfortable with, caring for others. Self-care, however, is an investment in yourself that pays high dividends and produces lasting effects. It is similar to tending a garden. The ground must be prepared to receive seed. Fertile soil is worked soil that allows seed to put down roots, experience robust growth, and produce a harvest. Build into yourself, not in a narcissistic way but in a way that allows you to function at your best—with plenty of margin for the things that matter.

The priority of margin in my own life is motivated by the fact that I am created in the image of God, and so are you. Yes, *you*, with your body shape, size, blemishes, beauty, wrinkles, and scars. You are a divine image-bearer, and don't let anyone tell you differently. That means that you are loved and valued simply for existing and for being the unique creation that you are. Your value isn't linked to a merit-based system of earning God's approval, for God loves all that God creates. Your value is intrinsic to your very being.

I dare you to stand naked as a blue jay in front of a full-length mirror. Look yourself up and down. Look closely at everything about you. If you focus on your flaws, the things you wish you could change, or aspire to be something or someone different, then you won't recognize what is staring back at you. That image you are looking at is nothing less than the divine image of God. Yep, you, all of you, and every blemish and imperfection you notice.

I'll bet you haven't looked at yourself through the eyes of God like that in a long time. Well, now is the time. You are not God, but because you are a divine image-bearer, God is in you. What you see in the mirror looking back at you is none other than the image of God in your Earth suit! How can you not love that? Realizing that you are indeed the image of God changes your self-image, and your self-image influences your sensitivity to divine whispers. Instead of seeing yourself as separate from God, corrupt and unworthy, you begin to see yourself in union with God, someone in whom God's nature dwells. This perspective changes everything.

Cast aside self-hatred and the "I don't measure up" shtick, for you are of immeasurable worth—highly esteemed by God. How could you not be, for in you dwells the very life, love, and presence of the divine. You are a partaker of the divine nature (Gen. 1:26–27; 2 Pet. 1:4). Understanding this changes how we see ourselves and how self-care is perceived. Now, it is framed within a larger and more meaningful context than beer, pizza, and football. Care must be taken with our image-of-God status, so refrain from all the negative self-talk that demeans the divine within you. If it helps, write yourself a cease-and-desist letter and pin it on the wall as a constant reminder. When you engage in healthy self-care, you are caring for that which God has declared good and valuable. You are caring for the very image of God.

It is readily apparent that none of us is perfect, to which I say, "Welcome to the human race, my friend." We are always in the process of becoming, never arriving. Divine intimacy transforms us, and when we see ourselves as divine image-bearers, then self-care becomes a holy pleasure and a sacred obligation. *Self-care* isn't a fancy word for selfishness or an advantage available only to the elite among us who can afford counseling, yoga, and lattes. Rather, self-care is a recognition of our nature, our value, and our identity, and because self-care takes many forms, it is available to all. When self-care is intricately linked to caring for the created image of God that we are, we begin to take the concept of margin a little more seriously, and creating space for God takes on greater significance.

Finding Your Way

You can create space in your life in countless ways, and because nobody knows you like you do, only you can discern where you are squeezed, where energy is lost, and where it can be gained. You know what depletes you and what energizes you. You are all too familiar with your specific life situations and the types of changes that are plausible. In other words, I trust you, and I trust the Spirit within to guide you toward awareness, honesty, and the difficult good, better, and best decisions. You just have to be honest with yourself and God, listen to the Spirit's voice, and be courageous enough to act.

Generating margin goes beyond strategically finding gaps in your day. If that were all it took, then intimacy with God would merely become an exercise in clock and calendar management. Finding gaps may be helpful, but discovering, securing, and safeguarding margin stems primarily from a fundamental choice about how you choose to live your life. It is a way of living according to what your heart treasures.

Let me share some ways that help me maintain margin in my life. They are not exhaustive or prescriptive by any means but are merely examples of how I safeguard the priority of margin. I share these examples with reluctance because I want you to be you and do you. In other words, care for the divine image that you are in your own way and as the Spirit leads. I don't want what works for me to be a stumbling block for you. So, take my examples as they are intended—mere examples from a fellow sojourner.

Simplicity

Living in simplicity is one way I engage in self-care and create margin in my life. I have addressed this topic earlier in this book, but the practice of simplicity has deep meaning for me. Simplicity of life, possessions, and values helps me orient my ship in the right direction, so that I am not wasting energy zigzagging around. Over the years, I have narrowed down what is important to me, what I treasure, what my gifts are, and how I desire to live. It has created a roadmap that I follow of what matters to me. That's pretty simple. If it doesn't fit on a 3×5 notecard, it is probably too much. I don't try to be all things to all people or do all the things this life offers. Instead, I take a narrow approach—one that God and I have agreed upon. This approach works to provide margin in my life, for I am settled in this regard.

This space for margin, of course, leads to personal contentment and satisfaction. I certainly have goals that are important to me, but they are narrow in scope, related to the simplicity of my life. I have come to accept that I am me, loved and valued by God for no other reason than that I am both the creation and partaker of God. My intrinsic worth stems from the divine imprint on my life rather than some arbitrary merit-based system. This perspective creates margin in my life because I can just be me and, at the same time, just be. I can simply exist as I am, because I am, and not worry about arriving at some destination. When you realize you are on a journey into mystery and have the inner security that you are loved and valued by God—imperfections and all—you can simply relax, love yourself, love God, love others, and embrace the journey as a divine dance with your creator. That is divine intimacy.

Balance

I seek to be in tune with myself because it helps stabilize me. Balance isn't equal portions of the pie, as though everything fits neatly together in some symmetrical and equal way. Rather, balance is akin to walking across Niagara Falls on a tightrope, always shifting the balance pole one way or the other to counter gusty winds, shifting weight, wire tension, the fear of heights, and other issues that arise. In other words, by being in tune with myself, my needs, and what is going on in my world, I am able to shift the balancing pole in my favor. I may need more rest on this day, more pondering on another day, more relational time on another day, and so forth. My pie is divided not into equal pieces but into pieces that are just right for the moment. Awareness helps me with tightrope balancing and ensures that nothing depletes the margin I have worked so hard to create. In this way, I make time for divine whispers.

Rest

Rest is important to me. I am not talking about sleep—I mean physical, emotional, and spiritual rest that rises up from deep within. In all honesty, I don't think that I have ever slept a full eight hours at one time. It just isn't how my internal clock is wired. But I do find internal refreshment of the soul that releases energy into me. I find pleasure and rest in pets. I walk outside in nature and feel the energy flowing into me. I close my eyes and listen to pleasing music that creates space for divine intimacy. I find rest in putting my hands, heart, and brain to work—when I am doing something that I was created to do. Even as I write this chapter, I sense God's pleasure in me. By doing what I feel called to do, I create margin, margin creates energy reserves, and through it all, I am refreshed and sensitized to the whispers of God.

Personal Sabbaths

Personal Sabbaths become another means by which I engage in self-care. It is not unusual for me to take a weekend, block off an afternoon, or schedule an entire day to recharge my batteries and get my mind right. I go for walks. I ponder. I converse with God. I read Scripture and other books. I take a nap. These personal Sabbaths are intentional, holy, and deeply meaningful. My spiritual, emotional, and physical health is worth it, for I am simply caring for the image of God that I am, something more valuable to me than gold and diamonds. Personal Sabbaths help me find, secure, and experience margin in my life, and in so doing, my sensitivity to God's presence is heightened.

Relationships

Finally, I discover margin through great conversation and deep relationships. Connecting with others on a soul level brings me life. I love and value all humans, but I connect deeply with those who are vulnerable and authentic. Being real with another human is priceless.

Taking Stock

Although margin takes many forms and travels many paths, it is an important element in our quest for divine intimacy. I encourage you to take stock of your life in an honest and genuine manner. What stresses you? How many hamster wheels do you have up and running? What needs to give? Where can you find margin? What gives you energy? How can you simplify? How serious are you about caring for the image of God that you are? Have you made a life choice regarding how you want to approach life? Good questions, wouldn't you say?

I often think of margin as those physical, emotional, and spiritual places I go to over and over again that (1) inspire me, (2) heal me, (3) energize me, and (4) bring me joy. Those are the places that instill life into my dry bones and draw me close to God, no matter the circumstances. Margin creates space for God, and when there is space for God, there is opportunity for divine whispering.

Challenge

Although margin creates the needed space for hearing divine whispers, challenge is an intentional step of faith that leads to personal growth. Quite simply, we experience God when we challenge ourselves, move out of base camp, and begin taking appropriate risks. La-Z-Boy faith and couch-potato Christianity are the paths of fear and complacency. Those who experience God, on the other hand, are spiritual explorers who get off their laurels and engage life with resounding gusto. They are not chained, constrained, restrained, or limited by anything, not even themselves. Life is one big adventure with God, and they are willing to engage with even the hard things.

Too many are satisfied with the safety and security of their little nesting box. After all, things are arranged just the way they like them, life is neat and tidy, and everything is predictable and safe. The thought of leaving the comfort of their nest to travel into the unknown is unsettling. It is something they are unwilling to do.

In essence, they choose to remain in Egypt while God orchestrates their journey to the Promised Land—if only they were willing to leave their bondage behind! But that kind of journey requires moving forward in faith and leaving the confines of comfort they have worked so hard to build. God is asking too much of them, and in predictable fashion, they limit their divine experience to one boring and routine hour on Sunday mornings. Did I actually say *boring* and *routine*? You bet I did. Because these people have risked so little, they also gain very little. They learn nothing, grow nothing, do nothing, become nothing, and experience nothing of God. Harsh? Maybe. But where is the journey part of moving toward wholeness? It is difficult to steer a parked car! They are missing the very element—the essential pathway that is necessary for experiencing divine intimacy. For them, the Promised Land is merely a story in a book, not something they will ever experience, and that is just fine, for the safety of the nest is always within sight.

Discovering New Things

At one time in my life, I thought about joining the military. I was required to register with the selective service system, although the draft was never operational in my day. In retrospect, I think it would have been good for me. It is not unusual to hear those who served our country say that their military experience helped them grow up and discover things about themselves they never knew. It was about challenge and growth, and it stretched them in a good way.

Although these veterans were filled with endless energy at such an early age, they lacked discipline. They were idealistic but not well grounded in values. Placed in arduous situations, they faced difficult decisions and demanding outcomes where attitudes had to be dealt with, risk was employed, and digging down deep was the order of the day. They learned a great deal about themselves. They learned a great deal about life, loyalty, and leadership. Their eyes were opened, and they were stretched beyond what they thought was possible. They rose to the challenge and became better because of it.

Unfortunately, we want the *benefits* risk can bring us without actually risking. We want to experience God while remaining in our cozy nesting box. We want the thrill of entering the Promised Land while remaining in Egypt. What in the world are we thinking? Nothing in life works that way. *Risk* is a scary word for many, so I use the more palatable term *challenge*. In essence, we experience God when we challenge ourselves, get off our spiritual laurels, and hit the road. It is the difference between surviving and thriving, and I want to thrive.

To flourish spiritually, I engage in self-challenges, and I do so often. It is a way of life for me. In fact, I make a point of identifying and addressing one significant challenge each year. I face my fears, recognize the limits I have placed upon myself, and foster willingness to be in uncomfortable situations for the sake of growth. My heart is always looking for opportunities to dance with the divine. With full intention, I often say to myself, "In this situation, am I nesting, or am I journeying with God?" Nesting gives me nothing. It is in the journey that my vision is expanded, my heart enlarged, and my skills enhanced. I want to be better than I currently am and more like the Christ I love. It isn't easy to be honest with myself in these challenges, for they are often painful and revealing. You lift up one rock only to find something you didn't expect to find, and yet it is life-changing and attitude-altering, the very stuff divine intimacy is made of.

Strengths and Weaknesses

One school of thought promotes enhancing your strengths rather than wasting precious time improving your weaknesses. Far greater success can occur when you are starting with something you are already good at. Take a strength and make it even stronger. It is called positive psychology. If you have artistic talents, then work to excel as an artist. The argument is that you will go farther and find greater success by enhancing your strengths. I struggle to even draw stick people, and no matter how many years I practice, I will never be able to draw like someone with natural artistic gifts who has invested the time and hard work to become even better. This theory also describes teamwork: When each person uses their strengths rather than their weaknesses, the team is enhanced.

I understand the concept and find much to like about it. Even Scripture notes that when our spiritual gifts (strengths) are used, the body of Christ is built up. The same cannot be said when we function from non-giftedness. I may have a strong desire to sing in the choir, but if I can't carry a tune in a bucket, harmonize, read music, or attend practice, then maybe that's not where I need to be.

However, on a deeply personal level, I don't discount weaknesses. I have thought quite a bit about this concept and have come to a modified understanding, one that feels right for me. To become my best self—not just my strong self or my gifted self—I find it necessary to enhance my strengths and minimize my weaknesses. A rock may be hard and strong (strengths and gifts) but still possess jagged edges (weaknesses) that make it difficult to grasp and use. In other words, I am strong in certain areas that build others up, but often those sharp, jagged edges make me unappealing and prevent my strengths from being maximized. I am compelled by Christ to improve my strengths and smooth out my rough edges.

When I function in my strengths, I am used by God and *others* are built up. When I work to smooth out the rough edges in my life, *I am* built up and become much more appealing and pleasant for others to experience. I experience God's pleasure when I am using my gifts, and yet I also deeply experience God in my challenge to smooth out those sharp, jagged edges that negatively influence my strengths.

Leaving the nest entails facing our fear; dealing with our shadow side; rising above the baggage of the past; moving on from victim mentalities; rethinking attitudes, behaviors, and values; and mustering up the courage to identify and address our jagged edges. I don't work on sharp edges to make them a strength; I work to smooth them down so others won't be harmed by them and so they will not hinder my strengths. Believe me, it is much safer in the nest where you will never be challenged, never be stretched, and never be placed in uncomfortable and uncertain situations. But then again, neither will you experience God to the degree you desire. No risk, no gain.

Are you a nester, or are you a spiritual traveler? Have you limited the movement of God in your life to the self-imposed boundaries of your nest? Think of a time when you challenged yourself to go beyond your comfort zone, rode out over the handlebars, survived the experience, and learned things about yourself you would never have discovered otherwise. Did you scurry back to the nest, trembling in fear, or were you pleased with yourself for having had the courage to venture out? Growth occurs in the journey, and the journey happens apart from the nest. Divine intimacy awaits just beyond your comfort zone.

Have you ever observed someone facing a difficult challenge head on? Have you witnessed the internal wrestling match that occurs within them or the many courageous steps of faith they have taken to address the challenge? You find yourself cheering them on, for they are exemplifying a path that is inspiring and honorable. They did what you wish you could do in your own life. They overcame. They persevered. They rose above their obstacles and reined in their fear. They experienced God and inspired others along the way. It takes great courage and energy to climb higher up the mountain of faith because you are dealing with yourself in so many ways. Yet the higher you climb, the more thrilling your views of God. Is there a place where God's presence is more precious than gold or silver? I say yes a hundred times over, but it is only found in the challenges of the journey—never in the nest.

Journey to Jerusalem

Each year, mainline denominations engage in the season of Lent. It is the time before Easter, and it symbolizes our own personal journey to Jerusalem. Beginning with Ash Wednesday, Lent is a time of preparation and self-examination—a time of ridding ourselves of that which holds us back. *Jerusalem* means "city of peace," and what we know about the city is that it was anything but peaceful. It was a place of tension and difficulty and, for Jesus, a place of death. He was arrested, tried, beaten, and crucified as a common criminal in Jerusalem. And much to our surprise, it was also the place of resurrection, new life, and rebirth.

Do you see the cycle here—the imagery that is before us? There is no resurrection without a journey to Jerusalem. Before we experience divine resurrections in our life, our own personal journey to Jerusalem must occur, where discomfort, pain, and the death of old ways of thinking and behaving take place. Death becomes the cycle of growth and the pathway to resurrection.

We must leave the nest to fly. We must challenge our ways of thinking, being, and doing in order to experience the freedom found in Christ. We must become like new wineskins, ready and willing to house the creative work of God in our life. In other words, what is in the way *is* the way. Jesus said it this way: "Very truly, I tell you, unless a grain of wheat falls into the earth and dies, it remains just a single grain, but if it dies it bears much fruit" (John 12:24, NRSVue). You can't hoard the seed, protect the seed, or expect the seed to produce fruit unless and until it falls into the ground, dies to its old self, and becomes something new. We want the fruit part without the dying part. It doesn't work that way. That kind of thinking is nesting at its finest, and it prevents us from experiencing divine intimacy.

I have faced this dying part of the resurrection cycle many times. It is never easy, but my resolve has grown, and my commitment remains solid. There was a particular individual in my life for whom I held disdain in my heart. This individual played a significant role in my life, and yet I held little respect for them because they always made excuses and chose to nest instead of taking action and facing challenges. They always chose the path of least resistance and allowed fear to reign supreme. A thousand opportunities presented themselves, but this individual preferred nesting to flying.

After digging down so deeply in my own life to overcome challenges, I found myself with little respect for those who refused to rise up and overcome. I would rather endure discomfort for a short season to enjoy payoffs that would last a lifetime! As you can see, my judgmental attitude needed some work. I was nice on the outside but resentful on the inside. It wasn't right, and it wasn't Christian, and I knew it. I was, in essence, doing the very thing I was accusing this person of doing—taking the path of least resistance and not facing my challenge. I was settling in my own nest of judgment.

So, I challenged myself to love this person, no matter what. I laid aside my woundedness and my holier-than-thou expectations to get to the heart of the problem—me. As is often the case, that's where most of our issues lie—within ourselves. I sought the help of a professional counselor, who offered sage advice and helped me see more deeply into myself and the folly of my ways. I still wish that more people would rise to the challenges before them because I believe so strongly in the cycle of resurrection, but I no longer hold their choices against them. Instead,

I want to cheer them on to persevere, for there is light at the end of the tunnel, and it isn't another freight train thundering down the tracks to run them over.

I no longer hold this individual in the prison of contempt. I released them so that I could love them better, and in so doing, I released myself and loved myself better. In choosing to love, I allowed God to love me. Like you, I am far from perfect, and like you, I have plenty of challenges that will keep me journeying for a lifetime. Like you, I am challenged to love my Judas, and like you, I seek to live for God and to experience the divine presence in my life. So, I took on the challenge, knowing that my continued nesting would get me nowhere. The learning, growth, and intimacy that come from the risk of spiritual exploration are always worth it. Are you willing to challenge yourself? Are you ready to fly? Now is as good a time as any.

Is That The Way You Ought to Be?

I was teaching a university course to adult learners when a young woman relayed to the class some in-your-face things about her life that were out of place and shocking. She concluded her rant by saying, "And that's just the way I am." Stunned, the class fell absolutely silent. How would I, as the professor, respond to such statements? I slowly walked toward her and asked, "But is that the way you ought to be?" It was an invitation for self-examination and self-challenge, for even though she presented herself as an out-there, in-your-face kind of person, it was nothing more than a classic posture of nesting. It was easier and far more comfortable to say, "That's just the way I am" than to ask, "Is that the way I ought to be?"

As churches mark their journey toward Jerusalem during the Lenten season, I often use a phrase that has become quite dear to me: "Lord, speak to me about me." It is a reminder to challenge myself, face my fears, leave my comfort zone, and listen for the still, small voice of God liberating me from my Egypt and leading me toward the Promised Land. What a thrilling journey it has been!

Our personal journey to Jerusalem isn't a one-time excursion, for we find ourselves traveling there over and over again, often multiple times in the same day. Many seeds in our life must fall into the ground and die. Jerusalem journeys aren't always made up of big, traumatic, dramatic circumstances. In most instances, they consist of many small acts of courage that require one step of faith at a time, and as we drop our seeds into the plowed soil, we reap a season of harvest in due time. By challenging ourselves in the small things, we gain practice and strength to face our mountains that lie just beyond the plains.

A Simple Truth

This chapter isn't difficult to understand, at least from a conceptual point of view. It discusses a simple truth that is much more difficult to implement. Yet margin and challenge pay huge spiritual dividends. Margin provides the necessary space for hearing the voice of God, while challenge renews our journey with God.

May I offer you a personal challenge? Try to do two things this week. First, find a way, however small, to create some margin in your life—a space where you can breathe, ponder, and soak in the peace, presence, and pleasure of God. It just has be simple at this point, but it serves as a good first step. Second, find one thing that brings you discomfort and face it head on. Challenge yourself in a way that moves you farther from the nest and closer toward a renewed journey with God. Become cognizant of God's presence and strength in your discomfort, and then release one seed into the ground to see whether it doesn't return amazing fruit back to you.

As I create margin in my life and challenge myself to move from base camp, I discover transformation, change, renewed strength, and a softer heart that is more ready than ever to receive from God. I actually make progress in my journey toward wholeness and become more sensitive to the journeys of others. As I am renewed, I become a renewing influence in the life of others. To me, that's fruit-bearing and a plentiful harvest. The margin I create and the challenges I face influence others to create margin and meet their personal challenges head on. It's all part of the harvest—all part of the resurrection cycle—and that is good and wholesome.

13

ODDS & ENDS

THIS CHAPTER IS A COLLECTION OF FURTHER thoughts regarding divine intimacy—another toolbox filled with valuable assets at your disposal. This isn't a chapter of "less-than" rusted gizmos hanging out in the spiritual shed with nothing to do. No, all the tools presented in this book are wholesome and profitable, even those listed in this chapter.

Additionally, I encourage you to create your own tools for the task at hand, if you are so inclined. The goal is divine intimacy, not hoarding, sorting, and analyzing gadgets in the shed. The point is to discover which ones work for you—which ones actually help you practice the presence of God. Tools find practical value only when used in practical ways, for they are merely the means to a greater end. Let's begin with the value of gratitude, another pathway for hearing divine whispers.

Gratitude

As I write this section on gratitude, it is 2:45 in the morning. Darkness has cast its long shadow over the land until the good morning kiss of the rising sun. As I sit in my comfortable leather chair, golden beams from the floor lamp create peaceful shadows throughout the room.

In this tranquil moment, as in every early-morning endeavor of mine, I am keenly aware of something within me that is immeasurable. It hangs about like the haloed glow of a light post in an early-morning fog, and I am lost without it. I am talking about gratitude—a treasured companion during my early-morning stirrings.

Yesterday afternoon, the inevitable occurred in my life: Cancer ran its hideous course, and after fourteen wonderful years, Lottie—my faithful furry friend, a beautiful brown-haired, amber-eyed rescue dog— departed this earthly world. She would typically have been near my side, offering up her comforting presence. I find myself looking for her, but she is no longer there. What a precious gift she was.

I shed tears, like all pet owners who understand the friendship that pets endear, but what I experienced most was gratitude. My heart is full—grateful for her presence in my life, and grateful that I could bring comfort to her, especially during her final days. I experienced God through my dog, Lottie. She taught me a great deal about love, acceptance, and the joy of being present. She added value to my life, and I am overcome with gratitude, for in some way, through Lottie, I experienced the divine. The comfort of God arose not from institutionalized religion or church doctrine but through the life and presence of a dog. Imagine that!

Gratitude colors our world, for it is a filtering device through which we can view life. It begins with a humility that recognizes our finiteness and lack of control, and it allows others, even animals, to become a healing presence in our lives. An attitude of gratitude rejects the paths of self-aggrandizement, cynicism, sarcasm, victimization, and free-floating anger often provoked by the apparent arbitrariness of life. Instead, gratitude recognizes that God is everywhere present. Gratitude colors our world in a way that helps us see God in even in the little things. The humility of gratitude recognizes simple pleasures, such as the taste of food, a bed to sleep on, the joy of friends, a breath taken, and the Lotties of this world. Being grateful adds color to an otherwise monochromatic world.

Receive the Day

One practice that promotes gratitude in my life is receiving the day. I welcome each morning and all that comes my way, and before I retire for the evening, I release the day with thanksgiving. Then, I close my eyes and sleep in the presence of God—or, in my case, get up in the middle of the night and write in the presence of God! This practice of receiving the day keeps me oriented toward gratitude and the sacredness of each moment. Last night, before turning in, I stood outside and marveled at the stars. They reminded me of the grandeur of God and the wonder of worlds unknown. I stood in awe of such beauty and it was great to be alive. It was a simple way for me to close the day with a grateful heart.

Have you known individuals with an attitude of gratitude? They are peaceful, positive, uplifting, and easy to be around. In fact, it really doesn't matter what comes their way, for they are always a "Steady Eddy" in a "Negative Nancy" world. The practice of receiving each day and all that comes our way helps steady our ship in the rough seas of life. It allows us to feel the warmth of sunshine and behold the colorful rainbows even on our worst days, for God is present with us even then.

Each morning, whether aloud or in my heart, I say something like this: "God, I humbly receive this day and all that comes my way. Help me walk with you in gratitude and awareness of your divine presence." In the evening, I might say: "God, thank you for this day and all that came my way. I received it, lived it, and am grateful for the lessons learned and the joy of your presence. I release this day with thanksgiving, for you were with me. Now, I sleep in your presence."

The point isn't to get your words down just right or to say what I say but to somehow, in your own way, be mindful of how you journey. Practicing the presence of God is intentional rather than haphazard. Beginning and ending each day with gratitude enhances our sensitivity to divine whispers. Although I do this routinely, it is merely a tool—it doesn't make me holy, spiritual, or special in any way. It is simply one practice that helps me recognize and receive God's presence.

How is your attitude these days? Do you receive each day as a gift from God, or is it just another drudgery to endure while you hang on until the weekend comes? What color is your world? Do you see life in black and white—absent the color of God? Does your ship sail through rough seas with the same gratitude as in placid waters? We could all do better in coloring the book of life—myself included. If we want to experience divine intimacy, then gratitude is a healthy way to begin. Receive and release each day with a grateful heart. You will discover the color of God in everything!

The Gift of Service

One of the things we easily discern about Jesus is his compassion and service to others. His other-centered perspective broke through cultural barriers, allowing him to speak with a Samaritan woman at Jacob's well—something unheard of in his day. Imagine, a Jewish male fraternizing with the opposite gender in public, and a despised half-breed Samaritan at that! Jesus wasn't constrained by bigoted cultural boundaries. Instead, he saw his role in service to all, especially those whom society despised.

Jesus healed many who came to him, and I imagine that a great portion sought him out not because of who he was, because of his spiritual wisdom, or because they had plans to become devoted followers. Many came for what they could get from him—healing, food, notoriety, and so forth. They were not interested in serving but in receiving and getting. They were posers and users whose chief aim was always for themselves.

Throughout my many years of ministry, I have met plenty of folks just like them. In fact, I have wrestled with this "tares among wheat" principle and don't find it appealing at all. Even more troubling is living with the many weeds in my own field of wheat. Religion, it seems, can become a great hiding place for pride—a place where the priority of self is clothed in the flowing robes of colorful religious attire.

My point is not to identify weeds in the wheat field, for we already know they are there. My point is to say that the priority of self is not the way of Christ. We don't see the mercenary promotion of self in his life, his work, his ministry, or his teaching. He taught that the way up is down, that the way of greatness is becoming the least of all, and that the way to being first is to become last. He not only taught it, he lived it.

Washing Feet

The gift of service Jesus speaks of is powerfully demonstrated in John 13, where he washed the feet of his disciples during their last meal together. In those days, it was common courtesy to wash the feet of guests arriving for a meal. In this case, no one was available to perform such customary service. Who would wash their feet? Who would play the role of servant? Which of them would humbly realize that the way up is down and actually practice what Jesus had been teaching them all along? Which of them would see this opportunity for what it was—a chance to live out the way of Christ, to serve others, and to experience the kingdom of God?

In typical fashion, it was Jesus who led the way and demonstrated his own teaching. It was Jesus who took a knee and began washing the feet of others. How embarrassed his disciples must have been! How glaring was the contradiction before them—that the master was serving the servants, for no one else would stoop to that level. Adding insult to injury, Jesus even washed the feet of Judas, the very one who would betray him. Such love! Such devotion! Such service!

What prompted Jesus to value and demonstrate an other-centered perspective when he could have easily used his notoriety for personal gain? What caused him to rise above the self-interest and disillusion-ment that can sneak up on us with so many tares among the wheat? What prompted his pursuit of passionate service? What caused him to risk his own life for other-centered causes?

To me, the most plausible explanation is exactly what others found so appealing about him—that he was intimately aware of, connected to, and empowered by the Spirit. When you realize the gift of divine pres-ence, as Jesus did, you see life differently, march to a different beat, and walk in step with the Spirit. You no longer pursue "*your* way," but "*The Way*." In other words, divine awareness enlarges our vision for seeing something bigger than ourselves, and service is nothing more than becoming the hands and feet of Christ to others. It is a foundational, other-centered approach to life.

In other words, service is living in the way of Christ—a by-product of being connected to the Spirit. It is not something we do as much as it is a way of being—an outgrowth of walking according to The Way. It is an outflow of the presence of God that is directed toward others.

Grounded in Divine Image

As a means of experiencing divine intimacy, service is grounded in the recognition that others are created in the image of God and, as such, are intrinsically valuable and worthy of our time and attention. It is one image of God (me) recognizing the image of God in another (you). When you have been deeply touched by the love and service of others, you see this great circle of divine image-bearers, all with other-centered perspectives, reaching out and blessing one another. When we serve others, we are actually loving God.

Intrinsic to all of humanity, the significance of this divine image can-not be overstated. Abraham Joshua Heschel, the famous Jewish author and scholar, used to ask his audiences whether they knew when God broke the Ten Commandments. Of course, this question confused them, for how could the originator of the great Ten Commandments actually break one? Isn't it interesting that we are commanded *not* to make an image of God, and yet that is exactly what God did? God broke the commandment and made an image of Godself. The divine image God set before us was humanity itself.

Although all of creation bears the mark of its creator, only humanity is expressly said to be created in God's image. To experience the Holy One is to live as divine image-bearers—to live in a way that attracts others to God and allows one image-bearer to serve another image-bearer. The pathway of service is grounded in the image of God, and when we live out that image in service to other image-bearers, we experience divine intimacy. It is humbling, difficult, and exciting all at the same time.

Anybody Can Serve

Within reach of the church's influence lies a tremendous opportunity for serving local communities. In a world of me-first mindsets, could there really be a place on this planet where humility reigns and other-centeredness frames our relationship with one another? What better place to differentiate between these get-or-give perspectives than in a place where following and serving are more highly valued than leading and getting?

Anybody can serve—even you. It takes no special training, education, or status, just a willingness to humbly recognize the divine image within others. There are a million ways to serve through our actions, our attitudes, and our words. My simple counsel is to serve with the currency you have available, such as time, talent, finances, encouraging words, a smile, your presence, and so forth. Whatever you have to give—relinquish. Whatever gifts and abilities you possess—share. No one expects you to sing your heart out for God in the church choir if you can't carry a tune in a bucket, but you can share from the various resources you do possess.

Love takes many forms, one of which is service, and because everyone is capable of loving, everyone is also capable of serving. Serving others is love in action—one way to exemplify the way of Christ. When love is expressed in service, we become beacons of light radiating hope amid darkened clouds of me-first mindsets.

My point is that the whispers of God can travel to you, through you, and on to others as acts of service. When expressions of love are other-centered and grounded in the image of God, the giving of ourselves is nothing more than the giving away of God to others.

The transformative nature of an other-centered approach to service is seen in the life of St. Francis of Assisi, who ministered to lepers—the shunned outcasts of his day. Serving lepers was a good and worthy avenue of service, but even service to others can become perfunctory if we don't guard our attitude. Francis had a heart for the downtrodden, but he initially saw them as objects of ministry rather than fellow divine image-bearers.

His perspective was divinely altered when he actually put his arms around a leper and hugged him. In that simple act, he saw them differently. In that moment, he was transformed on the inside. No longer were they mere objects of ministry but divine image-bearers—fellow human beings created by the hand of God in the very image of God. That's the transformative work of divine whispers traveling the pathway of service!

Prayer & Work

Something about the rhythm of work and prayer connects God with the real world in which we live. This concept has been known for centuries within Catholic monastic practice as *Ora et Labora*, which simply means "pray and work." Brother Lawrence, living in a Carmelite monastery in France, served in the kitchen, cleaning pots and pans and mending the sandals of his monastic brothers. This was the "work" part of monastic life. Instead of constantly praying on his knees before a crucifix or partaking of the Holy Eucharist, he worked. Monks and nuns view work and prayer as complementary components of a wholesome, balanced life. They understand that being close to nature, working the soil, and serving the community provide time and space for spiritual depth, insight, and renewal. It is their way of experiencing the presence of God.

To this day, men and women in monastic orders continue this valuable tradition. They labor in vineyards, bake fruitcakes, build caskets, teach, care for orphans, and perform a host of other *Ora et Labora* rhythmic endeavors. They get their fingernails dirty and engage in physical labor. They see work and prayer as wholesome. *Ora et Labora* gives them space and time for spiritual wondering, divine pondering, and discovering balance and harmony with God, nature, and others. Their work is a living prayer that enlarges the heart and opens them up to a whispering God.

When I speak of *work*, I am not referring to being a workaholic, a syndrome that affects so many twirling about on life's out-of-control hamster wheel. That isn't harmony, or balance, or any sort of healthy rhythm at all. It is nothing but routine chaos in which many are trapped.

I have always enjoyed working and began at an early age by detasseling corn in the huge cornfields of Iowa. Walking through the tall rows in the dew of the morning and the heat of the afternoon sun was hard work. We didn't have the mechanical comforts of modern-day detasseling—no, we walked those fields and used our hands while the corn leaves sliced into our neck and arms. We quickly learned to wear proper protection. An Iowa cornfield taught me the value of work.

My father was a blue-collar man—a master craftsman who repaired musical instruments for a living. He worked with acid, lacquer, and buffing dirt. His hands were cracked and rough, filled with the grime associated with manual labor. Day after day, I watched him traipse off to work in service to the family he loved. As a teenager, I even helped him out in the buffing room, and, quite frankly, I don't know how he did it for forty years.

He was a true craftsman who excelled at his trade. His dirty finger-nails became hero hands to me. He worked in rhythmic fashion year after year, loving his family and serving his church. He provided me with a solid perspective of work and prayer. He wasn't just repairing musical instruments; he was bringing balance and harmony to his own life, and if his work was the field upon which the seed of his labor was planted, I am the harvest he reaped. This book is a testament to his role in my life.

Intimacy with God involves the whole person—mind, heart, and body. We experience God in all of our humanity. I have sensed God in the intellectual aspect of my being as well as the physical embodiment of my senses and emotions. The heart is often associated with those emotional roller-coaster highs and lows that often get in the way of spir-itual discernment—where all too often, we are not honest about their deceptive nature.

But I am not referring to our emotions. Rather, I speak of that aspect within us capable of *directly* perceiving the nonphysical world. In other words, the heart is the trusted bridge that connects the intellect with the body. Sensitivity to the divine is heightened when the mind, heart, and body are working in harmony with one another, and that is the beauty of *Ora et Labora*. The rhythm of prayer and work helps sensitize us to divine whispers.

There are those who simply refuse to work and seek to avoid it at all costs. Let's be honest: Some people are just plain lazy. They are always late, always have an excuse, and do the bare minimum to get by while others take up the slack. Yet they show up for Sunday church services, extolling the work and ways of God in their life. Something is amiss, don't you think? This path belongs to users and posers who don't under-stand or appreciate the benefits that offered by *Ora et Labora*. They will not experience the harmony they seek through a life built upon a self-centered castle made of sand. Narcissism, in all its forms, is antithetical to The Way.

Work is a good and holy endeavor when embraced in the model of *Ora et Labora*. Prayer and work provide a proper space for pondering, enjoying nature, and living in the world of wonder while at the same time creating a rhythm to life that allows us to live in the present moment. It provides the three centers of knowing (mind, heart, body) with an opportunity to join the divine dance. Prayer and work, the dirty fingernails of divine whispers, sensitize us to the voice of the Holy One.

Attention of the Heart

The Western world places emphasis on the mind. As humanity progresses in its knowledge of the universe, our intellectual capacity rises to the occasion. Unfortunately, intellect is viewed as the "end all, be all," as such elite universities as Harvard, Yale, Cambridge, and Oxford enjoy an overabundance of competitive applications from the smartest among us. Although intellect may increase our knowledge of the physical world, it falls short when it comes to awareness of the nonphysical, spiritual dimension just beneath the surface. Jesus was an astute individual whose wisdom came not from a university diploma but from his perceptive connection to the world of spirit. In fact, his lack of traditional credentials was one of the criticisms leveled against him, for how could he be so wise and know so much when he didn't attend school, sit under a famous rabbi, possess a university degree, or obtain ecclesiastical training?

The mind focuses on what it perceives best—the physical world. Sensitivity to the world of spirit, however, requires that we see beyond the intellect and through the eyes of the heart. There is that pesky *heart* word again, confusing as ever. If *heart* means "emotions," then what is asked of us is to be mindful of our feelings, our emotions, how they affect us, and, more importantly, what triggers them and why we react emotionally in such predictable ways. That kind of self-awareness is essential for healthy living, but it is not what is meant by *heart*. If our connection with the divine were totally reliant upon our intellect, we would forever be tied to one limited, physical avenue of experience. On the other hand, if our connection with the divine were totally reliant on our emotions, the endless pendulum swings would cause constant confusion and spiritual dysphoria.

Although intellect and emotion are part of the equation, neither one of them alone allows us to correctly solve the intimacy formula. We are missing an essential third element: the heart, the part of us that directly perceives the dimension of spirit. Jesus was what he was, did what he did, and taught what he taught because of his connection to the power, presence, and peace emanating from the Spirit. He was paying attention to the heart—that internal element within us that connects directly with the Spirit and is able to bridge the physical, emotional, and nonphysical worlds.

Attention of the heart is a catchy phrase, but what does it mean, and how does it help us experience divine intimacy? We are simply talking about being consciously present toward the divine. As we pay attention to the heart, we become consciously aware of the Spirit in our life, which means that we are more likely to experience divine encounters. When our mind, our emotions, and all of life are tethered to the part of us that directly connects to the world of spirit, we are able to live in the manner of Jesus and experience a dimension of life beyond the limits of our physical, intellectual, and emotional senses. To live in the Spirit is to pay attention to the heart.

If the word *heart* is not to your liking, then find a more comfortable term. The issue isn't what we name it but rather our awareness of, and engagement with, the divine within us. In other words, to be present, aware, and engaged with every aspect of being alive is to be aware of the physical world around us and the divine presence within us. We do this by paying attention to that which connects our entire being with the

Spirit world. The heart allows us to be present to the physical and spirit dimensions of life, and this awareness makes all the difference in the world when it comes to divine intimacy.

The language of the heart is that of surrender—of letting go. To perceive divine whispers is to entrust ourselves (surrender) to the power, presence, and peace of God. Because the heart is the element within us that directly engages in spiritual perception, the degree to which we pay attention to the heart is the degree to which we encounter divine whispers. Awareness and surrender go together like lock and key, hand and glove. Surrender is the language that enhances awareness.

Living in the world of intellect or living in the world of emotion is an incomplete element in the divine intimacy equation. We experience God in the totality of our humanity when we pay attention to the heart, for it is the bridge between intellect, body, and Spirit. Jesus, our great example, lived in that awareness.

Helpful Illustrations

Sometimes when we speak of the spirit dimension, the language of surrender, and the heart being the bridge between the physical and spirit worlds, things can get a little murky, especially when we haven't had much experience with bridging the two dimensions. Let me try to make the point by using the example of love—a concept more familiar to us.

If God is love, then the more we are consciously aware of love in our life, entrust ourselves to love, and abide in love, the more we experience love, show love, and become an extension of love itself. It is not simply intellectual awareness of the concept of love or an emotional awareness of the strong and varied feelings of love, for love is much more than intellect and emotion. It is when we actually connect to love itself that intellect and emotion become active and alive, for we are uniting and aligning ourselves with love in such a way that love flows into us and out from us. Intellect and emotion are parts of the love equation but cannot solve it alone.

How do we live in the power, presence, and peace of God like Jesus did? We pay attention to the heart, which allows the Spirit to flow into us and out from us. We experience divine intimacy when we become aware of, present to, and engaged with the divine nature within us. The Bible refers to this very thing when it exhorts us to "become participants of the divine nature" (2 Pet. 1:4, NRSVue). In becoming alive to the divine nature of which we partake, we become an extension of the divine as it flows into us and out from us. This idea may be what Jesus meant when he said that the kingdom of God is within you.

This talk is difficult for traditional-minded Christians, who often see themselves as debased sinners, unworthy of anything at all, and in need of God's holy rescue operation through the sacrificial death of Jesus. That perspective is nothing more than worm theology. It leads to groveling rather than acknowledging and participating in the divine nature of which we partake and possess.

Lift up your head, my friend—you are not a worm! Quit groveling. Quit crawling. Quit seeing yourself as a dirty, sinful, good-for-nothing human being who simply takes up space on this planet. Plant the flag of self-acceptance and claim what is rightfully yours. Acknowledge the truth about yourself. You are holy, treasured, loved, and set apart as a possessor of the image of God, life of God, love of God, peace of God, and presence of God. How can you be a worm when you are a "participant of the divine nature" and possess the life and Spirit of God within you? Rise up to the measure of your created status and stop believing the lie of worms. Quit trying to get God to love you and recognize that God is already within you. To be a worm means that God would actually hate Godself, an impossibility!

Traditional Christianity focuses so much on sin that it has forgotten the life part. If I were standing on a beach near the Atlantic Ocean and scooped up a cup of ocean water, I would hold in my hand a part of the ocean. It would not be the ocean in its totality, for no single cup can contain all that the ocean is, and yet there I would be, in possession of the ocean. I would be not the ocean but a partaker of it. I realize that illustrations always fall short, but they help us ponder the great mystery—that we are partakers of the divine nature.

As incomplete as illustrations of mystery are, maybe another one would be helpful. You are the offspring of your parents. You are a unique individual, with your own personality, gifts, skills, interests, and passions, but you carry within you the DNA of your parents, to whom you are connected. They are a part of your very essence. Similarly, we participate in the divine life and Spirit of God within us—our spiritual DNA. We are not our parents (God), but something within us intrinsically connects us to the divine.

We are not the divine nature in its totality, for God is more than mere participation, but we are partakers of the life and nature of God within us. By participating in the divine, we become an extension of the divine. This is our love illustration, our ocean illustration, and our parent illustration. When we connect to love and allow it to flow into us, through us, and out from us, we unite with love and become an extension of love, even though we are not all that love is.

Let me repeat once again what the Bible proclaims: We are partakers of the divine nature. I didn't make that up; it is in the Bible. The key to being fully alive to God is becoming aware of, present in, engaged with, and connected to the divine element within us. That is what attention of the heart is all about. Our "partaking status" allows us to experience divine whispers and become an extension of God in this world and the life of others. It is time to light up this world!

Life Is Always Easter

Easter resurrection is most often thought of as a past event (Jesus's resurrection) or a future event yet to come (our resurrection). In reality, Easter resurrection is not limited to the past or the future but occurs unceasingly throughout this life. Life is always Easter when we see the great cycle of death and resurrection. To the surprise of many, resurrections occur in the ever-present now.

Jesus taught us about the great cycle of life. We read in John 12:24 (NRSVue): "Very truly, I tell you, unless a grain of wheat falls into the earth and dies, it remains just a single grain, but if it dies it bears much fruit." These words align with his paradoxical teaching that to be first, one must be last; that the way up is down; and that to be great, one must be a servant. He demonstrated these paradoxical truths in many ways and on many occasions, such as when he washed the feet of the disciples, humbled himself to the executioner's blows, and experienced resurrection after death.

Easter is about resurrection, not in a literal, bodily sort of way but in a metaphorical sense. Jesus was the grain of wheat that fell into the earth and died (crucifixion) and whose death produced a harvest (resurrection). Resurrections are about transformation, and life is full of them. These are life's aha moments where old paradigms fall by the wayside and new perspectives arise. We grow and produce only when we change from within. That is called transformation, and it is the great cycle of life.

We can apply this concept to just about anything. When an animal dies, it is transformed into food for other living things. An invention that once met a specific need at a specific time in history spawns an even newer invention that makes the old one obsolete. An outdated and nonsensical theological construct is cast aside in favor of new spiritual perspectives. What we once viewed through the lens of our own prejudice is suddenly altered when we realize just how wrong we were.

These transformational resurrections occur over and over again in life as we grow and change. They transform into our best selves. It is Easter every day. This transformational resurrection allows the divine nature within to claim new ground and influence us in a greater way. They help us become more Christ-like. It is the great cycle of life—something must first die for it to transform into something new. That is the essence of resurrection.

As one might imagine, this idea is very threatening to those who hoard seeds as though clinging to them were what divine intimacy is all about. Seeds are not meant to be collected, stored, admired, analyzed, or elevated in any way. Seeds are meant to die, to slip through our fingers and drop into the ground. They are something to let go of because they are good for nothing until they die and transform.

The past is comforting because of its familiarity. Faith, however, is a constant journey into the unknown mystery of God. Life is a constant surprise filled with ups and downs, twists and turns, highs and lows, straight roads and mountainous curves. Life is filled with the very stuff that makes divine intimacy real to us. In this continuous cycle of life and death, resurrection becomes the operative norm. Something new begins where something ends, and there is always an ending before a new beginning. That is the substance of resurrection and transformation—our journey into God.

We look for a type of stability that adds a dab of God here and there, and we want this at our own pace, in our own way, and in a manner that is under our control—without pain, of course. That is not how the great cycle of life happens. The twists and turns come unexpectedly, the mountains are higher and more rigorous than we envisioned, and the pain of letting go often seems more than we can bear. Yet through the mysterious twists and turns, death-defying mountain climbs, and excruciating pain, we discover the intimacy we have longed for.

This is when we remember the faith it took to navigate such sharp curves in the road of life—a faith that makes us stronger than we ever imagined we could be. We recall gasping for breath on the steep mountain, yet our heart treasures the incredible views we would never have seen without the climb. We are amazed at just how much courage we displayed when faced with letting go of someone or something that mattered deeply to us, amazed that through it all, we experienced resurrection life flowing through our veins. Because of life's many resurrections, we are now more alive than ever before. Although we had to dig deeper into ourselves than we ever thought possible, we are transformed people because of it.

This is life—one long continuous Easter—where the cycle of death and resurrection becomes the fertile soil in which our faith grows. We experience God in our specific life, whether we are walking the plains or traversing a mountain. God is there. God is present. God is real. Life is a moment-by-moment Easter experience of divine intimacy—one death after another is followed by one resurrection after another. The death of seeds becomes the sprouting of resurrected life.

Climbing Upon the Cross

The process of growth is good and holy, but it is not a path of ease, for it is most often accompanied by discomfort. After all, who wants to let go to the point of death in order to experience a resurrection? We like divine intimacy but would rather bypass the arduous routes that take us there. Death and resurrection are metaphors for the deep truths of transformation, and transformation is a means of experiencing God. Changing ourselves is always a process of letting go (dying) so that something new can be born within us (resurrection).

When we contemplate just how difficult it is to change ourselves, we realize the slim chance we have of ever changing anyone else. Yet when we think of change, our focus always seems to be upon others. It is a mind game we play that turns the illuminating spotlight away from ourselves. We insist that external things should align with our internal demands, but the great cycle of life is always a personal internal experience. We boldly call for change in others, for we readily discern all that needs to be fixed in them. We even try to help them along by criticizing them and nit-picking all their perceived shortfalls. If they can't see it themselves, we will just have to help them out! In essence, we put them on a cross and crucify them, and, like those who crucified Jesus, we excuse and justify our behavior. It is so much easier and far less painful to shift the spotlight to others than it is to deal with the blinding truth about ourselves.

However, we experience divine whispers not by playing God in the lives of others or by serving as their executioners. Rather, we experience divine intimacy when we seek change within ourselves. If anyone is going to be crucified on a cross, it will be us, and we will voluntarily climb upon the rugged timber with outstretched arms, knowing what must be done to experience a resurrection.

I am saying nothing new, for Jesus and Paul said the same thing. Aside from Jesus's seed illustration, he also said, "If any wish to come after me, let them deny themselves and take up their cross daily and follow me" (Luke 9:23, NRSVue). Paul noted in Galatians 5:24 (NRSVue), "And those who belong to Christ have crucified the flesh with its passions and desires." Again, in Romans 6:6 (NRSVue): "We know that our old self was crucified with him so that the body of sin might be destroyed, so we might no longer be enslaved to sin." Walking in step with the Spirit is associated with dying and rising, crucifixion and resurrection, ending and beginning, and letting go to grasp something new.

Whether it's an attitude, a behavior, a prejudice, a feeling—or whatever holds us hostage to our base self—we must nail it to a cross and allow that seed to fall into the ground and die. The cycle of death and life, crucifixion and resurrection, reflects the internal struggle each person goes through in progressing toward their best selves. Over and over again, something must die to transform. Something must end for something new to begin. In short, it is the process of surrender, change, and transformation that Jesus spoke of and demonstrated in his own ministry, death, and resurrection.

It is in this sense that Jesus told Nicodemus that if he wanted to experience the kingdom of God, he must be born again! It is in this sense that we interpret the miracles of Jesus, the raising of the dead, the healing of the lame, and the giving of sight to the blind. One of the greatest testimonies for having experienced divine intimacy is self-transformation—those Easter events throughout our lives that mark us forever. It is like seeing for the first time, being born again, and rising from the dead. Change! Growth! Transformation! Resurrection!

God Is Now

Ever listen closely to the lyrics of contemporary Christian music or to how Christians speak in general? In my experience, Christians are consumed with the past and the future. It seems to be their default orientation. The past is glorified in recounting what God once did at one time in history thousands of years ago, or even forty years ago at a tear-stained altar. Christians also glorify their hope of heaven with great anticipation. One day in the future, they will finally go home to be with the Lord, inherit eternal life, live in a mansion, walk upon streets of gold, and perpetually worship God. In other words, the past and the future are the opposite of what they experience here and now.

A starry-eyed gaze to the past implies that God is no longer speaking in the present and that divine intimacy is centered upon correctly interpreting a past-written holy book. It is a past orientation about a past God who spoke in the past through a collection of past writings. Needless to say, driving forward is very difficult when the car is always in reverse, for the present path is unseen by eyes fixed on the rearview mirror.

If constantly looking to the past isn't troubling enough, many Christians also have a tendency to focus on the coming future of a better day—a heaven to come. This view dismisses our world as corrupt and sinful—a place we need to escape to finally decontaminate ourselves. The great escape can't happen soon enough. Interestingly, everyone wants to go to heaven where pure perfection resides, but no one wants to be on the first bus there!

Not only is the world one large trash heap in this point of view; we ourselves are also corrupt and contaminated. There will come a day when we shed our corrupt bodies, escape this immoral world, and finally enter a glorious heaven. That's why we hear sappy Sunday sermons and emotion-laden contemporary Christian music that focus on getting us through this evil age by looking either forward to heaven or by looking backward to what God has done in the past. My point is not to denigrate contemporary Christian music or to criticize the past, for I see value in both. Rather, my point is that focusing our attention on the past or the future detracts from experiencing God in the present. God is found in the now. God speaks in the now. God is experienced moment by moment in the now of this life—the only now we have.

The past is nothing more than a once-present moment gone by—a present moment that once was and is no more. When we say that God was in the past, we are really saying that God was in the present moment of those who once lived. You see, God was actually in their present moment, even though from our view, it looks like the past. It reminds us that God is always in the here and now. When we say that God will be in the future, we must realize that tomorrow is never a present reality, as it is always ahead of the present moment.

The issue, however, is not where God was or where God will be, for God is everywhere present. The issue is where we are, and we are always in the here and now. That's where we live. We cannot go back to the past. It is gone. We cannot enter the future, for it is not here yet. We only have the present moment, and it is in this present life—our life, the life that so many seek to escape—that we experience God. That's why I say that God comes to us in our life disguised as life.

Many miss the reality of God because they are not living in the present moment. When you view this life as a cesspool of sin and a "grit-your-teeth-and-bear-it" endurance test until the perfection of heaven arrives, then experiencing God is always something that will occur at some point in a hoped-for future. In other words, if only we could go back to the glory days of the past or finally arrive at heaven's pearly gates, then we could finally experience God's presence. What a sorrowful shame to miss out on the still-speaking God of today because we limit the divine presence to a bygone past or a future tomorrow!

When our mind dwells on the past, we are using a precious present moment to live in the land of the dead. When our mind dwells on the future, we are using a precious present moment to live in a world that doesn't exist. The only thing that exists is the present moment. We experience divine intimacy when we look for God in the here and now.

The God of Imperfection

It sounds so unorthodox, so sinful and heretical, to speak of the God of imperfection. I am not suggesting that God is somehow marred with flaws and deficiencies. No, I am referring to God's *orientation* toward imperfection and God's *emphatic presence* in and among the imperfect.

Over and over again, we are told that we must attain absolute perfection to experience the divine, for God is perfect and can only look upon perfection. If that were the case, then God sure doesn't see much! We have turned this perfection myth into a "measure-up" standard for the granting of divine intimacy. Of course, what this "measure-up" standard means is interpreted in different ways by various ecclesiastical bodies and pompous, judgmental Christians unwilling to look at their own imperfection. Let me respond to the "measure-up" standard as resolutely as I can in the vernacular of the day: "What a load of crap!"

The "measure-up" standard is nothing more than spiritual abuse, religious bondage, and a pharisaical method of heaping heavy loads upon the shoulders of spiritual seekers. If we wait to experience God until we arrive at perfection's doorstep, we will never experience divine intimacy, for we will never reach absolute perfection, no matter who is doing the defining. This unfortunate piece of baggage must forever be left behind if we are to journey into the mystery of God—so, get rid of this debilitating myth now.

Do you see the juxtaposition here—the inconsistency and irony between a God who loves and accepts you just as you are and a God who demands perfection before divine whispers are allowed to flow your way? The many burdens placed upon us by institutionalized religion and holier-than-thou religious folks do nothing but portray God as some trigger-happy curmudgeon who withholds divine whispers. These human-made portrayals are both false and destructive.

If God imbues us with life, Spirit, and divine image and calls creation good, and if we partake of the divine nature, then are we really going to demean the truth of our identity with all sorts of crazy roadblocks? God is the creator of all that is. God created humanity and called it good. This belief means that *you* are intrinsically good! Take that to heart and hold it close. You are the divine image of God and a partaker of the divine nature. For God to be displeased with you, God would have to be displeased with Godself. Absurd!

Although I realize that I am intrinsically good, accepted, and loved, and that I carry within me the Spirit, image, and nature of my creator, I also realize that I am not perfect. This understanding is the very thing that irritates some, for they cannot accept that a perfect God could relate to imperfection. Interestingly enough, some see the Bible as the literal words of God to humankind, and view it as perfect, even while its flaws and imperfections are glaring. If something in the Bible were ever contradicted by science or reason, their faith would crumble like a flimsy house of cards.

They take what holds the life, Spirit, image, and nature of God (humanity) and treat it with disdain, while elevating an imperfect book written by imperfect people and venerating it as pure perfection. There is something wrong with that picture! These folks aren't willing to deal with reality. Instead, they are held hostage by their limited paradigm of God.

Divine intimacy is experienced by imperfect human beings through imperfect means, and this occurrence is readily apparent in Scripture. This picture of perfection that we have in our mind isn't real. Those who experienced God in Scripture weren't perfect people with perfect lives but regular folks like you and me. They journeyed with God, stumbled, fell down, did some bad things, got up, journeyed some more, stumbled, fell down, did some bad things, got up, journeyed some more, and on and on. David, the apple of God's eye, was a murderer and an adulterer. Rahab the prostitute was a woman in the lineage of Jesus. Jonah refused to share the words of God with the Ninevites, for he couldn't stand the thought of God showering grace upon those he despised. With his sharp sword, the prophet Samuel cut down the Amalekite king and dismembered him. The list goes on and on. And these are people who experienced God?

Do we really think that the many people who serve as examples of faith in Scripture actually lived their lives in perfection? Nothing could be further from the truth. They were fully human, and, like us, they wrestled with their shadow side. Yet they experienced God in all of their humanity. Despite their legendary and numerous missteps, they experienced the divine. The card of perfection isn't even in the deck we are playing with.

We have a tendency to see God only in the good and beautiful. A blazing orange sunrise set against an ocean of blue is absolutely stunning! The beauty of childbirth and the joy of creating new life is priceless! We see God in the pay raise, the promotion, the high test score, and the many privileges we enjoy and work so hard to attain. It is easy to sense God in the good things.

But life is imperfect. This world is imperfect. We are imperfect. Can God be experienced when we can't see the sunsets, when the birth of a child goes wrong, when we are passed over for a pay raise or promotion, or when we work hard but still don't enjoy the benefits given to others who have worked less? Can God be found in the beautiful sunset *and* the smoke-filled skies of a destructive forest fire? Can God be found in the massive earthquake or only in the gentle breezes of a tropical island?

People are imperfect. You are imperfect. Life is imperfect. The church is imperfect. Everywhere we look, we see deficiencies, flaws, and dark shadows. And yet God is profoundly present in the good as well as in the many imperfections we see all around us and to which we contribute. It is all part of our journey into the mystery of God. We don't get to control life, God, or much of anything. Our plate is full in dealing with ourselves, and that is exactly where God shows up. When you can see beauty rising from ashes, you are well on your way to experiencing divine whispers in your life.

The God of Paradox

Not only is life filled with imperfection; it is also packed with paradox and ambiguity. We are often forced to deal with opposites—contradictions that require us to breathe them in, ponder their meaning, and boldly set our course to follow the way of Christ that embraces them. Even Jesus used paradox to reveal profound truth. We seek linear, absolute, singular truth that holds no tension, requires no internalizing, and demands nothing of us. Just give us an ecclesiastical dictionary of supposed truths—a book of religious rules and regulations to follow so we won't have to deal with our inner selves or ponder too deeply! That escapist mindset doesn't allow us to journey with God.

According to Jesus, we save our life by losing it, a paradox that rubs against the grain of conventional wisdom. Something more than a literal losing and saving is going on here—something much deeper and more profound. We must wrestle internally with the contrast of opposites—a seeming contradiction that leads us further into divine mystery—rather than follow a set of religious protocols established by institutionalized religion.

According to Jesus, if we want to be first, we are to be last. It seems that greatness is found in serving rather than in being served. We must leave everything behind to follow the way of Jesus, and it is more blessed to give than to receive. These are but a few of the difficult teachings of Scripture where we wrestle with their underlying truth. The point is that God is found in the paradoxes and ambiguities of life because they require an interior journey to experience their truth, and it is in that journey that we hear divine whispers. We wrestle with ourselves, and doing so forces us to question, evaluate, ponder, listen, be truthful, and decide on the path we will take. If we are not embarking on inner journeys that require genuine introspection, then we miss out on divine whispers traveling the path of paradox and ambiguity.

Life Is Unitive

With two active children involved in sports, dance, church, and a host of other activities, I began to search for a minivan, the practical vehicle of young families back in the day. I never paid much attention to minivans until I needed one. Once awareness set in, I began to notice their presence everywhere I went. The same principle applies to divine intimacy; the greater our awareness, the more we notice the presence of God.

This book seeks to increase our sensitivity to the divine presence in two ways. First, we must realize that intimacy with God is a mystery we walk into rather than a journey we control. This perspective allows the winds of the Spirit to blow freely without constraint. It is a train set on the correct track for transporting us to our intended destination. Spiritual sensitivity is hindered by preset conditions, unrealistic expectations, and restrictive limitations on how that journey should unfold.

The second half of the book describes various pathways for moving us toward greater awareness of spiritual realities. They are means to divine intimacy rather than intimacy itself. Both parts of this book, the perspective and the pathway, are designed to increase spiritual sensitivities.

This final point in our Odds & Ends chapter may actually be the most important one to consider, for it increases the reach of our spiritual antenna in wonderful ways. In fact, I have alluded to it many times already, but it now deserves a fuller discussion.

I am referring to what has often been voiced in mystic writings as *nondualism* or *unitive consciousness*. These are unfamiliar terms to many Christians and may be confusing and off-putting because of their perceived New Age and Eastern religious connotations. I understand this knee-jerk reaction, for I experienced it until I realized that labels were irrelevant compared to the truth to which they pointed. Could this understanding be another helpful pathway enhancing our quest for divine intimacy?

Increasing spiritual sensitivity entails seeing differently—embracing new perspectives that allow us to rise above the limits of dualistic thinking. We begin to embrace the connection between God and humans and between humans and humans. It is similar to the *Magic Eye* concept presented in an earlier chapter.

Dualistic thinking sees things in "either/or" categories, such as sinner/saint, good/bad, heaven/hell, us/them, me/God, spiritual/nonspiritual, and so forth. If I need brain surgery, I seek out a trained brain surgeon. Either you are a trained brain surgeon or you are not. If I need legal representation, I seek out a licensed attorney to represent me. Either you are licensed to practice law or you are not. The brakes on my car either need to be replaced or they don't. This type of "either/or" thinking is often useful and necessary in navigating our physical world. But dualistic thinking also has a dark side that can be extremely damaging when used as a justification for racism, discrimination, genocide, and war. It is "us/them" exclusionary thinking that slips into the depths of destruction.

Duality is helpful in dealing with the physical world, but not at all helpful in seeing beyond it, for it has built-in limitations when it comes to experiencing the divine. The spiritual dimension seems to require a different type of seeing. For mystics, it is non-dual consciousness or unitive awareness that enhances our spiritual sensitivity. In other words, divine awareness sees no separation between ourselves and God and no separation between humans. Although this teaching isn't new, as some suggest, and is something Jesus spoke of and Scripture supports, it is fraught with misunderstandings that cause great angst among religious fundamentalists.

This dualistic entrenchment of the physical dimension hinders us from seeing the connectiveness that exists between God and humanity and between humans. We continually seek to separate God from ourselves when a union exists between humanity and divinity. Most Christians view God as a separate being sitting on a heavenly throne actively running the universe. To them, God is separate from us and dwells in a separate place. To speak of non-separateness challenges this traditional dualistic theology. In light of this confusion, an explanation is in order.

When we speak of oneness with God, as Jesus spoke of it, we are not implying *equivalency* with God. In other words, we are not saying that we *are* God. Rather, we are saying that we are *in* God and that God is *in* us. In fact, Jesus made a similar statement that got him in trouble with the religious elite of his day: "The Father and I are one" (John 10:30, NRSVue). He was claiming not equivalency but mutuality—something that every human being could also claim. He used the vine-branch illustration to drive his point home in John 15 where he is the vine, and we are the branches, and if we abide in him, he abides in us. Jesus restates the concept in John 14:20 (NRSVue): "On that day you will know that I am in the Father, and you in me, and I in you."

Jesus is teaching the principle of mutuality (oneness, connectedness, union), where we abide in God and God abides in us. The vine and the branch coincide together in a relationship of blissful mutuality. It is the abiding oneness principle—not equivalency but mutuality. This abiding principle is also seen in 2 Peter 1:4, where we are said to be partakers of the divine nature. Again, God is in us and we are in God. The Spirit of God, the life of God, and the presence of God make us participants in the divine exchange. The author of 2 Corinthians 1:21 (NRSVue) says it this way: "But it is God who establishes us with you in Christ and has anointed us, who has put his seal on us and given us his Spirit in our hearts as a down payment." Even Acts 17:28 (NRSVue) reminds us, "In him we live and move and have our being."

When we speak of nondualism or unitive consciousness between God and humans, we are referring to the fact that God is in us and that we are in God. It is awareness and oneness that we are after when it comes to divine intimacy. Dualistic thinking doesn't recognize this divine exchange that is so essential to practicing the presence of God. Nondualistic thinking is essential to divine intimacy, for it recognizes the interconnectedness between humanity and divinity, between humans and God. We are participants in the divine dance rather than spectators. The divine element is not just beyond us but also within us, and that is what we are recognizing.

When it comes to human relationships, dualistic thinking advances an "us/them" mentality that seeks exclusion when, in reality, we all share in the same life and Spirit endowed upon us by virtue of creation. All humans are created in the image of God, which gives them dignified standing. Jesus affirmed this perspective when he exhorted us to love our neighbors as ourselves. In other words, our neighbor is simply another human being imbued with the life, Spirit, and divine image of God, just like us. They are, in essence, an extension of ourselves and should be treated with the same dignity. Again, there is no separateness, only mutuality and connectedness.

By incorporating nondualistic thinking into our spiritual repertoire, we are better able to perceive divine whispers. Awareness is heightened when we consider our union with the divine—our participation in the divine nature referred to in Scripture. Jesus's prayer that we would all be one is the realization and living out of our vine-branch relationship of connected mutuality. That is what we mean by unitive consciousness and nondual thinking. It is simply living in the awareness and reality of the Christ presence within.

This Odds & Ends chapter is not odd, nor is it the end. It does, however, lead us to our final chapter, which presents a most excellent way for experiencing divine whispers—the pathway of love. The primacy of love truly helps us experience what we have been searching for all along! On to the last and final chapter.

14

THE PRIMACY OF LOVE

LET ME SAY IT LIKE A 1960S HIPPIE: "IT'S ALL about love, man! Groovy!" If love were a wild animal, it would be at the top of the food chain, for it has the power to overtake all other apex wannabes. If love were a mathematical formula, it would be the equation that unlocks every other equation. If love were a fire, it would rage with such ferocity as to consume everything in its path. Love isn't an animal, an equation, or a raging fire, but the force of its influence has the power to shake us from the core, change us from deep within, and consume us with the overwhelming presence of God. Love is powerful beyond measure.

Boiling It Down

If we could boil Christianity down to its bare essence and place it in a clear bottle for all to see, we would discover that the only thing inside the bottle is love. Love is the heart of the matter because God is love—the essence of the matter. Jesus boiled things down in John 13: 34–35 (NRSVue): "I give you a new commandment, that you love one another. Just as I have loved you, you also should love one another."

As the very heart of Christianity, love is the hallmark of what it means to follow The Way. That sentence exasperates all who make Christianity out to be about right beliefs, religious rituals, precise statements of faith, preferred Bible versions, the proper length of women's skirts or men's hair, and all the other meaningless minutia elevated to a biblical standard. The author of 1 John 4:8 (NRSVue) draws a line in the sand: "Whoever does not love does not know God, for God is love."

Even Paul got in on the action by devoting an entire chapter to the greatness of love. In 1 Corinthians 13:13 (NRSVue), Paul declared, "And now faith, hope, and love remain, these three, and the greatest of these is love." The greatness of love has nothing to do with correct doctrinal statements, religious rituals, preferred Bible versions, and all the other nonsense we send up the religious flag pole and salute Sunday after Sunday. No, it is about love, for what better reflection of God is there, and what better pathway to know God, live for God, and experience God than the reality of love in our life?

If there is any doubt as to the primacy of love, the teaching and ministry of Jesus ought to convince us. When a scribe asked Jesus to identify the greatest commandment, he did so, but he also threw in a second one. The greatest commandment is to love God with our whole being, and the second is to love others as we love ourselves. According to Jesus, loving God, loving others, and loving ourselves fulfill the law and the prophets. Jesus was merely boiling things down to the bare essence and placing it in a clear bottle for all to see. That's it. Bottle it up for all to see!

The great commandment has nothing to do with theology, right doctrine, attending church, adhering to ritual, tithing, or a host of other things we elevate as significant concerns of God. No, of all the things Jesus could have said, he purposefully boiled things down to love—the very nature of Godself.

In my best hippie voice, I say again, "It's all about love, man! Groovy!" To follow The Way is to follow love, and to follow love is to follow God, and to follow God is to experience divine intimacy. To love is to reflect God. To love is to allow God, who is love, to flow into us, through us, and out from us. To love is to connect with the divine. To love is to experience divine whispers. Love is the heart of the matter because God is love—the essence of the matter.

A Fruitful Tree

Imagine a magnificent, flowering fruit tree in a large open field—placed there by God so that all might admire it, climb it, photograph it, enjoy its shade, and taste its succulent fruit. Its flowers never fade. Disease cannot touch it. Its shade is cast wide, and its fruit never runs out. Always available, its beauty and abundance are for all who seek it.

The tree represents God—who is filled with all love, all goodness, and all benevolence, and who extends a divine invitation for all to enjoy what the tree offers. Those who eat of its fruit and enjoy its beauty and benefits are filled with awe, joy, peace, contentment, and gratitude. The tree analogy is breathtaking, isn't it? We can imagine such a wondrous tree—gigantic and gorgeous—standing with stately poise in an open field that is accessible to all, waiting for all, and free for all to experience and enjoy.

Now, let's obstruct the magnificence of this mental picture and disfigure its beauty as religion has done to God over the centuries. Let's imagine that giant skyscrapers have now been built upon the land—so many, in fact, that the tree is obscured. Human construction began with erecting fences around the tree as a means of protection and control. Fees are now charged to catch a glimpse of this obscurity, and only certain kinds of people are allowed through the gate to get up close and personal—those with money, prestige, power, and status or those who have graduated from skyscraper-and-fence-building school.

The masses yearn for the simple beauty of the tree and desire to eat its succulent fruit. They sense a calling deep within to experience the tree, but it is now difficult, for the tree is obscured and "protected," and access is given only to the privileged few. Instead of visiting an open field with open access to a tree filled with free and abundant fruit, people must now enter skyscrapers built by human hands, sit in sterile rooms, and listen to others tell stories about the tree instead of experiencing the tree for themselves.

In fact, a different tree story is told within each skyscraper, and each has its own entrance fees and requirements for attending the tree talk. The problem is that no one ever gets to actually see and experience the tree anymore. Instead, this religious hijacking merely offers cheap substitutes that are nothing more than the advancement of human ego. What should be simple and free is turned into a complex scam that fleeces the flock and profits skyscraper and fence builders. The story told is never as thrilling as the real adventure.

Does the destruction of such beauty give rise to anger and frustration? Is the obstruction of fences and skyscrapers an internal irritant for you? I sure hope so. Does your heart yearn to return to the open field and experience the beauty and benefits of the tree itself? Do self-serving stories told *about* the tree from 38th-floor skyscraper dwellers feel like divine intimacy to you?

Jesus faced a similar situation. He said of the religious elite of his day: "They tie up heavy burdens, hard to bear, and lay them on the shoulders of others, but they themselves are unwilling to lift a finger to move them (Matt. 23:4, NRSVue). They were skyscraper and fence builders when Jesus's simple message was: "Come to me, all you who are weary and are carrying heavy burdens, and I will give you rest" (Matt. 11:28, NRSVue). Obstructions to God were the frustration of the Old Testament prophets, and we can see this problem reflected in our own age. Obstruction. Disfiguration. Smoke and mirrors. Everything about the tree but the tree itself.

We take what is simple and make it complex. We turn a beautiful tree into a circus, complete with sideshows, admission tickets, tilt-a-whirls, cotton candy, and pickpockets. Quite simply, God is love, and to love is to experience God. Pretty simple! God is like a tall tree standing in an open field, inviting all to sit under its shade. That is divine intimacy.

But, alas, rather than leading people to the tree, religion comes along to obstruct the view and set itself up as the tree's proxy. Religion is in the business of self-preservation and erects all sorts of barriers and fences around a God-given tree designed for all. Religion seeks to protect the tree, control who gets close to the tree, and be the sole arbiter of what the tree means and how it is to be properly experienced. But fences and skyscrapers cannot hinder the wind of the Spirit that blows without restraint. The tree still whispers, and hearts are still drawn to it. It is the yearning we feel within us. As the tree beckons, spirits are moved, fences are climbed, and skyscrapers are bypassed. The draw of the tree will not be denied.

Organized religion doesn't trust people to have their own tree experiences, for to do so would diminish its controlling power and gatekeeping activities. When people seek the tree itself, question the presence of fences and skyscrapers, and initiate tree explorations, they are quickly excoriated, shamed, kicked out of the skyscraper, and labeled a heretic or troublemaker.

Well, enough of this story—you get the point, and I am getting riled up just writing about it. All we want to do is see the tree, touch the tree, climb the tree, eat its fruit, enjoy its shade, and sit under its branches in awe and wonder. That is the essence of divine intimacy, and if God is love, as Scripture notes, then experiencing love, living in love, and showing love become the heart of the matter. If we want to experience divine intimacy, then we must get back to the tree of love. Love is the heart of Christianity, the essence of God, and the best way to experience divine intimacy. Let's stop taking what is simple and making it complex. Let's just love and, in so doing, experience God. The alternative is a preoccupation with nonessentials—a religious chasing of the tail that leads to dizzying circles.

Universal Language

As a universal language, love is well known, well respected, and readily understood around the globe. Isn't it interesting—we have thousands of denominations, untold religious beliefs, and countless ways of speaking of God, and yet God is love, something every human being on this planet can grasp and experience? Maybe divine intimacy has nothing to do with denominations, religious beliefs, or the myriad ways God is articulated in human language. Instead, maybe God is best articulated in a four-letter word that everyone on the planet can share.

Love, it seems, is the language of God, for it speaks to everyone. That makes sense, given that God is described as love and that we experience divine intimacy best through receiving love and giving it to others. If God is love, then we best experience God by loving extravagantly, fully, and abundantly. Love isn't an ancillary sideshow but the very expression of God, and its primacy is predicated upon this very basis, for when we love, we are interacting with the reality of God.

I am constantly amazed at how quickly religious people dismiss the simplicity of love or treat it as some high-falutin' theological treatise. They make it out to be another proper doctrinal statement of faith rather than a lived experience with a still-speaking God. It is one thing to talk about love, preach about love, and believe wholeheartedly in love, and quite another thing to actually love.

The calling card of theological liberals is to lovingly accept everyone, except, of course, those deemed to be intolerant and unaccepting. Conservatives Christians, on the other hand, speak of the love of Christ for everyone, except, of course, those who disagree with their "correct" theological perspectives. Both sling mud, and both get dirty. Both salute the flag of God's unlimited love while placing barb-wired boundaries upon that love. It is the same unloving posture from opposite sides of the fence, with each side justifying their exception to love.

Sadly, I can name plenty of churches, denominations, and individual Christians who readily abandon the principle of love for a cause they believe justifies non-loving behavior. The incongruence is glaring and is nothing more than another end-justifies-the-means scam. The church, it seems, operates on the same principles as secular society, except its blows are cushioned by fluffy and palatable religious jargon. And we wonder why people are turned off by Christianity and struggle to experience divine intimacy!

When we rise above the mudslinging and begin to actually love those on the other side of the fence, we come face to face with the transforming power of the living Christ. One of the hardest things you will ever do is to love well, love fully, and love abundantly. To do so is to reflect God, and that requires a courageous inward journey, for love requires more from us than slinging mud at our enemies under the guise of religious justification. To love well, we must come face to face with ourselves—the good, the bad, and the ugly. The deep inward journey of self-examination brings God closer than a brother. It is part of the love process.

One of the reasons we talk a good love game but practice so little love is because our perspective is skewed. We view life through the lenses of culture, upbringing, personality, education, theological bent, life experience, emotional reaction, pain, and so forth. We are always seeing "through" various lenses rather than allowing the Spirit to see through us. In other words, until and unless we actually put on the lens of love, even when it is difficult, the intimacy we yearn for will bypass us. The Spirit helps us recognize the skewed lenses that filter our perspective and cause us to place boundaries upon our love. But when we allow God to love us, when we experience God's love, and share that love with others, divine transformation becomes a well-worn mark of divine intimacy.

The Primacy

Love is the premier pathway to experiencing God for a number of reasons, many of which I have already addressed. Let me list a few of these reasons just to be on the safe side:

- Through love, we engage in divine experiences, for we are emulating a key quality of God. God is love, and when love flows into us, through us, and out from us, it is the moving of God.

- To love is to experience God, for the fruit of love is patience, kindness, humility, forgiveness, hope, and the like (1 Cor. 13:4–8a).

- Through love, we participate in and operationalize the greatest of all the gifts (1 Cor. 13:13).

- When we love what God loves, that love becomes real to us, for we begin to see life through the eyes of God.

- Love is the hallmark of following Christ and speaks to the transformative effect divine intimacy has upon our life (John 13:35).

- Recognizing its premier status, Jesus commanded his followers to pursue love (John 13:34).

- The absence of love is a sure sign that we do not know God, regardless of how much we claim otherwise (1 John 4:8).

- Loving well requires an inward journey that challenges us and transforms us. We experience God when the limits of our love expand beyond what we thought possible.

However, one reason for love's primacy towers above all others, and it has to do with why we love—our motivation. Unfortunately, love is often conditioned upon value and return. If I offer you some form of love, all the while expecting a return on that investment, then love is nothing but a transactional exchange. I give you love, and, in return, you give me what I want. Rather than something that is given freely, it is offered with expectation and strings attached—a quid pro quo cost of exchanging relational business. That kind of love isn't transformative at all, for it requires nothing of us—no inner journey, no following a new path, and no going deeper into ourselves.

We merely play a relational game where love and acceptance become marketplace commodities. It is the way of the world, not the way of Christ. It is the way of transaction, not transformation. But when love is freely given, without expectation of return or strings attached, it becomes transformational, and that is pretty amazing in a quid pro quo world. That kind of love requires an inner journey, and that inner journey becomes a well-trodden path to divine intimacy. You want to experience God? Then love without expectation of return. That will take you on a journey full of twists and turns—the very stuff divine whispers are made of.

The primacy of love also has to do with value. Unfortunately, love is often extended only to those we deem valuable enough to receive it. Rather than being given freely and without expectation, this kind of love is based solely on the object itself and our personal assessment of its value to us. We size it up; assess its quality; quantify the amount of love, attention, and acceptance it deserves; and offer up only what is deemed proportional to its value.

The well-behaved child, for instance, is afforded more love than the renegade because she has earned it and is regarded as more valuable. We are used to making judgments of worth and value; we do it every day while shopping for clothes, cars, houses, churches, and even soulmates. We are assessing value. Is the object worth my time, attention, acceptance, finances, and love?

The decision of whether to offer love, and if so, how much, is solely conditioned upon the value we place upon the object itself. We become the supreme judge of another and determine who is inferior and who is superior. It is the basis of society's ranking system, where some hold worthier title. Some are always picked first when forming dodgeball teams, and others are always chosen last. It is hurtful and places people into us/them, worthy/unworthy categories.

This type of ranking system has been with us since the beginning of time, and yet we don't see Jesus engaging in this behavior. The way of Christ is the way of love. In fact, Jesus hung out with the "less-than" people within his culture's ranking system. It was his way of seeing value in every person and revealing just how destructive ranking systems of human worth can be.

The greatness of love isn't dependent upon reciprocity or the value we attach to the object itself. We love because God loves. We love because the love of God is within us. We love others because they exist and are bearers of the image of God. They possess the same life of God within them that we possess. How can we value them any less than ourselves? Love is grounded in God, is a reflection of God, and becomes the impetus for loving God back.

Progression, Not Perfection

Let me be the first to confess that I have not always loved well and that I fail miserably at times in my pursuit of love. I have extended love while expecting something in return—something that advances my personal agenda. I am guilty of playing the love game under the ruse of religious beauty when it was nothing more than an ugly gesture of self-centered living. I imagine that you could confess to the same thing.

Let me be the first to confess that I have placed differing values upon people so that my love was selective. I became the sole judge of another person's worth and, in so doing, cast my lot among the highest order of modern-day Pharisees. Numerous times, I have opted to give my time and attention only to those whom I perceive as holding worthier title while casting shadows of dispersion upon those who weren't picked for my dodgeball team. My love was corrupted and prostituted, for I was seeking something in return and judging the value of human dignity. My actions weren't loving at all but were the strategic advancement of my cause, my judgments, and all things me. The hidden core of my love was self-centeredness, even though it was adorned in religious form.

I can beat myself up a thousand times over for my imperfections, or I can learn from my failures and rejoice at my progress. I choose the latter! We are not perfect people but *progressing* people, who journey toward wholeness and our best selves. Try as we might, when perfection becomes the standard by which we measure ourselves, we always fail, for who of us can attain the impossible?

Perfection isn't our goal; progress is. Your progress is different than mine, for we are on different paths at different times. Yet as we both seek to follow Christ, we realize just how far we have come in our journey toward love. I try to be honest about my failures and my self-interest; there is no need to sugarcoat it. I am not fooling God or myself. How will I ever progress in love if I am unable and unwilling to admit even my shortcomings? The difference is that I don't wallow in my shortcomings. I journey beyond the rut of my failures and, in looking back, see how far I have journeyed. Progress, not perfection!

Our journey toward love is a journey toward God, for God is love. In the journey, we experience divine intimacy: no journey, no intimacy. With courage and authenticity, we must each acknowledge that we have used people, treated them poorly, manipulated them, judged them, and viewed them as either obstacles or pathways to selfish ambition. But let's not get stuck there; let's move forward from where we are and where we have been. That is the blessedness of the journey: We are always in movement toward becoming, toward loving more like God loves and loving the things that God loves. That is the primacy of love and the ultimate pathway to divine intimacy.

Why Should We Love?

Now that we have all 'fessed up to being imperfect, we can embrace the fact that our movement toward love is really a movement toward God and that this movement toward God is a journey of introspection. Loving well isn't a matter of checking the boxes of Christianity but a way of being, seeing, and living. It rises from within, not from without. It is not something we acquire but something we are. It is not an obligation of duty but a way of being. It is allowing the divine within us to love through us.

Our journey into love provides powerful, life-changing experiences that shape us, break down barriers, and tenderize our soul. As the premier pathway to divine intimacy, love always leads us to greater love and more powerful God encounters.

As with most pathways, we turn it into a duty, an obligation, a badge of superiority, or a means to earning God's approval, but the primacy of love is none of these things. In fact, no pathway to God is! This pathway is merely loving God back, and the more we love, the more we emulate the source of that love. Loving well is a universal pathway to God—the aim of all spiritual practice that leads to divine intimacy.

When we love, we dip into the eternal mystery of God. Oh, we catch glimpses and snippets of God throughout life that inspire us, but until we make love the aim of our spiritual endeavors, our divine experiences are like shooting stars—amazing, but short-lived. Without intentionality, we struggle to abide in God's love that is so transformative—a love that makes the mystery of God real to us, moment by moment.

Love is the path to enlarging our neighborhood and widening our welcome. In other words, it is the summation of all that Jesus taught, all that the prophets taught, and all that the law teaches. Love is the main thing, the primacy, and what Christianity is all about. Love is the heartbeat of God—the divine DNA within us. When we love well, we open wide the gates of invitation for all to experience divine whispers. In reality, people most often experience God as loving when they experience our love. Love is the gift we give to ourselves, to others, and to the world.

Choosing to love is creating our own divine experience. Love always leads to God, and by choosing love, we choose God, which leads to divine whispers. It is the premier pathway for opening our heart, enhancing our hearing, and acting in loving ways. The choice to love is always before us, for God is always in the present moment.

What Is Love?

Is love an act or an emotion? Folks pick a side and argue one way or the other—in love, of course. The church I grew up in told me that love was an action, not an emotion. But without the feeling component, love can become cold and mechanical. Others equate love with the emotion of a Harlequin romance novel—a hot and steamy volcano of passionate eruptions. With the ever-changing nature of emotions, love becomes hot or cold, depending on the fleeting feelings of the moment.

Why does it have to be one or the other? Why can't love involve action *and* emotion? Why can't it include intellect as well? For me, love involves my whole being, not just one part of it. At times, my feelings inspire me to love, for emotion can be a powerful motivator. At other times, I intentionally engage in loving acts, not because I feel like it but because I know that it is the loving thing to do. I pursue love whether my feelings are up or down or all tangled up like spaghetti on a plate. There are times when I love in my mind, especially when action and emotion are not possible or appropriate. I hold loving thoughts toward others.

I simply love with all of me—my mind, my emotions, and my actions. If we wait to love until all three are in perfect alignment, we will never get around to loving. Love with all of you, even when all cylinders aren't firing in correct order. Sometimes, you act your way into loving, and sometimes, you love your way into acting. Either way, love.

As I write this chapter, my mind is filled with love for you—yes, you! There is a good chance that we have never met and may never meet, but I wrote this book for you. I love you in my thoughts as I uplift all who take time to engage with the fruit of my labors. I love you with my feelings, for I know what it is like to search for divine intimacy. My heart goes out to you. I love you through my actions. Writing this book hasn't been easy, for it has entailed an investment of time and effort on your behalf. Love involves all of me. Sometimes, everything lines up, but most often, it does not. Sometimes, love is an action. Sometimes it's a feeling or a thought. Sometimes, all three are in alignment and sometimes they are not. Regardless, I move toward love one way or another—always.

If you wait to love until you feel like loving, then you might as well kiss divine intimacy goodbye. If you wait to love until some action is needed, then you discredit the capacity to love with your emotions and your mind. If you wait to love until you compute a cost-benefit analysis, then you have already lost the battle.

Call me silly, but I have a simple idea that just might work: How about we just love? If you don't feel like it, act like it, or think like it, then love anyway. In other words, love your way into feeling love. Love your way into thinking love. Love your way into doing love. Sometimes, we overanalyze things to death, and my humble advice is to simply love, and to love simply, without the angst of overanalysis. Love with all of your being and love what is before you, not what you wish you had, what might come in the future, or what you loved in the past. Just love now in the present moment, and by doing so, you will encounter God in powerful ways.

To love well is to experience God, and when we experience God, we leave the world a better place. Through love, we sow seeds of kindness, forgiveness, and hopefulness. Wherever love is sown, a consistency of harvest is produced, according to 1 Corinthians 13:4–8a (NRSVue):

> Love is patient; love is kind; love is not envious or boastful or arrogant or rude. It does not insist on its own way; it is not irritable; it keeps no record of wrongs; it does not rejoice in wrongdoing but rejoices in the truth. It bears all things, believes all things, hopes all things, endures all things. Love never ends.

How to Love Well

Even though love is a universal language, not everyone speaks the language with the same degree of fluency. We know how to love ourselves without much instruction or practice, and yet many even struggle with that. I suppose that some elements of loving come as natural as breathing, while others must be learned and experienced before they are ingrained into our soul. We love much better when we are surrounded by love, experience love, allow God to love us, and see love modeled for us. Love is like a muscle that grows, develops, and becomes stronger the more it is used.

Nothing transforms the heart and uplifts us like love. It has a way of bringing out the best in us while opening the door of our heart to the blowing winds of God. That's why love is the hallmark of the community of faith. Where love abounds, transformation occurs. When the church embraces love, lives love, and extends love, it becomes a healing community where the whispering God of love is experienced.

Although plenty of books advance various perspectives on the topic of love, I would like to offer a few ideas that have been helpful to my own journey into the love of God. As always, take what is helpful and discard what isn't, or, if you are so inclined, create your own highlight reel for loving well. The point is to do it—to actually love and make it a prized aspect of your life's purpose. Let's not permit the false reality of Hollywood or social media to dictate what love is from behind the curtain of fame, fortune, makeup, avatars, video games, computer screens, and cell phones. Instead, let's bypass the hype and get to where the rubber meets the road—where we actually have a chance of hearing the whispering winds of God.

Major Life Purpose

Many pursuits vie for top-billing in our lives, but extending love to others doesn't seem to rank highly on most of our lists. It is not seen as important, essential, or worthy of a major life purpose. Rather than concerning ourselves with learning how to love, giving love, and engaging in acts of love, we are more concerned with receiving love and being loved—a perspective of getting rather than giving. Love is considered a "thing" rather than a way of being, seeing, and living.

I preach in churches that often use a prayer of confession followed by an assurance of pardon, and it makes me cringe. The prayer is nothing more than a collective groveling over how bad, corrupt, and unworthy we are, followed by a brief statement that God has pardoned us unworthy worms. I sometimes rewrite this prayer to soften the sadistic blows upon the congregation, and most often, I leave it out of the service altogether. Who wants to be reminded Sunday after Sunday of how wretched they are?

Instead, I opt for what I call the Great Affirmation. I don't do this every Sunday, but when I do, the congregation soaks it up like a sponge. People often weep during its recitation. For the first time in their church experience, they sense the power of affirmation. I tell the congregation how wonderful they are, how loved they are, and how God is with them, and I affirm them in their journey. I shower the love of God upon them, and the moment is palpable, powerful, and memorable.

It goes to show how harmful the typical Sunday berating can be and how thirsty we are for love—gulping it up like a parched camel. But when do we move toward being the one showering love upon others rather than the dehydrated camel packing in water? We need both, but the more we shower love upon others, the more love returns to us. When love rains down upon us, we are more apt to be loving ourselves. The church is in dire need of people who love well. Will you rise to the challenge and rain blessings upon others?

May I encourage you to move from being solely a love-receiver to becoming a love-giver, from camel-gulping to being the cloud that rains love drops upon parched ground? We often withhold love until we receive it first. To our surprise, however, the by-product of being a love-giver is that, in return, we discover love, experience love, and are transformed by love. In a sense, we love our way into divine intimacy.

With this idea in mind, I ask: What place does love have in your life purpose? Is it a major element of who you are and how you live? It is, after all, nothing more than following The Way, loving God back, and loving what God loves. It is nothing more than the summation of the Christian faith. When love becomes a conscious, intentional life goal, we cannot help but experience God, for God is love. We cannot fail, for we are engaging in love while also moving toward greater love. How do you love well? You make it a major life purpose.

Love the Ordinary

Shiny objects that sparkle in the sun capture our attention as though nothing else is worthy of our consideration. If the bling doesn't razzle, dazzle, and frazzle us, then surely it is incapable of rapturing our heart. We should know by now that not everything that glitters is gold.

Love is an end unto itself and needs no reciprocity, no adjudicated value, and certainly no bling to be desirable. Jesus wasn't fooled by the colorful robes of the self-righteous Pharisees. He loved the smelly fishermen and the sweating crowds searching for God; He loved despised tax collectors and his executioners; He loved the half-breed Samaritan woman, his female disciples who supported and sustained his ministry, and so forth. He had a love for the ordinary, the commonness of life.

How do you love? Love the ordinary, and in so doing, you will unearth the extraordinary. The fact that it exists as the creation of God is enough to make it loveable. Every person, whether of high stature or lowly class, is the creation of God, the image of God, and a possessor of the life of God. Love the animals. Love the environment. Love your coworkers. Love your job. Love life. Love every moment. Great love consists of loving the ordinary and doing ordinary things in loving ways. Whether garbage collector or castle king, do everything in love and with love.

I'm reminded of employees who seek out leadership positions for power, prestige, and pay, all the while treating their current job as though it is beneath them. Leadership in the small things can build to leadership in the big things. It is the same with love: If you don't love the small, ordinary things, what makes you think that you will suddenly be able to love the big, extraordinary things? How you love one thing is how you love all things!

When you discover the extraordinary in the ordinary, you are well on your way to experiencing the whispers of God. You love God by loving everything, and when you love everything, you realize that love is becoming a way of being, living, and seeing for you. How do you love well? You love everything, and by doing so, you turn the ordinary into the extraordinary.

Love What Is Before You

Ever witness someone searching for their glasses when they were already wearing them? It has happened to me. I have even stepped into the shower with them on. I missed what was right before my eyes. The same thing can happen with love. While scanning the environment for shiny objects worthy of our attention, we miss what is loveable right before our eyes—the people, things, and circumstances in our zone of love. Love what is in your zone, within your reach, and right in front of you.

In other words, bloom where you are planted. Become the yes to someone's no, love the ordinary before your very eyes, and view the people, things, and circumstances in your zone of love as gifts from God. Remember, God comes to you in your life as your life. If you miss these precious moments to love, you are merely looking for spectacles already on your head. How do you love well? You love what is right in front of you.

Put Your Oxygen Mask On

Before takeoff, airline personnel review required safety procedures with cabin passengers. Parents are instructed to put on their own oxygen mask before assisting their children. The one helping must first receive life-giving oxygen before enabling others to breathe; otherwise, both will be gasping for air. This instruction makes perfect sense and is a good metaphor for life.

It is difficult to give to others what we don't possess or haven't experienced. I can't give advice on stocks and investments, for that is not the world in which I live. I can't help with interior design, for I don't know much about color schemes, perspective, and the latest trends. I wouldn't be much help in constructing a bridge, repairing electronics, digging a well, or doing a host of other things. I don't possess the knowledge or experience for such endeavors. We would both be gasping for breath, for I cannot share what I do not possess.

But love, on the other hand, is something I know about, possess, and have experienced. When it comes to love, I ensure that my own mask is on, and in so doing, I am able to assist others with their own breathing. I put my oxygen mask on first for numerous reasons.

One reason is that love is the main way I participate in the life of God. I don't experience God through doctrinal statements, religious dogma, or boring rituals. No, I experience God in the realm of love. How can I exemplify and share the life and love of God if they aren't operative in my own life? As I practice loving well, I become a better lover of God, others, and myself. In other words, the greater my love, the greater my experience of God. Love produces love, which produces more love. As I put my own oxygen mask on first, I ensure my own participation in the life of God.

By putting my own oxygen mask on first, I become the love in another person's life that I wish I had experienced in my own life. It is one way I become the yes to another person's no. By putting my oxygen mask on first, I ensure that love becomes a way of life and a common practice. It becomes the lens through which I see God and others. In other words, love begins to take over because it has taken me over. It isn't so much that I now have love but that love now has me. You experience God to greater degrees when love becomes so ingrained in you that it simply becomes the way you live, process, and view the people, things, and circumstances right in front of you. The more we love, the more we grow in love, and greater love equates to greater sensitivity to divine whispers.

Finally, I put my oxygen mask on first because it is an important way for me to love myself as God desires. I am not referring to a self-referential, narcissistic, me-first mindset that is destructive and antithetical to the way of Christ. To be full of yourself is to be empty of God. Instead, love emanates from the hills of humility and is devoid of self-aggrandizement.

Loving God, self, and others is not only a simple and successful formula for life; it is also a simple and successful formula for experiencing God. We love others as we love God and ourselves. Loving ourselves is difficult for many. They either demean themselves to be worthless or esteem themselves to be God's greatest gift to humanity. Neither extreme is helpful or accurate. Loving yourself is being comfortable in your own skin, with your own gifts, talents, interests, and personality. You realize and accept that you are who you are, and that is enough. You embrace you. You love yourself when you accept yourself while also working to become your best self. It is one way we allow God to love us.

We are intimately aware of our many shortcomings, immoral thoughts, and corrupt motivations. If people had an inkling of all the skeletons in our mental closet, they would turn away, shocked and appalled, all the while realizing that we are just like them. We are not perfect, for we are not God. But we are on a journey to wholeness, and in that journey, we experience divine intimacy. Learning to love yourself, warts and all, is a journey in itself that will make you more loving. How do you love well? You put your own oxygen mask on first so you can then help others breathe.

Love Is the Way of Christ

We are always tempted to turn the simple path of following Christ into a complex, labyrinth walk of nonsense. You must do this! You must do that! You must believe this way! The many "you musts" become so prevalent that following God turns into a confusing set of nonsensical rules that sucks the life right out of us. Our focus is diverted from the simple to the complex and causes us to be preoccupied with trivial, non-essential matters. The simple is never enough for us. We always want to add something, when the main thing is to keep the main thing the main thing.

Jesus simplified things pretty well: He summed up the entire law and prophets with directions to love God, others, and self. That's it. He invited us to follow him in this simple approach to life with his "come unto me" welcome. There are no requirements, no preconditions, and no litmus tests. Just come and follow The Way. In other words, his way is the way of love. To follow the way of Christ is to love God, love others, and love yourself.

This idea is simple to understand but much harder to practice because it requires that we look inward and deal with ourselves. It initiates an inner journey. Jesus knew this, and that is why love is entirely transformative. It breaks us, molds us, marks us, and alters our limited view of the landscape around us. It takes us on an inner journey of becoming our best selves, and our best selves are always a reflection of the divine within us. The journey allows the image of God within us to shine forth like the welcoming beauty of the rising sun. How do you love well? You keep it simple and constantly choose the way of love.

An End in Itself

We speak of the transformative nature of love, and it is absolutely true. To love well brings about transformation, and transformation is nothing more than divine intimacy at work. Love is the conduit through which transformation flows. Although I can personally speak of the transformative nature of love in my own life, and although I continue to uplift its value and importance for divine intimacy, it must be clearly stated that we pursue love not because of its effect upon us but because it is an end unto itself. In other words, to love is to follow the way of Christ, whereas transformation is the effect, result, or by-product of our following.

We seek divine intimacy, and so we love. That is true, and the more we love, the more we experience God. Why is that? I suggest that love is an end unto itself because it reflects an important element of God's very nature. To pursue love is to pursue God, and to pursue God is, indeed, an end unto itself. It is to our advantage that love is transformative and has the effect of making us more loving, but that is the *result* of following The Way, not the end itself.

My point is that love should not be viewed as another check box on our "pleasing God" list. Love is the very heart of the Christian faith, and the pursuit of love is the pursuit of God. How do you love well? You realize that pursuing love means pursuing God, which is an end unto itself, and that its resulting effect transforms us to be more loving. And that, my friend, is divine intimacy.

Live, Love, Be

Episcopal Bishop John Shelby Spong often spoke of an approach to life that involved living, loving, and being. If God is the source of life, then we best honor God by living life fully. If God is love, then we best honor God by loving wastefully. If our existence (our being) is directly linked to the existence of God, then we best honor God by being our best self. Living for God is simply living life fully, loving wastefully, and being all that we can be.

Individuals often seek to know what the will of God is for their life. In essence, they want to know what specific steps and decisions adhere to

God's will for them. Tell me what to do, whom to marry, what job to accept, when to have children, how to deal with a difficult child, how much to donate, whether to go bowling tonight, and on and on and on. To me, these kinds of questions are fruitless and reveal a fundamental misunderstanding of our relationship with divine mystery. Instead of being connected to the source of life itself that leads us in all things, we want a "how-to" manual—a Google map that precisely routes our travel, as though God is our divine concierge. From my perspective, nothing could be farther from the truth.

Darn, I ate scrambled eggs, bacon, toast, and orange juice for breakfast when God's will was that I eat oatmeal and blueberries, skip the bacon, and drink skim milk. Darn, I fell in love with this person and got married when God wanted me to marry a different individual. I experienced the loss of a spouse, and it sure was painful. God must be punishing me for not following the divine plan laid out for me. Nonsense!

My advice is to simply love God with all your heart, soul, and mind and do what you want. Live life, love wastefully, and be all that you can be to the honor of God. Simple. Precious. True. If love is the heart of your way of life and love is a key element in the nature of God, then to love is to do the will of God. Simply love and live your life. It is that simple. That is the will of God.

Does it really matter to God what you eat for breakfast? I hardly think so. Does God have a specific person for you to marry, whereas all other potential matches are sinful endeavors? I doubt it. Are difficult circumstances the punishment of God or simply life happening like it always does? That would be one creepy God who gets divine jollies from seeing people suffer. Maybe love is a way of being, seeing, and living that allows us to enjoy life, see God in this life, and experience all of life's events with a constant connection to the Spirit. You want to love well? Then live, love, and be with all your might and do what you want, for when love becomes the heart of the matter, it becomes a matter of the heart.

The Jonah Syndrome

I realize that loving well is no easy task. Yet if practicing love is the primary way we experience God, we must not abandon the pursuit because it is challenging. Loving is difficult because it forces us toward introspection and self-examination. Love does not allow us to hide from our self-serving prejudices. The inner unwinding of ourselves moves us to love beyond the boundaries of our own limits.

We all experience the Jonah syndrome sooner or later. The story of Jonah is about boundaries and limits. Jonah's disdain for the Ninevites flowed from a tarnished perspective. God asked Jonah to confront his own prejudices, but Jonah did everything he could to outrun God's call to expansive love. Instead, he nursed his disdain into stubborn disobedience. He preferred to watch the destruction of an entire group of people rather than become a conduit of grace upon his enemy.

His love had limits, while God's love is limitless. When the limits of our love run into the brick wall of self-imposed boundaries, we must rely upon the limitless love of God to take us farther. Ultimately, Jonah sulked and dragged his feet in relaying God's message. His prejudice and intransigence caused him to miss out on participating in the life of God. To his loss, he refused to trade in his hatred for the gift of divine intimacy.

At times, we will run into the brick wall of our own limits, and that is when we must rely upon the limitless love of God to supplement our need. That is when we grow. That is the inward journey I speak of—dealing with oneself. In this journey of love, we experience divine intimacy in powerful and life-changing ways.

The End Has Come

This book has been a joy and a challenge to write. It has helped me process and clarify my own thinking. It has challenged me to seek God with all that I am, to live with intentionality, and to practice the presence of

God as a way of living, loving, and being. I hope that it has done the same for you.

We began with perspective—getting our mind right about God and divine intimacy. We followed that with pathways for hearing divine whispers. Perspectives and pathways work together to unlock our pursuit of God. May your quest for a closer walk with God be experienced beyond your wildest expectation. May your journey lead to a deeper understanding and acceptance of yourself, a greater love for God, and a richer experience of the Spirit. May practicing the presence of God become as common to you as breathing. Live life with all you've got, love extravagantly, and be all that you can be to the glory of God. Joy and peace are yours for the taking. Grab them, smile, and help others find them. Amen.

Other inspiriting books by Dr. Wise

Titles are available online and through your local bookstore.

Leaving Religion Finding God: Rediscovering a Faith Worth Believing and a God Worth Following
ISBN: 978-0-9860613-4-9

Every Scar a Treasure: Wisdom for Life's Journey
ISBN: 978-0-9860613-3-2

Mentoring Relationships: Investing In Others
ISBN: 978-0-9860613-2-5

Big But Christians: Overcoming Our Excuses
ISBN: 978-0-9860613-1-8

Tiny Bubbles: Biblical Teaching on Alcohol
ISBN: 978-0-9860613-0-1

You may contact Dr. Wise for speaking, conference, ministry, mentoring, or consulting services at:
servantcom.tswise@gmail.com

Printed in the USA
CPSIA information can be obtained
at www.ICGtesting.com
LVHW051051190224
772186LV00001B/190